Seeing to See

A VOLUME IN THE SERIES
Becoming Modern: Studies in the Long Nineteenth Century
Edited by
Elizabeth A. Fay

Seeing to See

**THE NON-TELEOLOGICAL POETICS
OF DICKINSON AND THOREAU**

DANIEL A. NELSON

University of Massachusetts Press
AMHERST AND BOSTON

Copyright © 2025 by University of Massachusetts Press
All rights reserved

ISBN 978-1-62534-856-2 (paper); 857-9 (hardcover)

Designed by Jen Jackowitz
Set in Minion Pro
Printed and bound by Books International, Inc.

Cover design by adam b. bohannon
Cover illustration by John James Audubon, *Brown-headed Nuthatch*, c. 1827.
Engraving. etching. and aquatint printed in black ink. colored by hand on wove paper.
Plate: 19 5/8 × 12 3/8 inches (49.8 × 31.4 cm). CC.0.

Library of Congress Cataloging-in-Publication Data

Names: Nelson, Daniel A. author
Title: Seeing to see : the non-teleological poetics of Dickinson and Thoreau / Daniel A. Nelson.
Description: Amherst : University of Massachusetts Press, 2025. | Series: Becoming modern: studies in the long nineteenth century | Includes bibliographical references and index. |
Identifiers: LCCN 2024058171 (print) | LCCN 2024058172 (ebook) | ISBN 9781625348562 paperback | ISBN 9781625348579 hardcover | ISBN 9781685751326 ebook | ISBN 9781685751333 epub
Subjects: LCSH: Dickinson, Emily, 1830–1886—Criticism and interpretation | Thoreau, Henry David, 1817–1862—Criticism and interpretation | LCGFT: Literary criticism
Classification: LCC PS1541.Z5 N45 2025 (print) | LCC PS1541.Z5 (ebook) | DDC 811/.4—dc23/eng/20250326
LC record available at https://lccn.loc.gov/2024058171
LC ebook record available at https://lccn.loc.gov/2024058172

British Library Cataloguing-in-Publication Data
A catalog record for this book is available from the British Library.

A version of chapter 2 was originally published in *The Emily Dickinson Journal*.

A version of chapter 3 was originally published in *Arizona Quarterly*.

To God, and to one who served Him:
Mustafa Rafat Zaman (1983–2025)

Contents

Preface ix
Acknowledgments xiii

INTRODUCTION
Seeing to See
1

CHAPTER 1
The Uncanny Return of the Ordinary Thoreau and Dickinson
13

CHAPTER 2
"Distance – be her only Motion"
Dickinson's Poetics
45

CHAPTER 3
"Between Poetry and Natural Fact"
Thoreau's Journal
74

CHAPTER 4
Two Models of Disinterestedness, Part 1
Thoreau
101

CHAPTER 5
Two Models of Disinterestedness, Part 2
Dickinson
127

CONCLUSION
150

Notes 155
Index 169

Preface

Emily Dickinson and Henry David Thoreau loom large in the history of American literature, in large part because of the enigmatic nature of their lives and works. With both authors, the enigma is owing as much to what they did not do and did not write, as to what they did do and did write. Dickinson did not publish more than a few poems. She did not title her poems. She never wrote a long poem. She never wrote a statement articulating her aims as a poet or her theory of poetry. Thoreau, in the middle of his life, wrote one masterpiece—*Walden*—but did not write anything like it again; apparently he did not even try. Instead, he wrote more and more in his private Journal (the capital "J" is his own). He spent a great deal of time outdoors, studying nature, but he did not identify as a scientist. Although in his later years he occasionally wrote and lectured on scientific subjects, he did not join any scientific associations, and devoted most of his energies to his private routine of walking, looking, and writing. This routine, it seems, became for him an end in itself; it needed no justification.

Why did Thoreau and Dickinson, who were aware of their considerable literary powers, put those powers to such unconventional uses? Or, to put it negatively, why did they put their powers to such little use? This book proposes an answer to this question. It suggests that to understand why Thoreau and Dickinson did what they did—and did not do what we might expect them to have done—we must try to think as they thought, based on the evidence provided by their writings. Only by immersing ourselves in their manners of thinking and seeing can we appreciate simultaneously the smallness and the greatness of their achievement. In particular, through this effort of imagination we begin to understand how Dickinson managed in as few as twenty—or eight, or even four—lines of elliptical verse to make striking, even unforgettable statements on such vast subjects as God, immortality, life, death, love, pain, nature, and poetry; and how Thoreau, despite having devoted his later career almost entirely to painstaking observation and description of natural subjects, managed through that practice of observing and describing to articulate, and to put into practice, a coherent philosophical and artistic vision.

I began this study because I trusted that Dickinson's poems and Thoreau's Journal had something to teach me: something quite different from what other literary works seemed to offer. I sensed, for instance, that both bodies of writing were intensely concerned with everyday life—both the life of humans and the life of plants and animals and other phenomena—but that they challenged us to discard our everyday ideas and attitudes toward those subjects. ("Joy and sorrow, success and failure, grandeur and meanness, and indeed most words in the English language do not mean for me what they do for my neighbors," writes Thoreau.)[1] And I sensed that both writers were too vast in their thoughts and ambitions to be hemmed in by a single category of endeavor—whether literature or philosophy or science or religion—even as they adopted some of the methods of each of these disciplines. I have given the name "non-teleological" to their poetics (that is, to their theory and practice of literature) not because they had no ambitions or goals, but rather because their aims did not align with those of any discipline—not even with the more open-ended aims of religion. And also because one thing that is consistent across their writings is a resistance to what I call teleological ways of thinking and writing: the tendency to evaluate things in terms of their consequences rather than in terms of their intrinsic merits. If we are to think like Dickinson and Thoreau, the first thing we must try to do, as my Dickinson-borrowed title suggests, is "see to see": look at a poem, or a page of prose, or a natural object, and try to locate value in the words of the text or in the details of the object, as well as in the act of seeing it, interacting with it, puzzling over it. This might seem commonsensical, yet Dickinson and Thoreau put our powers of seeing intrinsic value and meaning—of seeing for no other purpose but to see—to the test, because many of their texts are strikingly devoid of extrinsic value. What is the point of a poem about "Four Trees . . . / Without Design / Or Order," about which all that can be said is that they "Maintain,"[2] or of a pages-long description of the process by which the author obtained maple syrup? (J 8:216–18, 3/21/56).

Part of the point, I will suggest, is to alert us to how difficult it is to see the value in such texts and in their subjects. Their texts are reminders, in other words, of how little we are able, as a species, to separate the concept of "good" from the concept of "good for." Looked at in this way, Dickinson and Thoreau, far from seeming like oddly under-accomplished writers, come to seem heroic in their feats of non-teleological thinking and seeing. They impress us, that is, not merely with their literary talents, but with their ability to see value and meaning where most would see little or none. Dickinson defined a poet as one who "Distills amazing sense / From Ordinary Meanings" (F446); Thoreau, as one who "needs to have more stomachs than the cow, for for him no fodder is stored in barns–He relies upon his instinct which teaches him to paw away the snow to come at the withered grass."[3] How Dickinson and Thoreau live up to these idiosyncratic definitions—what unhabitual ways of thought enable them to make so much of so little—is the subject of this book.

Acknowledgments

My first debt, as the grateful author of this book, is to God, "the One who taught by the pen" (Qur'an 96:4). The second is to my parents, who have given me so much, and who continue to give. The third is to my wife Nasheed, who has long been my first reader, and on whose surefire advice and loving encouragement I have counted through every step of writing this book (right down to the drafting of these acknowledgments); and to our three children, Hanaan, Nadhar, and Ishmael, whose responses to literature and to life have been nothing short of enlightening for me. The fourth is to my dissertation advisor, John Michael, second reader (and long-time teacher), Kenneth Gross, and master's thesis advisor, Susan Eilenberg. All three of these individuals were kind enough to take an interest in my rough ideas, and so made it possible for me to take an interest in and learn from their own polished ideas. Next, I must thank the dedicated faculty and staff of the English Department of the University of Rochester, especially then director of graduate studies, Katherine Mannheimer, for making my time there so much more pleasant and productive than I could have reasonably expected. More recently, I have been blessed in the generous support I have received from Brian Halley, Elizabeth Fay, and Mary Dougherty of the University of Massachusetts Press, as well as from the anonymous readers assigned to my manuscript, the copyeditor Kellye McBride, and the indexer Amy Murphy. I also owe debts to James Guthrie, former editor of *The Emily Dickinson Journal*, and to the editors of the *Arizona Quarterly*, as well as to both journals' anonymous readers, for agreeing to publish, and for helping me to improve, earlier versions of chapters 2 and 3, respectively. Finally, I wish to say a word of thanks to the people whose scholarship is discussed in these pages—in particular, Sharon Cameron, Anne-Lise François, Paul Fry, and François Specq. Without the instruction and inspiration that I received from these authors, from my teachers and family members, and above all, from God, I could not have written this book.

Seeing to See

Introduction

SEEING TO SEE

When Emily Dickinson, at the end of one of her many poems about dying, speaks of no longer being able to "see to see," she seems to mean at once nothing much and a great deal: "And then the Windows failed – and then / I could not see to see" (F591). On the one hand, this second seeing is no different from the first, and the line states a tautology: one sees in order to see, just as one hears in order to hear, or even, lives in order to be alive. On the other hand, there is the hint, and the hope, that this second seeing is somehow different, even categorically so: a kind of seeing to which physical perception is merely a preliminary. So, while the poem records how these windows "failed," there is hope in their having once functioned—hope, if not for the speaker, then at least for the poet and her readers.

Henry David Thoreau, too, expressed hope that perception would not merely give him access to the material world, but would save him from the "quiet desperation" with which he famously diagnosed his society.[1] To see the world but not to see its meaning; to possess life only to find that it is a "life without principle";[2] to have "walked a mile into the woods bodily, without getting there in spirit"[3]—these were symptoms of that desperation. While he had no doubt that the natural world was alive with meaning, Thoreau did not take for granted that he would perceive this animation, and be animated by it in turn. On the contrary, he considered that it would be his "greatest success" just to perceive that the things around us really "are" (J 12:371, 10/4/59). Pursuing this seemingly modest aim was his version of seeing to see, while warding off the failure of the senses to awaken the spirit was the object of his daily walks, as well as of the record he made of those walks in his Journal.

Many would argue that Thoreau was decidedly more hopeful than Dickinson about the transformative power of perception. Indeed, it would be possible to read the poem quoted above as an expression of just such "quiet desperation" as Thoreau dreaded. The poem begins, "I heard a Fly buzz – when I died," and at no point does the fly's presence seem to lend meaning or beauty to that death; on the contrary, the fly "interpose[s] . . . // Between the light" and the speaker just before that final failure of "the Windows." But if the fly seems to minimize the significance of the speaker's death, and by extension her life, by taking center stage in a scene she naturally thought was set for her alone, it also unexpectedly lightens the scene of her dying, taking the spotlight itself rather than simply blocking it out:

> and then it was
> There interposed a Fly –
>
> With Blue – uncertain – stumbling Buzz –
> Between the light – and me –
> And then the Windows failed – and then
> I could not see to see – (F591)

As a result of this awkward, "uncertain" interruption, the poem is not so much melancholy, much less despairing, as it is bizarre, thought-provoking, and even—depending of course on the reader—mystical, or at least mysterious. Reading it and contemplating it, and searching in vain for something to say about it that would not be simply a description of it, one gets an inkling of what Dickinson herself might have felt one day as her eyes involuntarily followed a fly about the room, or of what Thoreau might have felt when he suddenly "perceive[d] that such things are," or when he exclaimed, "The bream, appreciated, floats in the pond as the centre of the system, another image of God" (J 11:359, 11/30/58). In each of these instances, meaning has imperceptibly seeped into the experience of mere seeing that the writer records. Perhaps that is why, in ending this poem which is about both the end of life and the end of sight, Dickinson felt that what was ended was not mere seeing after all, though she had no word to denote what was different about it—a failure of language that is embodied in the redundant final phrase "see to see."

Like the fly, and like Thoreau's redundant-seeming verb "are," as well as his bathetic association of God with a bream, this "see to see" is not pretty; it doesn't sound like how a poem should end, even to our jaded twenty-first-century ears. These writers' cavalier attitude toward their seeming failures, toward the very linguistic medium in which they were so skilled, scares away many, but it is thrilling because we sense that it originates in a corresponding reverence for their protean subject matter, which eludes both direct approach and elegant figurative speech. John Donne's "The Flea" is an excellent poem, but it is not about a flea in the way that Dickinson's poem is about a fly. And while a number of naturalists' writings are clearly "about" nature, they are not *poems* about nature in the way that Thoreau's prose descriptions manage to be. Balancing between these poles of prose and poetry; between the "aboutness" of the one and the seeming arbitrariness of the other (which may in fact be more faithfully "about" the elusive subject matter than the more straightforward approach); between mere seeing and seeing to see, is, I will argue, a defining feature of Dickinson's and Thoreau's poetics.

NON-TELEOLOGICAL POETICS

This book is about two authors who are notoriously hard to classify. Rather than try to overcome this interpretive obstacle, I look for its roots in their writings (primarily, Dickinson's poems and Thoreau's Journal), where I find evidence of a determined avoidance not only of generic conventions that would aid in classifying these texts, but also of some of the most basic features of literary texts. Both Thoreau's Journal and Dickinson's poems avoid teleological structures of writing and thinking, whereby a thing's—or a word's, or a text's—value hinges on its participation in a larger system; this explains the fragmentary nature of both bodies of work. Stanley Cavell remarks, "A book of philosophy suitable to what Thoreau envisions as 'students' would be written with next to no forward motion, one that culminates in each sentence."[4] This vision of a non-teleological book is realized in Thoreau's last and longest project, his Journal, which is less a personal diary than a meticulous, if unstructured and seemingly aimless, catalog of the author's observations of nature, day after day, year after year. It is a text in which no sentence is more or less important than any other, because each accomplishes the same non-teleological task of recording a momentary perception rather than a large-scale vision or idea. The Journal came into its own around 1851, a time at which Thoreau felt "uncommonly prepared for *some* literary work, but [could] select no work" (PJ 4:50–51, 9/7/51). Soon, however, this very lack of a project became itself a project: to write not in order to fulfill personal or professional purposes, but as an aid to pure perception, unadulterated by ulterior motives. "Your greatest success will be simply to perceive that such things are," he writes in 1859, "and you will have no communication to make to the Royal Society" (J 12:371, 10/4/59). The Journal, then, is not a report or "communication," least of all to a professional entity with distinct, discipline-specific objectives, but rather a kind of endless poem, whose individual descriptions aspire to an immanent, self-contained, even "absolute" significance, rather than a significance contingent on some greater future discovery: "Unconsidered expressions of our delight which any natural object draws from us are something complete and final in themselves . . . and who knows how close to absolute truth such unconscious affirmations may come" (J 14:117, 10/13/60).

Dickinson likewise eschews teleology, preferring isolated, small-scale reference points (a single bird, four trees, a fly), or else reference points so vast (death, distance, immortality, light) as to permit an extreme vagueness and indirectness of treatment, which enables an avoidance not only of familiar ideas but also of recognizable rhetorical goals—indeed, of the articulation of ideas altogether. Hers is a word-based poetics, the rationale of which is glimpsed in a remark preserved by a friend of the poet's: "We used to think . . . that words were cheap & weak. Now I dont know of anything so mighty. There are [those] to which I lift my hat when I see them sitting princelike among their peers on the page. Sometimes I write one, and look at his outlines till he glows as no sapphire."[5] While of course the individual word derives its power from the myriad contexts in which it has been employed, Dickinson in her poems does not so much create a new context for words to work in—and a new purpose for them to work toward—as play their individual auras off each other; that is why her poetry is built not around sentences but around two- to five-word phrases, and sometimes around single words. The poem beginning "Sweet Mountains – Ye tell Me no lie" (F745), for instance, is in my reading encapsulated not only in the first line but in the first two words—"Sweet Mountains"—which seem to pit human desire and vulnerability against natural coldness and durability. If according to some critics Dickinson's poems often begin strongly only to disappoint expectations, this is not an accident but a necessary consequence of a non-teleological poetics, whose goal is not to create texts with a beginning, middle, and end, but to take repeated, instantaneous stabs at truth and beauty.

In this book I use "non-teleological" to refer to a mode of thought and of writing in which the concept of telos—the ancient Greek term for purpose or final goal—is, not rejected outright, but bracketed. A good example of this ambiguous philosophical stance is Thoreau's idea of "sauntering," a word which he uses to evoke the feeling of being without a home or destination (*sans terre*, i.e, landless) yet at the same time in search of something great beyond conceptualizing ("going *à la Sainte Terre*," i.e., to the Holy Land).[6] In a similar vein, Dickinson writes of "Salubrious Hours . . . / Which, if they do not fit for Earth – / Drill silently for Heaven" (F1087), evoking a kind of experience that has no purpose, no goal that can be arrived at, or even conceptualized, in this world—a privation which helps explain why this poem is only four lines long. And in another poem Dickinson writes of the "Reportless" joy she feels in "reportless places" (F1404), echoing Thoreau's intuition that one's highest achievement would leave one with "no communication to make" to others (J 12:371, 10/4/59). By bracketing the concept of telos, or by envisioning a telos so abstract and vague as to be almost unthinkable (not "fit for Earth," *sans terre*, "reportless," and incommunicable), Thoreau and Dickinson seem to be able to set aside all thought of distinct personal and professional goals, by whose means we typically try to make an overarching sense out of, and to derive some form of profit from, disparate experiences, events, actions, and feelings. Further, they seem to be able to get outside of the worldview according to which the value and meaning of something, be it a natural object, a word, an experience, or a text, is a function of its participation in a larger system: an ecosystem, taxonomic system, or syntactic system; a writer's career, or life, or philosophy; even a single poem or journal entry. This negative capability, the ability to escape almost irresistible habits of thought, is what makes Thoreau's Journal and Dickinson's poems thrilling in spite of the absences for which both bodies of text are notable: the absence of narrative and of sustained argument; the absence of character and conflict; the absence of a fully fleshed-out, biographical "I"; the absence, above all, of telos, a discernible overriding purpose.

Despite their forays into non-anthropocentrism and their evident affection for the minute particulars of the natural world, the Dickinson and Thoreau that I present here do not belong to the materialist tradition as it's been variously reformulated in such recent works as Branka Arsić's *Bird Relics: Grief and Vitalism in Thoreau*, Jane Bennett's *Vibrant Matter: A Political Ecology of*

Things, Mark Noble's *American Poetic Materialism from Whitman to Stevens*, and Rochelle Johnson's "'This Enchantment is No Delusion': Henry David Thoreau, the New Materialisms, and Ineffable Materiality."[7] The distinction between "non-teleological" and "materialist" (or "new materialist") is worth unpacking. First, the non-teleological approach to writing, thinking, and living is not centrally concerned with material objects; when I speak of a "thing" being valuable in itself for Thoreau or Dickinson, that thing could be an experience, a word, or a text just as well as it could be a hill, a tree, or a bird's nest. Second, whereas new materialism seeks to correct a perceived overemphasis on the socially and linguistically constructed aspect of lived experience, and in this respect is a preeminently academic endeavor (it is, in large part, a reaction against the so-called linguistic turn in academia), the non-teleological as I understand it is much broader and more transhistorical in its concerns and its scope, as well as, by definition, less concerned with particular aims. The non-teleological might best be described as a phenomenon rather than a program or project. It is something one experiences, like Dickinson's "Salubrious Hours" and "Reportless" joy and Thoreau's spontaneous "delight," and while one can cultivate an attitude that is receptive to such experiences, one cannot codify them into a set of practices or ideas. "Non-teleological" is an adjective that cannot easily be made into a noun.

It is true that both writers turned to nature in search of alternative ways of being, of thinking, and even of writing. But whereas new materialism seems to suggest that this turn to nature need not entail a turn away from culture (since, according to its critique of binaries, nature and culture are not separable), but can be practically realized in the form of new scholarly and philosophical approaches, Thoreau and Dickinson were more aware of this turn's inherently transgressive, impractical quality. Dickinson, for instance, describes herself as "Disdaining Men, and Oxygen" (F319); as having "on"—not in—her hand "Branches . . . full of Morning Glory" (F605); as, most famously, one who has already died. A new materialist approach would likely have us take literally these statements' denials of binaries such as nature/culture, plant/human, and dead/alive, but to me they are obviously to be taken figuratively: as figures for the experience of alterity that is one of Dickinson's central subjects. Dickinson, like Thoreau, inherited a romantic tradition, and anticipated a modernist one, of celebrating experiences of alterity: encounters with the strange and incommensurable, both in the self and its artistic creations and in nature. The point was not to escape culture or the human (or the binary oppositions without which concepts such as "culture" and "human" are virtually meaningless) and somehow immerse oneself in the alterity of either the material world or inchoate artistic media, but rather to contemplate and comment on human experience and artistic practice from the perspective of an outsider—one who has turned away, toward otherness. That is why so much of William Wordsworth's poetry, for instance, adopts the perspective of a child, or a recluse, or even of a "mad mother" and an "idiot boy." Only by adopting the perspectives of such marginalized figures, or, in Dickinson's case, by foregoing altogether the orienting perspective of a clearly defined speaker, can the poet imaginatively achieve the transcendence of binaries—in particular, the immersion of the self in its material surroundings—that new materialism seems to propose can be practically achieved by us all. As Theo Davis puts it in her review of Noble's *American Poetic Materialism*—a book that neither embraces nor refutes the claims of materialism, but instead highlights its "aporetic" or unrealizable quality—"Apparently, aporetic materialism in all of its forms (philosophical, scientific, and poetic) is either a poetics or leads to a call for poetics, because it identifies aspects of reality that can only be described or responded to in poetic practice."[8]

If Dickinson shows us that poetry is the exception that proves the rule of the tenacity of binaries, and especially of the tenacity of the self's claim to centrality, Thoreau spells that rule out in his Journal: "man is all in all, Nature nothing, but as she draws him out and reflects him" (J 9:121, 10/18/56). New materialism would call our attention to the material object's "draw[ing] out" of the subject—i.e., to the agency of the thing observed or experienced—but Thoreau emphasizes that the material object is "nothing" unless it manifests itself in the experience of the observer who is "draw[n] . . . out and reflect[ed]" by it. This passage of the Journal paints a very different picture of the subject than is rendered by materialism's notion of the "atomized human subject—the person conceived as its relation to a field of objects."[9] It is not that Thoreau did not challenge binaries, or that he exalted the human self at the expense of physical matter. But for Thoreau, the opposition between nature and human, and the singularity of human consciousness, were axiomatic, and it was from this point that his experiments in thinking and writing about nature—his efforts to be "the scribe of all nature . . . the corn & the grass & the atmosphere writing" (PJ 4:28, 9/2/1851)—took their departure. As I explain in a later chapter, it is not quite accurate to say, as Alfred Tauber does, that Thoreau tried to "escape the web of his own self-consciousness" and overcome the "divide between nature and man";[10] the quotation from the Journal above ("man is all in all, Nature nothing") makes it plain that he was fully aware of the impossibility of this. The Journal, like Dickinson's poems, does not deny the human/nature binary, but neither does it accept as final humans' ignorance of nature. In this respect Thoreau and Dickinson distinguish themselves from new materialism on the one hand and skepticism on the other, and locate themselves squarely in the "nowhere" space that Maurice Blanchot named "the space of literature"[11]—that space which Dickinson called "Possibility – / A fairer House than Prose" (F466), and which Thoreau called "*Extra vagance*": "somewhere *without* bounds," suitable for "a man in a waking moment, [speaking] to men in their waking moments" (W 18:580).

If the non-teleological Dickinson and Thoreau were not materialists and not skeptics, what were they? What is gained by labeling them "non-teleological," which is, after all, more of an anti-label than a label? Perhaps the chief benefit of this approach is that it alerts us to the interdisciplinary, or simply non-disciplinary, nature of the texts under discussion. It is one of my main contentions that Thoreau and Dickinson, refusing to channel their energies into a preexisting discipline with its attendant protocols and aims, expended their creativity on circling a subject too broad to be the domain of any one discipline, and too ephemeral to lend itself to premeditated methods or to yield discrete discoveries. At present this subject often goes by the name "the ordinary," and is generally acknowledged to be equally the domain of poets and philosophers. Perpetually revolving around their ephemeral subject, Dickinson and Thoreau practiced philosophical thinking by means of poetic language, and innovated poetic language by thinking philosophically.

My main points of engagement, therefore, are with theorists who bridge the divide between philosophy and literature, and who have addressed, whether explicitly or implicitly, the concept of the ordinary, such as Sharon Cameron, Stanley Cavell, Angus Fletcher, Paul Fry, Anne-Lise François, and Martin Heidegger. One of this book's ambitions is to pursue the implications of Fletcher's insight, in *A New Theory for American Poetry: Democracy, the Environment, and the Future of Imagination*, that "there is an almost genetic connection between poetry and natural fact."[12] This insight echoes Thoreau's remarks, "Mere facts & dates & names communicate more than we suspect" (PJ 4:296, 1/27/52), and "A true account of the actual is the rarest poetry."[13] Despite the ostensibly matter-of-fact, prosaic manner of the Journal, Thoreau records there "unconsidered," seemingly disproportionate "expressions of . . .

delight" over the natural objects he describes, because he believes that "such unconscious affirmations," when coupled with simple notations of "mere facts & dates & names," may come as close as humans can to expressing the "absolute truth" about those objects (J 14:117, 10/13/60). Similarly, Dickinson "Distills amazing sense / From Ordinary Meanings," transforming what at first seem like simple descriptions into gnomic utterances that defamiliarize their subject, or else call unwonted attention to it without denying its familiarity, its ordinariness: "Sweet Mountains – Ye tell Me no lie" (F745); "A Sparrow took a Slice of Twig" (F1257); "There interposed a Fly – // With Blue – uncertain – stumbling Buzz – / Between the light – and me" (F591); "Four Trees – opon a solitary Acre – / Without Design / Or Order, or Apparent Action – / Maintain" (F778). In both cases humility is coupled with ambition, for if Thoreau bases his Journal on "mere facts" and Dickinson bases her poetry on "Ordinary Meanings," they nevertheless challenge readers to see beyond this mereness and ordinariness to another order of meaning which yet is inseparable from the first: "Mere facts . . . communicate more than we suspect"; "From Ordinary Meanings" can be distilled "amazing sense." In this way Thoreau and Dickinson disrupt the experiential boundaries separating the ordinary from the transcendent, as well as the generic and disciplinary boundaries separating poetry, which is said to aim at beauty, from philosophy, which is said to aim at truth, or from science, which is said to aim at fact.

A non-teleological poetics is a minimalist poetics—a mode of writing that aspires, in Dickinson's phrase, to report "The simple News that Nature told" (F519), or, in Thoreau's phrase, to convey simply "that such things are"—which is nevertheless deeply concerned with the meaning of things. This is a kind of writing about nature that foregrounds and lingers not over the question of "why" but over the question of "what," as if that were all that mattered, or as if that were fantastic enough. It decontextualizes and isolates the ordinary subject matter, in order to put to the test the bold hypothesis that the ordinary is already interesting—that its interest is intrinsic, and not in need of embellishment: "But are not all Facts Dreams as soon as we put them behind us?" writes Dickinson (L, prose fragment 22). Curiously, however, this very confidence in facts' and names' self-sufficiency, which might be read as part of a modest evasion of poetry and philosophy (what need for either if nature speaks for itself?), feeds into the idea that facts and names, in their gnomic starkness and suggestiveness, can double as answers to the question of "why": that prose is capable of doubling as poetry, and poetry, of doubling as philosophy, or science. Sharon Cameron says it best when she writes that Thoreau's "progressive refusal to interpret the observations recorded" in the Journal makes it seem, not as if the author doesn't care what significance his observations hold, but rather "as if the significance of the description of a tree were the description of that tree."[14] The lack of frame, of apparent function, and of sequence (hence, of consequence ordinarily conceived) in Thoreau's and Dickinson's statements about things lends to those statements an inordinate potential for meaning; yet this meaningfulness can vanish, like an optical illusion, in an instant, taking along with it the literary value of the statements and indeed the reasonableness of the writer's undertaking. Like gnomes, their texts seem at once fragmentary and self-sufficient; they risk appearing meaningless yet evoke a plenitude of meaning too great or too knotty to be elucidated.

The near impossibility of selecting a name for the project of Thoreau's late career (the period during which he wrote the bulk of the Journal) and for the project of Dickinson's career generally is the subject of my first chapter, which locates the connection between these two authors in their difficulty. This is a difficulty not so much of understanding as of categorizing. It is virtually impossible, I argue, to identify consistent rhetorical, ideological, or professional goals in pursuit of which Dickinson's poems and Thoreau's Journal were written. In the chapter's final section, I revisit the groundbreaking critical works on Dickinson published in the late 1970s and early 1980s by Sharon Cameron, David Porter, and Susan Howe, as well as earlier studies of Thoreau such as Cameron's and John Hildebidle's. The former group of monographs emphasized the sui generis Dickinson (maker of "a modern idiom," according to Porter; "founder" of a new "poetic form," according to Howe),[15] while the latter emphasized the iconoclastic Thoreau, who sought to avoid the constraints of genre, of discipline, and of profession by seeking refuge in what Hildebidle calls "a naturalist's liberty" and what Cameron simply yet paradoxically calls "writing nature."[16] Far from being outdated, these books are much closer to the truth about Dickinson and Thoreau than recent depictions of the two writers as products of their time and place, I argue.

Chapters 2 and 3 describe how Dickinson and Thoreau, respectively, place an inordinate amount of trust in the building blocks of their texts: for Dickinson, isolated words; for Thoreau, isolated facts. Chapter 2 proposes that the defining feature of Dickinson's poetics is its non-teleological use of language. The primary semantic unit of her writing is the word or short phrase rather than the sentence or stanza. Dickinson foregrounds the building blocks of her poems rather than any larger overarching structure they might be thought to be in the service of. She favors a hands-off, non-teleological presentation of language, because to impose a telos on the words of a poem would interfere with the hoped-for emergence of a mysterious, innate meaningfulness in the words themselves. What Dickinson named the "Circumference" or curvature of her writing ("My business is Circumference"),[17] its refusal to travel in a straight line from subject matter to statement about that subject, makes the unfolding of her language the central event of each poem; yet this linguistic event frequently mirrors the odd, apparently purposeless events of nature that are so often the subject of her poems, suggesting that her concern is not just with exploring the meaning of words but with exploring the meaning of nature as well.

Countering the trend of arguing for the scientific usefulness of Thoreau's Journal, chapter 3 classifies the Journal as a non-teleological work—a kind of endless poem. I describe how the Journal's lack of an object (besides perception) apparently puts into question its status as literature, yet also earns Thoreau a place in the company of modern poets such as Dickinson, for whom a "poem" is a highly indefinite item—more a unit of perception than a unit of meaning. Thoreau deliberately turns away from forms of human communication (addressing an audience, contributing to a discourse community) in order to explore the equivocal communicativeness of natural phenomena. This turn, I conclude, places the Journal both within and outside of poetic tradition.

Borrowing from an insight of the poet-critic Susan Howe, chapters 4 and 5 characterize Thoreau and Dickinson, respectively, as disinterested writers: writers who eschew what Howe calls "calculations of interest" and "representations of calculated human order." Thoreau declines to "select a work" in his late career, he says, because he is conscious of "a mere fulness of life, which does not find any channels to flow into" (PJ 4:50–51, 9/7/51). On January 28, 1852, he writes: "Perhaps I can never find so good a setting for my thoughts as I shall thus have taken them out of," that is, as the setting which is furnished by the Journal's undiscriminating record of each day's observed phenomena (PJ 4:296). This setting, he writes in the previous day's entry, explaining why he does not "bring the related thoughts [articulated in the Journal] . . . together into separate essays," is "the proper frame for my sketches," because within it "my thoughts are now allied to life–& and are seen by the reader not to be far fetched" (PJ 4:296, 1/27/52). Thoreau doesn't want to lift his "sketches" out of the Journal framework and into "separate," closed off "essays," I argue, because he is convinced of a mysterious relation between *hors-texte* and text, contingency and artistry, nature and the mind. His aim is not any one thing or text but a way or process in which life and art, perception and thought, nature and humans are interdependent and immediately, invisibly fruitful ("I grew . . . like corn in the night," he says in a passage on meditation in *Walden* [W 4:411]), rather than subordinated one to the other for the purpose of some imagined future good.

Chapter 5 examines three of Dickinson's lyrics—"I am alive - I guess" (F605), "This was a Poet - it is That" (F446), and "It would have starved a Gnat" (F444)—and finds in them a subtle protest against conventional ideas about meaning and value. I read these as poems about poetry in which Dickinson identifies her craft as an ethical, not just an aesthetic, endeavor, whose object is to liberate words, things, and the self from the deadening familiarity which attaches to ordinary objects as well as to what she calls "Ordinary Meanings." Dickinson does not simply celebrate what Yvor Winters condescendingly termed "the small subject"; she challenges the hierarchical, teleological structure of conventional signification, and refutes the unwritten law that insects and flowers and words are not significant in their own right, but must play a subordinate role if they are to mean at all.

The conclusion recapitulates my argument while suggesting that the shortcomings I identify in recent scholarship on Dickinson and Thoreau are symptomatic of a teleological prejudice in contemporary thought. This prejudice favors the definite products of thinking and writing (Dickinson's and Thoreau's texts are celebrated only after they have been categorized: recognized as contributions to a particular idea, discipline, tradition, or cultural phenomenon), and undervalues strange modes of thought and expression which may yield no fruit but their own unique example.

CHAPTER 1

The Uncanny Return of the Ordinary Thoreau and Dickinson

The return of what we accept as the world will then present itself as a return of the familiar, which is to say, exactly under the concept of what Freud names the uncanny.

—Stanley Cavell, *In Quest of the Ordinary*

For life is like a poet, and on that account is different from the observer who always seeks to bring things to a conclusion. The poet pulls us into the very complex center of life.

—Søren Kierkegaard, *Purity of Heart is to Will One Thing*

B.—The only thing disturbed by the revolutionaries Matisse and Tal Coat is a certain order on the plane of the feasible.
D.—What other plane can there be for the maker?
B.—Logically none. Yet I speak of an art turning from it in disgust, weary of puny exploits, weary of pretending to be able, of being able, of doing a little better the same old thing, of going a little further along the same dreary road.

—Samuel Beckett, *Three Dialogues with Georges Duthuit*

TURNING AWAY

Emily Dickinson and Henry David Thoreau occupy a unique place in literary history. They come just after American authors had begun to carve a niche for themselves and to dispel the charge of unoriginality under which they had long suffered. In respect not just of its literature but in nearly every respect, America was fast becoming a "great" nation. Thoreau, born in 1817, and Dickinson, born in 1830, came of age at a time when the US, at the expense of Native American (and Mexican, and African American) lives and rights, was aggressively expanding westward and southward, building canals, railroads, and telegraph lines, and discovering immense stores of valuable resources. It was under these circumstances that Thoreau felt called upon, not to help establish America's greatness by contributing to its literary output, but to undercut it by (in Stanley Cavell's words) "refusing it his voice":[1]

> When I think of the gold-diggers and the Mormons, the slaves and slave-holders, and the *flibustiers* [i.e., perpetrators of military land grabs], I naturally dream of a glorious *private life*. No–I am not patriotic; I shall not meddle with the gem of the Antilles; Gen. Quitman cannot count on my aid [in conquering Cuba],–alas for him.! nor can Gen. Pierce.[2]

Ralph Waldo Emerson, in his eulogy for his young friend and sometime mentee, complained that Thoreau preferred leading a huckleberry party to "engineering for all America."[3] This was no joke; it was both literally and metaphorically true. Thoreau, born fourteen years after Emerson, was for all his strangeness part of a generation—perhaps the first generation—of Americans who could afford to look askance at American "greatness," as well as to look away from it toward the very different greatness—but also smallness—of nature.

Dickinson, judging from one of the two stray references she makes to Thoreau in her correspondence, was evidently sympathetic with his wry attitude toward American culture: "The fire-bells are oftener now, almost, than the church-bells. Thoreau would wonder which did the most harm" (L691). She, too, kept aloof from her mentor, the prominent editor and writer Thomas Wentworth Higginson (who after her death in 1886 would be, with Mabel Loomis Todd, her first editor and publisher). What Susan Howe calls Dickinson's "self-imposed exile, indoors" resembles Thoreau's self-imposed exile, outdoors, and was motivated by a similar "sense of being eternally on intellectual borders."⁴ "In prose and in poetry," Howe writes, "she explored the implications of breaking the law just short of breaking off communication with a reader."⁵ As with Thoreau, there is a sense of belatedness or of reaction in Dickinson's poetics: to turn away, one must have something to turn away from; there must be a law before one can break it. Yet what distinguishes Dickinson and Thoreau from the modernists who in many ways they prefigured is that there was very little to turn away *to*, besides nature and themselves. Dickinson seems in many poems to be constructing a sense of self from scratch—as if she were reinventing language, and even reinventing thinking, so that the page could be truly blank, permitting her to start afresh. This is part of the excitement created by her explosive openings—for example, "Conscious am I in my Chamber – / Of a shapeless friend" (F773B), or "I am alive – I guess" (F605). The sense of undaunted innovativeness that Howe identifies in Dickinson's writing is owing in large part to the poet's evident desire to start totally anew, as these two non-sequitur openings do so brilliantly.

Dickinson was aware that her explosive strength was inconsistent with the kind of "organiz[ation]" needed to achieve success on Higginson's terms ("when I try to organize – my little Force explodes," she wrote to the editor [L271]), yet she appears not to have tried to remedy this situation. Notoriously, she chose privacy over publicity, brevity over expansiveness, fragmentation over organization; yet her lyrics are often triumphant in tone, even when they appear to describe experiences of devastation. In one poem the speaker describes herself as "Defying Men, and Oxygen, / For Arrogance of Them" (F319). The line reminds me, oddly enough, of Thoreau's defiance of his neighbors' attitude toward his vegetarian diet: "There is a certain class of unbelievers who sometimes ask me such questions as, if I think that I can live on vegetable food alone; and to strike at the root of the matter at once,—for the root is faith,—I am accustomed to answer such, that I can live on board nails" (W 1:373–74). In both cases, the writer is evidently delighting in his or her freedom to say and think (and in Thoreau's case, though not quite in Dickinson's, to do) as he or she pleases, having turned his or her back on "common sense" in general, and on Americans' ideas of wisdom in particular. The "natural dream" of these two writers was, in Thoreau's characteristically suggestive phrase, "a glorious *private* life." Life was glorious for Dickinson and Thoreau to the extent that it was private; and to the extent that it was glorious, it was private even to the point of foreignness, inscrutability: "for if [a writer] has lived sincerely, it must have been in a distant land to me" (W 1:325); "All men say 'What' to me" (L271).

Thoreau and Dickinson are well-known for having declined to publish much or most of their writing during their lifetimes. But their indifference (or to be more precise, their efforts at indifference) to publication was part of a much broader rejection of product-oriented value systems, as I will try to show in this chapter. Many of Dickinson's and Thoreau's texts display what we might call the meaning of not meaning. They try to represent or give voice to things, especially natural objects and phenomena, that have no signifying power in the ordinary sense; and they seem to emerge from an intentional repudiation of intention (using "intention" in the broadest sense to refer to the pull of goal-oriented modes of thinking and writing). We might say that to seem to have no purpose, or to seem to have a purpose as obscure and elusive as nature's, is the purpose of Thoreau's Journal and of many of Dickinson's poems. Hence Thoreau says that he would have "a shrub oak for my coat-of-arms" (J 9:207, 1/7/57), though it (the shrub oak) is "well-nigh useless to man" (J 9:147, 12/1/56), and that he hopes his writing possesses at least some of the "obscurity" that characterizes the ice of Walden Pond (W 18:581). And Dickinson writes in a late letter, "Nature is a Haunted House – but Art – a House that tries to be haunted" (L459a), as if the function of art were to imitate, not the nature that we see and understand, but the nature that we cannot see or understand but only suspect, receive intimations of, the way one suspects and receives intimations of the presence of a ghost, or of God. Art tries, in this view, to be ephemeral and inscrutable, yet inhabited momentarily—at some moments and not others, it may be, or for some observers and not others—by meaning.

In subsequent chapters I will be discussing specific instances of this non-teleological poetics. In this chapter, however, my goal is simply to establish the point that an aversion to teleological modes of writing does characterize Dickinson's and Thoreau's work, and to point out the ways in which interpretations that search for distinct authorial purposes fall short in their representation of that work. In the chapter's fourth and final section I discuss three critics—Sharon Cameron, Susan Howe, and David Porter—who have highlighted non-teleological aspects of Dickinson's poems and Thoreau's Journal, and explain briefly how the present study will build upon and depart from these authors' contributions.

WHY DICKINSON AND THOREAU
ELUDE CLASSIFICATION

What makes Dickinson and Thoreau hard to classify? First, both writers are reticent, cryptic, or simply negative when they are asked about, or when they volunteer to discuss, their artistic goals. Neither of them specify the place—in a culture, a tradition, a library—where they hope their writings will eventually arrive. They are clearest when stating what they *don't* want. "I smile when you suggest that I delay 'to publish,'" Dickinson tells Thomas Wentworth Higginson, "that being foreign to my thought, as Firmament to Fin" (L265). And again: "My Business is Circumference" (L268)—which, whatever else it means, announces the author's determined waywardness, her sense of herself as "hav[ing] no Tribunal," being marginalized and alone with her eccentric, unauthorized genius (L265).

Though of course she rejects his advice, it is important to remember that Dickinson appeals to Higginson—who had just published an article in *The Atlantic Monthly* titled "Letter to a Young Contributor"[6]—not just to appraise her poems, but also to help her get some kind of a handle on them. For that they are difficult to handle, let alone to classify, Dickinson knew at least as well as Higginson did: "I had no Monarch in my life, and cannot rule myself," she writes in her fifth letter to the writer-editor, "and when I try to organize – my little Force explodes – and leaves me bare and charred" (L271). Certainly there is an element of play-acting here: with her letters to Higginson as with the mysterious, undelivered "Master" letters, one is never sure whether and to what extent Dickinson is putting the reader on. But she is also telling the truth about her poems: that they are incorrigibly short, and that they tend toward abrupt, unpredictable, potentially baffling movements of language and of thought. David Porter may be exaggerating when he says that the Dickinson–Higginson correspondence reveals a poet "without a project or a path."[7] But it is only reasonable to take Dickinson at her word when she says in 1861 that she is unsure what to do with her poems: how to "organize" and "rule" them, how to assess them ("Are you too deeply occupied to say if my Verse is Alive?" is her first question, indeed her first sentence, to Higginson [L260]), and how to present them to the public without denaturing them (as if one were to ask a fish to fly). In any case, those are certainly the questions that have troubled a significant number of critics in the decades since they were finally, partially published, four years after the poet's death in 1886—despite the determined efforts of Dickinson's first editors, Higginson and Mabel Loomis Todd, to winnow, "rule," and "organize" the poems into presentability.

Thoreau's self-reflective statements are generally more positive-sounding than Dickinson's (if Dickinson affects modesty, Thoreau affects confidence) but are in fact no less ambivalent and evasive. The sentence, "The man of genius knows what he is aiming at; nobody else knows" (J 11:380, 12/27/58), for example, sounds like the statement of a writer with definite aims—that is why his latest biographer uses it as the epigraph for a chapter subtitled "Thoreau's Turn to Science"[8]—but what it actually says is that the genius's aims are too indefinite to be stated, communicated. Though certain that "My work is writing" (J 9:121, 10/18/56), Thoreau was never certain exactly what kind of text his "genius" was urging him to write. "We are stimulated, but to no obvious purpose," he says in 1851. "I feel myself uncommonly prepared for *some* literary work, but I can select no work" (PJ 4:50–51, 9/7/51), which is why instead of bringing his thoughts "together into separate essays," he began around this time to leave them "in the same form" in which they originally came to him, that is, as entries in his Journal (PJ 4:296, 1/27/52).

When, in 1853, the Association for the Advancement of Science asked him which branch of science particularly interested him, he responded with something of Dickinson's perverse aloofness. "I am an observer of nature generally," he wrote back, and named as his particular field of interest an Indigenous American people unknown to and unknowing about "the Civilized Man." (Compare Dickinson's reply to Higginson's first letter: "You ask of my Companions Hills - Sir - and the Sundown - and a Dog - large as myself, that my Father bought me - They are better than Beings - because they know - but do not tell" [L261].) Thoreau's phrase, "an observer of nature generally," sounds innocuous enough, but if we consider that the trend of nineteenth-century science was, according to Michael Granger, toward "specialization and professionalization," the self-description seems deliberately against-the-grain.[9] In the Journal entry concerning this incident Thoreau is more candid but, if anything, less explicit. He writes that in fact he is "a mystic–a transcendentalist–& a natural philosopher to boot," and unlike the Association believes in "a science which deals with the higher law," but that he prefers to keep this to himself lest he become "the laughing stock of the scientific community" (PJ 5:469–70, 3/5/53). He declined to join the Association.[10]

The first reason, then, for the difficulty of classifying the writings of Thoreau and Dickinson, is that they refuse to state their purpose—to say, as

Thoreau puts it, "what he [or she] is aiming at." A second reason is that they are, to a degree perhaps unmatched by other nineteenth-century American writers (even including Walt Whitman), what we might call process-oriented rather than product-oriented writers. We see this in many features of their careers. First, there is their reluctance to publish and hence to finalize any given text. That this is the case with Dickinson is so well-known as to make elaboration unnecessary, at least for now. As for Thoreau, although in his early career he was evidently eager to publish, he is notorious for the number of drafts (seven) through which he put *Walden*, while many later works as well remained unfinished at his death because of his preference for accretion as opposed to organization and completion (not to mention his apparent willingness, in his mature years, to mostly forego the approbation of his peers). Second, there is the authors' penchant for revision. This is evident in Dickinson's practice of providing variant words and phrases in the margins of poem drafts, many of which she worked at off and on for months and even years, and in Thoreau's habit of going back, sometimes years later, to Journal entries and confirming or negating hypotheses made therein.

At a subtler level, too, both writers reveal their commitment to revision in their willingness to stick to more or less the same subject matter (and, in Dickinson's case, the same form) throughout their careers, as if what they sought still eluded them after so many attempts, or as if they continued to find satisfaction, if not success, in performing variations on the same themes and method. Thus, Dickinson never strays far from the hymn or ballad meter to which she primarily confined her verse, and after 1850 Thoreau seldom departs from his work routine of walking and observing through the afternoon and writing up the results of his excursions and observations in the morning. Dickinson's predominant concerns—insofar as they can be excavated from beneath her experiments in language—continue throughout her career to be (among others) loss, love, time, death, God, immortality, and the abiding strangeness and intermittent closeness of nature. Thoreau becomes increasingly devoted to studying the cyclical processes of diurnal and seasonal change, which simultaneously lend to the Journal its structure and its freedom from structure, that is, its license to proceed non-hierarchically and endlessly, beginning anew with each new season, indeed with each new day. An endpoint, as François Specq observes in "Thoreau's Journal or the Workshop of Being," eludes him in the Journal not because he dies too soon but because it was in the nature of the Journal to lack an endpoint: "[the] Journal is premised on the notion that nature is forever unknowable, in the sense that it resists its fitting with or into boundaries and classifications. It structurally and thematically presents itself as an alternative to hierarchical organization of knowledge."[11]

A third reason why Dickinson and Thoreau are hard to place is that their writing tends toward implicitness, ambiguity, non-closure, and even, most strikingly, absence or negation, in particular absence or negation of meaning. This last feature of Dickinson's and Thoreau's writing, which I will elaborate on throughout this book, is the main characteristic of the mode of writing I have labeled "non-teleological." It is, I think, the cause rather than the effect of the two features described above (namely, their uncertain statements—and sense—of purpose, and their process-oriented bent). And it is tied, I will suggest, to these authors' manners of approaching not just writing but also experience, in particular experience of the natural world. Resisting interpretation—trying to encounter nature without attributing a particular meaning to the encounter or its object—is for Dickinson and Thoreau a recurring, not to say a constant, endeavor. It is an endeavor that can never be completed, and indeed one that it would not be desirable to complete, since part of its point is to bring into fruitful contact the human urge to make sense of things, on the one hand, and nature's opacity, its resistance to the imposition of meaning, on the other. If we find it impossible to finally classify Dickinson's and Thoreau's efforts, it is in large part because they point in opposite directions: toward meaning, and away from it. Their art, to quote some ambiguous lines of Paul Celan, is one of

> Pursuing
> meaning, fleeing
> meaning.[12]

Recently, John Michael has added to our understanding of the resistance to meaning in Dickinson's poetry. Along with Edgar Allan Poe and Whitman, he argues, Dickinson was one of the first American poets to register in her writing the effects of secularization, that is, the loss of "a reliable (or naïve) common belief in transcendent or spiritual realities."[13] Michael finds in Dickinson as in Poe and Whitman a commitment to a kind of non-teleological thinking and writing, which poses and provokes questions but provides no answers, and demonstrates the value inherent in the processes of language and thought, rather than compelling those processes to yield a demonstrably valuable product: "Each [of these poets] is very good at provoking thought but increasingly uninterested in delivering the results of thinking as meaning or truth. Reason can lead to meaning, and usually meaning's determination appears to be reasoning's end. These poets tend to resist the arrival at that end, the end of conclusion or certainty."[14] Because my focus will be on the application of this non-teleological poetics to Dickinson's descriptions of nature, which she wants both to represent and to leave alone in its non-signifying strangeness, I am more interested than Michael in the referential quality of Dickinson's writing. Whereas Michael describes how Dickinson "emphasizes the materiality of her words, the potentialities of the signifier, rather than their spiritual import or the delimitation of the signified,"[15] I find that in many poems the potentialities of the signifier, of the linguistic medium—its strangeness and unpredictability, its seeming autonomy of the writer herself—lends a quality of mystery and even of "spiritual import" to the signified, whether the signified is a physical object or a metaphysical one. While "delimitation of the signified" is clearly not the object of Dickinson's poems, neither do they dispense with the signified altogether. Michael seems to equate "meaning" with "certainty," or at least to suspect that the former leads all too quickly to the latter. For the average person and even the average writer, this may indeed be the case. But Dickinson is a writer for whom meaning begins—that is, for whom things become meaningful—when certainty ends; for whom, to borrow Celan's terms again, the pursuit of meaning and the flight from meaning are inseparable.

TELEOLOGICAL INTERPRETATIONS OF DICKINSON AND THOREAU

Whereas the present study seeks only to account for the difficulty of identifying the aims and accomplishments of Dickinson's poems and Thoreau's Journal, by tracing this difficulty to the authors' investment in a non-teleological poetics, much of recent Dickinson and Thoreau scholarship has been directed at trying to resolve the classification problem. That there is such a problem has been widely acknowledged in both fields. The Journal, Thoreau's two-million-word long record of witnessing, whose only consistent subject is nature and the mind in contact with nature, and whose making was arguably the author's chief occupation from around 1850 until his death in 1862, has not attracted extensive critical attention. Stanley Cavell, who mentions Thoreau's Journal only twice in his 1972 book *The Senses of Walden*, describes it both times as "mysterious," as though the Journal were as yet unexplored.[16] In a sense he was right. Although the high quality of its prose and its importance as source material for Thoreau's other works have long been recognized, the Journal's status as an integral work of literature remains ambiguous at best even now.

The first major attempt to unravel the mystery of the Journal was Sharon Cameron's 1985 study *Writing Nature: Henry Thoreau's* Journal.[17] According to Cameron, not only did "Thoreau c[o]me to think of the Journal as his central literary enterprise," he also succeeded in that enterprise sufficiently to produce "the great nineteenth-century American meditation on nature."[18] But the Journal defies readers and scholars, Cameron argues, because it refuses to subject nature to any organizing structure or vision, and refuses, in turn, to organize its own prose. "The wholeness of nature and the wholeness of the Journal," she writes, "will come to be identical. Yet Thoreau's idea of totality is . . . predicated not on connections but on the breaking of connections. In fact, discontinuity could be described as the Journal's dominant feature, for no thought is ever entirely jointed to or separated from any other thought."[19] Thoreau represents nature's "totality" and "wholeness" not by drawing connections between its parts and rendering a complete picture or interpretation of nature, but by foregoing the drawing of overarching connections and thus conveying the essential obscurity of nature, even as he records discrete perceptions of and insights into its operations. For Cameron, then, the mysterious, problematic quality of the Journal is not an accident, but rather an integral element of Thoreau's project: "The *Journal* itself prohibits the use of many interpretive procedures ordinarily taken for granted."[20]

Dickinson scholars have been similarly troubled by the apparent lack of an overall structure or trajectory uniting the nearly eighteen-hundred poems of Dickinson's oeuvre, as well as by the uncertainty clouding any attempt to define what these myriad short texts are collectively, primarily *about*, in both the formal sense of "concerned with" and the colloquial sense of "up to" or trying to accomplish. Although few critics today would openly state, as J. V. Cunningham did several decades ago, that Dickinson's poetry lacks "scope and structure," many would agree with him that "it is easier to hold in mind and sort out the plays of Shakespeare or the novels of George Eliot" than it is to hold in mind and sort out the poems of Dickinson.[21]

While scholars in both fields have considerably improved our understanding of Thoreau and Dickinson by trying to solve their respective problems, I believe that they have also made the mistake of glossing over or underestimating those problems, and in turn of offering inadequate solutions for them. The attempt to fill up the absence that we find when we look for and try to name the overarching goals of Dickinson's and Thoreau's writing is itself misguided, I would argue, since that absence or indeterminacy is an essential element of their writing.

Granted, we cannot say for certain that Dickinson or Thoreau intended their texts to lack definite goals (though paratextual statements found in Dickinson's letters and manuscripts and in Thoreau's Journal do support that view, as we've already begun to see). But we can say that there is a lack of sufficient grounds for drawing the kinds of conclusions that recent critics have drawn about Dickinson's and Thoreau's goals, and about the place in a culture, tradition, or discipline which the pursuit of such goals earn them. Performing that sort of negative survey of the criticism is the object of the present section. Once this has been done, the path should be cleared for the kind of textual analysis to be found in the ensuing chapters, which locate in Dickinson's poems and Thoreau's Journal a profound curiosity about nature's resistance to meaning, and a commitment to simultaneously honoring that resistance and bearing witness to nature's strange powers of fascination. For this fascination is, according to the texts under discussion, not the opposite of nature's resistance to meaning, but a function of it. What draws Thoreau and Dickinson to nature, in particular what attracts them as writers, is the allure of a meaningfulness which is always concealed and unexpressed, contingent and even, it may be, illusory. They learn from nature the complementarity of meaningfulness and meaninglessness, purposefulness and purposelessness, which is the principle on which their non-teleological poetics is premised.

Gary Lee Stonum opens his 1990 book *The Dickinson Sublime* by remarking that "An astonishing and apparently unprecedented gap exists between the certainty that [Dickinson] is a major poet and the uncertainty about what her business as a poet might be. . . . We remain particularly unable to define Dickinson's general literary enterprise or even to be certain that her poetry manifests any coherent set of aims and accomplishments."[22] Porter, a decade earlier, writes: "Although there are many instances of larger structures in her work, the norm is small segments rather than carefully organized contexts of magnitude. The body of 1775 poems is the exhibit of this fragmentation, defying most avenues of critical approach. It seems an extraordinary privation, this absence of any sustained, architecturally intricate, carefully unfolding poem."[23] In *Choosing Not Choosing: Reading Dickinson's Fascicles*, her second book on the poet, Sharon Cameron (like Stonum just before her) makes a formidable effort to overcome the hurdle to criticism that Stonum and Porter describe. She argues that Dickinson's fascicles, the forty hand-sewn packets in which she grouped over eight hundred of her poems, provide larger, organizing structures for her writing to inhabit. Through the construction of these fascicles, Cameron suggests, and through the less definitive construction of the "sets" containing three hundred more, unbound poems, Dickinson furnished posterity with a unique method of reading, interpreting, organizing, and puzzling over her life's work. Cameron goes so far as to say that poems of the same fascicle are not in fact discrete texts, both because "words that are variants are part of the poem outside of which they ostensibly lie," and because "poems in the same fascicle may sometimes be seen as variants of one another."[24] In this view—which, as Cameron emphasizes, calls into question the very identity of Dickinson's poems, by undermining the definiteness of their boundaries—each of the fascicles can perhaps be seen as Porter's "sustained, architecturally intricate, carefully unfolding poem." As Cameron puts it, "in Franklin's edition [i.e., *The Manuscript Books of Emily Dickinson*], the unit of sense is not the individual poem but rather the fascicle book."[25]

The sheer lack of evidence about Dickinson's intentions has made it hard for Cameron's argument to gain traction among subsequent critics. As Cameron would probably be the first to admit, one can read the poems of a fascicle as though they made up a single, meticulously designed unit, or not. Much insight and stimulus can be derived from the former approach, especially if one is allowed (though increasingly one is not) to sit down at the Harvard or Amherst archives in front of the actual booklet Dickinson created.[26] For it is hard to read a fascicle from cover to cover, as it were, without agreeing with Cameron that here is no random or convenient grouping, but a product of design, enabling a particular way of experiencing Dickinson's abrupt, enigmatic utterances. But, of course, much can also be gained from reading the poems as though each were a self-sufficient creation of its own, taking the poems' apparent absences to be significant, part of how the poems mean, rather than gaps that can be filled by knowledge of the fascicle context.

The fact that these two options are equally viable means that the fascicles, though rich grounds for the drawing of inferences, are not sufficient grounds on which to base conclusions about Dickinson's artistic goals. Even if one grants that the poems of a given fascicle function as a meaningful unit, one would still have to ask whether that is their primary function or a secondary one—whether, in other words, the poems' assembly as a fascicle did not occur after their identity as individual lyrics had already been established. Cameron herself remarks on "the extraordinarily complex, perhaps even conflicted, set of beliefs, intentions, and desires that are registered when Dickinson's poems are read in the fascicles in which she copied them."[27] Her book's title, *Choosing Not Choosing*, is meant partly to evoke Dickinson's decision not to make definite or obvious any decision she may have made with regard to her poems' textual identity, their ordering and relation to one another, or even (when we consider the variants) their wording. Despite Cameron's attempt to resolve this dilemma as far as the evidence will allow, we cannot finally know whether Dickinson's poems should be seen as permanently inhabiting the fascicles into which she sewed (some of) them, or whether they should be seen as simply squatting there.

A number of further examples of revisionist arguments about Dickinson could be cited; I will limit myself to mentioning four. Curiously, even as Thoreau-the-scientist is increasingly the figure one encounters in scholarly texts, at least one recent critic, Robin Peel, has asked whether Dickinson, too, might not be considered a scientist rather than a poet. "What happens," Peel asks, "if we shed all the assumptions we normally bring to the work of Emily Dickinson and read her not as a poet, but as a concealed natural philosopher/scientist, using parallel methodologies and inspired by the same questions as her contemporary scientists?" Undaunted by the possibility that this "might seem to be a ridiculous question, for which the answer is clearly no," Peel proposes to "asses[s] to what extent we might regard [Dickinson's] poems as scientific, and as examples of writing that partakes in a scientific discourse no less, or even more, than the religious or literary themes with which Dickinson's work is normally associated."[28]

How one answers Peel's question, or the question of whether the fascicles are in fact books, or Virginia Jackson's similarly assumption-shedding question (discussed below) as to whether Dickinson wrote lyric poems, is not the main point here. My contention is simply that it is unusual to find critics so radically divided in their judgments of a major author's work as to be unsure of what she wrote (books or lyric poems, or something else altogether?) or even of what discipline she worked in (literature or science?). This uncertainty is owing not just to the positive content of Dickinson's texts but also to the absence from those texts (as well as from the author's paratextual statements and interventions) of clear evidence of the author's intentions and goals.

Obviously, one does not expect from a poet a statement of purpose. But one does expect his or her poems to articulate—if only in the aggregate, once stock has been taken of their collective rhetorical or philosophical force—a certain orientation toward a tradition, that is, an inherited set of themes, concepts, symbols, and methods. A major writer is expected to contribute to the elaboration and development of these latter, and in such a way that his or her contribution can be meaningfully compared with the contributions of other writers in the same tradition. Unlike Jackson and Peel, respectively, I do not doubt that Dickinson's texts are lyric poems, or that her concerns are overwhelmingly literary and (in a broad sense) philosophical rather than scientific. Nonetheless, what she wanted her lyrics to accomplish—what she wanted finally to say with regard to such themes and concepts as death, love, sex, marriage, poetry, time, nature, God, Jesus, and the afterlife, as well as the motivation behind her choice of meter, stanza structure, and method of punctuation—is considerably more obscure to us than it is to readers of, say, William Wordsworth, or Gerard Manley Hopkins, or one of her own favorites, Elizabeth Barrett Browning. Consequently, we are unsure with which literary tradition, school of thought, discipline, or other cultural phenomenon Dickinson ought to be associated; debates over this question occupy us inordinately. This is what Porter calls "the central phenomenon" of Dickinson's poetry: "Although Dickinson is a major poet, she provided almost none of the expected discourse that our great poets have furnished."[29]

My third example of revisionist Dickinson scholarship warrants more extensive discussion than the previous one, because it has had a rather dramatic impact on its field. It is a remarkable and suggestive fact that in the twenty-first century a critical study of Dickinson can seriously pose the question "How do we know that Emily Dickinson wrote poems?"[30] The study I mean is Virginia Jackson's *Dickinson's Misery: A Theory of Lyric Reading*, which suggests that the obscurity and sense of absence pervading Dickinson's writing is owing not so much to the writing itself as to the way in which it has been willfully divorced from its originary scenes: the places in, the people, practices, and traditions among, and the things with which it was produced. According to Jackson, what is so often said of the grammatical and rhetorical structure of Dickinson's poems—that, as critics have variously put it, the poetry is "sceneless," is "a set of riddles" revolving around an "omitted center," is a poetry of "revoked . . . referentiality"—can more aptly be said of the representation of the poems as such. Once gathered as the previously ungathered, reclaimed as the abandoned, given the recognition they so long awaited, the poems in bound volumes appear both redeemed and revoked from their scenes or referents, from the history that the book, as book, omits.[31]

Jackson claims that Dickinson's poems have been wrested from their contexts and coerced into serving literary critics as exemplary—because contextless, ahistorical—lyrics, indeed as tools in the nineteenth and twentieth centuries' "lyricization of poetry." As a result, the peculiarities and intricacies of these texts' involvement in cultural phenomena, ranging from letter-writing and stationery to the variety of forms that the reading and writing of poetry took in mid-nineteenth-century America, have been glossed over, if not entirely lost sight of. The "contextless or sceneless, even evanescent nature of Dickinson's writing" is according to Jackson an "(only) apparently" accurate fiction used by editors, publishers, and critics to pigeonhole Dickinson as a lyric poet, in a way that reflects how in the nineteenth and twentieth centuries poetry as a whole was increasingly pigeonholed as lyric.[32] "Lyric," in this contentious view, refers less to a kind of writing than to a kind of reading: "From the mid-nineteenth through the beginning of the twenty-first century, to be lyric is to be read as lyric—and to be read as a lyric is to be printed and framed as a lyric."[33] More specifically, "whereas other poetic genres (epic, poems on affairs of state, georgic, pastoral, verse epistle, epitaph, elegy, satire) may remain embedded in specific historical occasions or narratives, and thus depend upon some description of those occasions and narratives for their interpretation," lyric poetry "is thought to require as its context only the occasion of its reading."[34] Lyric poems, in other words, are less the historically embedded creations of writers than they are the creation of readers who suppress, either deliberately or unwittingly, the histories of the texts that they read. Indeed, that act of suppression is for Jackson the quintessential feature of "lyric reading"; it is how poems become (known as) lyrics.

Jackson is right in saying that Dickinson's poems have suffered from readers' ignorance of their material, personal, and cultural contexts, as well as from critics' avoidance of the vexed questions that these contexts sometimes raise. But her argument that Dickinson's texts have been mislabeled as lyrics is undermined by the fact that, far from having been unequivocally welcomed into the lyric tradition, these poems troubled many critics and poets who approached them with the expectation that they would read like other lyrics, and who were not shy about announcing their dissatisfaction or perplexity when the poems did not. Yvor Winters criticized what he saw as Dickinson's "countrified eccentricity," "silly playfulness," ubiquitous "crudities," and penchant for "nonsense,"[35] while R. P. Blackmur accused her poems of possessing a quality of disjunctiveness, or "cruel freedom," so great that one could rearrange the lines of some poems "without [much] damage" to the sense.[36] Yet both critics (Winters more freely than Blackmur) professed deep admiration for some of her poems, and both made allusion to her "genius."[37] Jackson acknowledges such criticisms, but she seems, with some justification, to think them merely instances of academic gatekeeping, not serious responses to the difficulties and peculiarities of Dickinson's texts.[38] Thus, rather than giving Winters and Blackmur credit for noticing Dickinson's difference from other lyric poets, Jackson focuses on these critics' extravagant, though selective, praise of Dickinson's rare "lyric" qualities, in order to support her claim that Dickinson was forced into the role of lyric poet.

For example, in a discussion of Winters's close reading of "Further in Summer than the Birds" (F895), she writes that "the important thing about his formalist, somewhat picky reading of Dickinson is that its aim is to establish her as 'one of the greatest lyric poets of all time.'"[39] Certainly that is the important thing for Jackson, but it is not the only thing worth noting in Winters's reading. For Winters, as Jackson glancingly notes, does attend to the thorny details of Dickinson's poem: its unusual but "fine[ly] modulat[ed]" slant rhymes; the "meaningless inversion" of the line "Repose to typify"; its "intense strangeness"; and its "personal grammatical shorthand."[40] Winters, like the other New Critics Jackson singles out, had it wrong, perhaps, but he was seeing the same, difficult poems that Jackson sees, not the illusory, "retro-project[ed]"[41] Dickinson lyric that Jackson suggests he saw.

Blackmur also comes under fire in *Dickinson's Misery*: for "divorcing poetry from the sources of self-expression, rendering the poem a pure text to be read by the scientifically detached observer of linguistic 'facts'"; for "fiddl[ing] with [the] parts" of poems; and for treating Dickinson's texts as though their "intersubjective function" were "not to reflect Dickinson's own intellectual culture or to reflect the individual taste of the reader but to create academic culture" by providing grist for the "professional," "scientifically detached" reader's mill.[42] Yet Jackson's question "How do we know that lyrics are what Dickinson wrote?"[43] is very similar to the question that Blackmur raised in 1937: "Without benefit of comparative scholarship it is impossible to determine whether a given item is a finished poem, an early version of a poem, a note for a poem, a part of a poem, or a prose exclamation."[44] Such observations and complaints, which show that Dickinson has long been a problem or limit case in the lyric tradition, are strong counterevidence for Jackson's claim that Dickinson was pigeonholed as a lyric poet. Jackson, however, would argue that Winters's and Blackmur's criticisms express their frustration at the challenges Dickinson poses for "lyric reading." "For Winters," she writes, the poem beginning "Further in Summer than the Birds" (F895) "is an instance of Dickinson's lyric power, *not* the sort of thing that the public would appreciate, and the sort of poem Dickinson herself rarely achieved."[45] And Blackmur she faults for "want[ing] Dickinson to be a professional" (in his words, one who "control[s] the means of objective expression") and yet denying her right to that title.[46] Still, this is rather slippery grounds for a polemic, since what Jackson is saying and what her opponents are saying is strikingly similar: Dickinson's texts resist (or, pejoratively put, fail to consistently achieve) inclusion in the genre of lyric poetry. As for Jackson's description of lyric as an "abstract genre," it seems unlikely that Winters or Blackmur would have baulked at this, though of course they would have denied having "created" that genre.[47]

Jackson notes that more recent scholarly readers have celebrated rather than criticized the sceneless, centerless quality of Dickinson's poems of revoked referentiality. However, she sees this development as only a further instance of the "abstract personification" of Dickinson that the New Critics were guilty of.[48] It is hard to see what is gained by thus conflating negative or ambivalent mid-century assessments of Dickinson's poetry with positive late-century assessments. Whatever the limits of late twentieth-century critics, their more respectful efforts to identify and analyze the most difficult features of Dickinson's writing have made it possible to view her idiosyncrasies— which mid-century critics often attributed to naiveté, immaturity, perversity, or simple incompetence—in a new light. We acknowledge now, for instance, that what Blackmur considered Dickinson's "cruel freedom" and what Winters considered her susceptibility to nonsense are elements in her "word-centered" poetics,[49] which aims as much at an inquiry into language—especially language's double-edged relation to meaning—as it does at an inquiry into the world. Likewise, a contemporary critic such as Timothy Morris can now grant the truth of Blackmur's accusation that Dickinson "revolv[ed] in a vacuum," but at the same time explain this isolation as a deliberate effort to create a poetry turned in on itself:

> R. P. Blackmur accused Dickinson of "revolving in a vacuum" when she wrote her unconventional verse, and the accusation is true. She never adopted conventional technique, but started very early with something idiosyncratic and then revised her own idiosyncrasies.... Picasso is supposed to have said that he didn't care who influenced him, so long as he didn't influence himself. Dickinson proceeded oppositely; she was vigorously anti-eclectic.[50]

We do not need to agree with the New Critics' assessment of Dickinson, or with that of their successors, the post-structuralists, in order to grant that the features of her poetry which they struggled to describe and account for are indeed present in the poems.

Pace Jackson, such features as those just described have not always—even during the years when post-structuralism predominated among critical frameworks—been seen as exemplary of lyric. Equally if not more often, they've been considered marks of Dickinson's radical difference: her talent for coming perilously close to writing what aren't poems at all. Porter, for example, claims that "Dickinson wrote at the extremes of linguistic tolerance, and seemingly without a discernible reason for doing so";[51] that her poems often consist of "three or four dozen words at a threshold state of organization that can just barely be called a poetic event";[52] and that the poems have baffled and been ill-served by a critical industry which tends to view poetry as a vehicle for the expression of personal feeling rather than as a site of linguistic experimentation.[53] Howe considers Dickinson's poetics closest to that of Gertrude Stein, who like Dickinson "explored the implications of breaking the law just short of breaking off communication with a reader."[54] Even Cameron's *Lyric Time*, though it argues that Dickinson's poems bring into relief certain defining elements of lyric, suggests in its very subtitle that they nevertheless exist at "the limits of genre."[55]

Building upon these post-structuralism-influenced assessments, John Michael has recently argued that Dickinson's resistance to "the commonalities of sense that are sedimented into the common language," and even at times to "making sense altogether," far from being a mirage seen only by the anachronizing lyric reader, partakes of an important nineteenth-century trend which he calls "the secularization of the lyric," or alternatively, "the modernization of the poem." Along with Poe, Whitman, and other writers of the "secular lyric," Dickinson "employs language as the vehicle of thinking that seeks to disrupt what is commonly thought," thus "tak[ing] a distance from meaning and truth as commonly understood."[56] In this view, to deny or gloss over the fact that Dickinson's writing was, as Michael affirms (speaking of Poe and Whitman as well as of Dickinson), "often purposively at odds with traditional genres and the expectations they represented, including the lyric traditions that they took as their points of departure,"[57] is anachronistic in its own way. For "in certain circles" in nineteenth-century America, England, and Europe, "poetry was quickly modernizing in the sense that it was becoming particularly lyric in the modern sense that [Virginia] Jackson and others criticize."[58] In a later chapter Michael elaborates on what the modernization of lyric meant for Dickinson: "Lyric offers Dickinson, as it did Poe and Whitman, a means of engaging with and resisting the discourses of the world on the fundamental levels of signification and significance, on the fundamental level of language and the materiality of the sign."[59] If Dickinson matters to us today, then, it is not because lyric readers have wrested her verses from the mid-nineteenth century into modernity, but, in part, because she herself helped to wrest poetry from its nineteenth-century condition into its present, lyric condition. If her poetry can in fact be called quintessentially lyric, it is in the special sense that lyric itself, at least for readers of such challenging modern poets as Hart Crane, Paul Celan, and Susan Howe (each of whom acknowledged Dickinson's influence), has come to be associated with the irreducibly strange—that which engages with "the discourses of the world" but at the same time resists those discourses "on the fundamental levels of signification and significance." It is a kind of writing that, in Dickinson's metaphor, "ha[s] no Tribunal" (L265), no final justification besides the author's wit and whim for being the way it is.

My fourth and last example of revisionist Dickinson scholarship, Cristanne Miller's *Reading in Time: Dickinson in the Nineteenth Century*, is perhaps the most representative, since it exemplifies more than Jackson's theoretical polemic does the historicism that is arguably the dominant mode of Dickinson criticism today. One of the main contentions of this criticism has been that despite her physical seclusion, Dickinson was deeply, if subtly, engaged with contemporary culture and politics, read avidly and clipped frequently from newspapers and magazines, and conducted an extensive and vibrant correspondence with friends, relatives, and neighbors—a correspondence that often served as the context or referential framework of her poems, many of which appeared at one time as either enclosures or as passages embedded within the text of a letter. To these claims, Miller adds the more controversial idea that Dickinson was not as original and innovative as we had thought, or rather, that her originality and innovations partook of a well-established nineteenth-century poetic tradition that valued "wildness" in verse, and viewed poetry as a vehicle for experiments in sound, rhythm, and rhyme as well as a vehicle for the subjective expression of thought and sentiment. Miller writes:

> Antebellum American verse cherished originality, often described as wildness, and encouraged what we might call a fluid relationship between European or traditional forms and innovative poetic practice. Dickinson grew up reading poetry of (for that time) experimental and at times markedly irregular forms; her own numerous variations from standard ballad and hymn meter are in tune with this aspect of her contemporaries' poetry, although they push farther in the degree and frequency of the irregularity and combine these features with a strikingly original compression of syntax and meaning.[60]

I will return to Miller's book (as well as to her earlier study *Emily Dickinson: A Poet's Grammar*) in later discussions. For now, I am interested chiefly in pointing out a similarity in the thrust of its argument with the thrust of Laura Dassow Walls's argument in *Seeing New Worlds: Henry David Thoreau and Nineteenth-Century Natural Science*, which has set the tone for Thoreau criticism of the last two and a half decades. It is striking, and even a little alarming, that Miller and Walls, two of the most prominent contemporary scholars of Dickinson and Thoreau, respectively, both characterize these least imitative of authors as, for all their "distinct[ness],"[61] writers working from "models." Thoreau's "reconciliation" of "the idealist's move" toward universal principles with "the limited and methodically realized aims of the scientist's methods," Walls argues, was "modelled for him by much of the discourse of the time, which sought to bring together polar opposites into new, progressive, higher unities."[62] Miller, somewhat more trenchantly, describes Dickinson as having "exaggerat[ed] . . . her individuality," and warns readers against "seeing her as unique or anomalous to a culture that in fact seems to have provided her with profuse and powerful models."[63]

Although there is truth in both of these statements, they can be misleading if taken to mean that the preexistence of "reconciliation[s]" between idealist vision and scientific methods, or of innovative verse forms and techniques, explains the existence of Dickinson's and Thoreau's writings. For the claim that Thoreau and Dickinson are sui generis figures does not rest solely on the fact that Thoreau employed scientific techniques in his study of what he calls "the higher law" (PJ 5:469, 3/5/53), or on the fact that Dickinson produced irregular "variations" on "standard ballad and hymn meter."

Walls and Miller both try to solve the problem of Thoreau's and Dickinson's resistance to classification by finding parallels between their methods and endeavors and those of contemporary writers and thinkers. (Walls goes so far as to name the category to which Thoreau belongs: he is "a Humboldtian naturalist," she avers.)[64] In doing so, however, they open themselves and their readers up to a bias against dwelling on whatever is strange, unaccountable, or unclassifiable in these authors' work. What Thoreau and Dickinson have in common with their contemporaries is foregrounded, while their deviations are downplayed as being differences in degree rather than in kind—a matter of "push[ing] farther in the degree and frequency of the irregularity," to use Miller's phrase. As Michael puts it, discussing a number of historicist readings of Dickinson, Poe, and Whitman (including Jackson's and Miller's readings of Dickinson),

> there is in each of these readings a tendency to normalize the poets discussed by demonstrating how they exemplify generic features and publishing practices typical of their time.... But focusing on the anachronisms of lyric reading and the ways it can vitiate a contemporary reader's appreciation of the occasional, sentimental, elegiac, and political aspects of nineteenth-century poetry, can, in turn, obscure the abiding strangeness of the poetry that Poe, Whitman, and Dickinson wrote, and that only a close consideration of their idiosyncratic language can capture.[65]

Some of us will be persuaded by Miller's version of Dickinson and Walls's version of Thoreau: here at last, it may seem, is "Dickinson *in* the Nineteenth Century," "Thoreau *and* [the] Nineteenth-Century Natural Science" which served him as both impetus and goal. Others, though, will feel that revolutionary figures are being passed off as merely prominent contemporaries: contributors rather than originators. Some will even feel that weariness which Samuel Beckett describes: a weariness of art that consists "of pretending to be able, of being able, of doing a little better the same old thing, of going a little further along a dreary road."[66]

The parallel between Miller's and Walls's claims is reflective of a broader consensus among contemporary Dickinson and Thoreau scholars. Arguments such as Miller's and Jackson's—with which recent work by scholars such as Alexandra Socarides, Martha Nell Smith, Vivian Pollak, and Mary Loeffelholz may be loosely grouped, given these writer's shared investment in tracing links between Dickinson's poetry and nineteenth-century history and culture—have much in common with the claims made by such Thoreau scholars as Walls, William Rossi, Bradley Dean, Kristen Case, and Henrik Otterberg. The latter group sees Thoreau's seemingly exceptional blend of poetic (or idealist, or transcendentalist) and scientific sensibilities as responsive to and reflective of the diverse ways in which science was practiced in the nineteenth century, when the "two cultures," science and the humanities, had not yet definitely parted ways. Thus Rossi, in an article titled "Thoreau's Transcendental Ecocentrism," acknowledges that "the sort of 'science' Thoreau sought to practice [in 1851] was one that, contrary to the positivist trend gaining ground in professional science, persisted in referring 'phenomena to the human situation.'" But "oddly enough," Rossi contends, "Thoreau's twin commitment to the metaphysics of correspondence and to a densely empirical knowledge of nature positioned him at the flashpoint of attempts to radically reconceive relations between physical and 'moral' nature."[67]

Likewise Bradley Dean, editor of two collections of Thoreau's late natural history writings, points out that Thoreau's crucial decision to minutely study the phenomena of seasonal change was apparently formed in 1851, the same year that "the Smithsonian Institute sent to scientists across the country a circular titled 'Registry of Periodical Phenomena,' which invited 'all persons who may have it in their power, to record their observations [of "periodical phenomena of Animal and Vegetable life"], and to transmit them to the Institution.'"[68] Whether or not this was coincidental, scholarship such as Dean's shows that Thoreau's decision to make a laborious record of his nature-observing was not in itself extraordinary for a man of letters in mid-nineteenth-century America. However, the decision to make such a record his "central literary enterprise,"[69] devoting the bulk of his time and energy to it for over a decade, after having begun his career as a poet and the author of two meticulously constructed books of lyrical prose, is one that did, and still does, set Thoreau apart. It is a decision that remains mysterious to us, and so demands further inquiry.

Arguments about Dickinson such as Cameron's, Peel's, and Jackson's, and the profound hermeneutic uncertainty that they reflect, are on a par with the claim recently put forth by Kristen Case and Henrik Otterberg, a claim that reflects a similar uncertainty about how, and why, to read the Journal. According to these scholars, the production of Thoreau's Kalendar was the Journal's "goal" and a "crucial part of its rationale,"[70] for it was the final stage of the "comprehensive process" of which the Journal was a "par[t]."[71] The Kalendar (so named by Thoreau himself) condenses several years' worth of observations into several dozen lists and charts of briefly described data points, allowing the writer and his future readers to compare the dates on which various natural phenomena, described in both objective and subjective terms, occurred across several years. The fact that it is manifestly incomplete obliges Case and Otterberg to qualify their claims for the Kalendar's importance, but it also allows them to speculate about what the Kalendar "would be" had Thoreau not died at the age of forty-four. If the charts presented by Case in her internet archive of Thoreau's "phenological manuscripts" seem insufficient to account for or provide "a crucial part of [the] rationale" for the Journal's seven-thousand pages, we are reminded in the archive's introduction that while "we can't know exactly what Thoreau's intent was for the Kalendar project, [the] evidence supports Dean's view that the Kalendar would be a massive work tracking Concord's seasonal phenomena through an 'archetypal' year, organized, like *Wild Fruits* and *The Book of the Seasons*, as a sort of encyclopedia."[72]

Notwithstanding such disclaimers and speculations, and depending on whether one defines the "Kalendar" as a set of charts or as a "massive" but unfinished project, the claim that the Journal was meant to eventuate in the Kalendar begs the question of the Journal's *intrinsic* worth; it rests the justification for a literary text/project (the Journal) on a non-literary text/project (the Kalendar). The inordinate importance attributed to the Kalendar is thus a prime instance of the teleological, product-oriented bent of criticism on the Journal. Of what other major author could it be said that thousands of pages of his or her prose, rather than constituting its own, "isolated wor[k],"[73] is only one part of another, more important project?

What this ends-oriented approach to the Journal seems to discourage is close textual analysis of individual Journal passages—as if to perform this kind of open-ended analysis were to second-guess Thoreau's own judgment about what use should be made of his writing; to treat as final and self-sufficient what was for him intermediate. That there is on the contrary much to be learned about Thoreau's understanding of and relationship with nature from doing close readings of the Journal, as well as about the possibilities for achieving poetic effects by means of prose, not to mention much to be gained in the way of aesthetic enjoyment, is one of the things the present study hopes to prove.

Whereas Case and Otterberg seem to value the Kalendar equally with if not more than the Journal (or at least, to make the Journal's value contingent on that of the Kalendar), in that they view the Journal as fragmentary and the Kalendar as tending to a whole ("a sort of encyclopedia"), H. Daniel Peck seems to take the opposite view:

> The charts Thoreau drew up between 1860 and 1862 (his Kalendar) are the literal expression and outcome of his effort to create a truer calendar, but these fragmentary documents are merely a token of what he was trying to achieve. The Journal itself is the calendar that Thoreau actually made, and to understand its purposes we must turn to its daily business of revising the seasons.[74]

Still, like Case and Otterberg, Peck effectively denies the self-sufficiency of the writing of the Journal, and instead describes its parts—which is to say, the sentences actually comprising the Journal—as opposed in form and nature to the whole toward which they vainly aspire: "The Journal—so open and apparently provisional in form—always awaits closure, which, because of the immensity (and ultimate impossibility) of the task, never comes. Yet, despite its provisional form, the Journal's overriding object is closure."[75] This statement, which boils down to the claim that the Journal has an "overriding object" which it fails to achieve, is strikingly similar to the one that Otterberg makes two decades later: "The apparent formlessness of his later Journal conceals a crucial aspect of its larger rationale, one that is easy to forget. Thoreau had as his explicit, if admittedly long-term, goal to compile a comprehensive phenological 'Kalendar' of the natural events taking place in Concord and its environs."[76]

Walls, too, characterizes the Journal as a preliminary or auxiliary work. Much as scholars of an earlier generation agreed that the Journal served

Thoreau as a place in which to draft material that could then be used in published works such as *Walden*, Walls sees the Journal—both the daily practice of making it and the observations and insights it records—as the chief source on which Thoreau drew when he finally came to write his mature works of natural history. If on one page she acknowledges the "value of the *Journal* as an accumulating timescape of experience in the land, coherent by virtue of its totality,"[77] on the next she undercuts that value by representing the Journal as merely a preliminary stage in the production of "clusters" of scientific writing that were the true focus of his late career:

> As Thoreau admitted in a letter of 1856, "I am drawing a rather long bow." It would take years of dedicated labor before he could have much to show. But by 1860, he was forming the mass of writing around a series of clusters, and beginning to draft his answer to what would come after *Walden*.[78]

This paints a rather sad picture of Thoreau's career, given that in 1860 he had only two years more to live. In her more recent work, Walls's view of the Journal as the precursor or supplement to something greater is still apparent, even as she continues to refer to its intrinsic value:

> Without announcing it, Thoreau simply stopped using his Journal as the means to the "real" work of art somewhere else, and started treating the Journal *itself* as the work of art, with all the integrity that art demands. Or, perhaps all the integrity that *science* demands: in this new mode, his Journal volumes were something like scientific notebooks, laboratory records whose value lay precisely in their regularity and completeness.[79]

This contradictory passage reflects a larger trend in Thoreau criticism, of simultaneously acknowledging the Journal's artistry and ascribing a scientific function to that artistry. Also symptomatically, it posits that the Journal can be viewed as "a work of art" without going on to defend or explore the implications of that claim. Indeed, Walls here immediately seems to change her mind about the Journal being an artwork, preferring instead to compare it to "scientific notebooks" that depend for their value on their "regularity and completeness." Yet Thoreau, as we've begun to see, has a different idea of completeness than the scientist's. For him, even irregular, fragmentary outbursts of the writer's feeling for his subject—"unconsidered expressions of our delight which any natural object draws from us"—possess a quality of being "complete and final in themselves," regardless of the role they might play in a larger record (J 14:117, 10/13/60).

NON-TELEOLOGICAL INTERPRETATIONS OF DICKINSON AND THOREAU

Both of the sets of arguments I've been describing, those concerning Thoreau and those concerning Dickinson, have obvious merit in that they illuminate the important connections between what Dickinson and Thoreau were doing and writing and what was being done and written around them. Dickinson, for instance, had good reason to think that she was not alone in conceiving of poetry as governed in part by abrupt, indeed "spasmodic," "Bolts – of Melody" rather than by orderly, stylistically genteel narratives or arguments. And Thoreau was, we now see, clearly interested in contributing to the scientific thought of his day, even if he was not, or not always, willing to abide by scientific norms or to pursue scientific discoveries that would be recognizable as such. For example, his lecture on "The Succession of Forest Trees," one of the texts found in Bradley Dean's edition of Thoreau's "late natural history writings,"[80] had a clear, immediate objective: to change its audience's ideas about and behaviors toward the nascent, endangered forests which, Thoreau warned, were growing unsuspected beneath their feet and next to their more cherished farmland.[81]

However, by focusing attention on the historical, contextualized Dickinson and Thoreau, the critics named above downplay, ignore, and in some cases deny other aspects of these author's work—as Jackson does when she claims that absence and elision are not so much features of Dickinson's writing as they are features of its presentation in books and critical studies.[82] While there are bound to be, so to speak, several different Emily Dickinsons and several different Henry David Thoreaus, it is not necessary that these figures be presented as mutually exclusive. There is no reason why "Dickinson in the Nineteenth Century" cannot coexist in our imaginations with the Dickinson who inaugurated what Porter calls "the modern idiom," and who named as her "Books" not contemporary Americans but "For Poets . . . Keats – and Mr and Mrs Browning. For Prose – Mr Ruskin – Sir Thomas Browne – and the Revelations," while as her "Companions" she named "my Lexicon," "Hills . . . and the Sundown – and a Dog – large as myself" (L261). Nor should knowledge of "Thoreau and Nineteenth-Century Natural Science" prevent us from learning more about the Thoreau who, when asked to describe his studies to the Association for the Advancement of Science, reflected that "a true account of my relation to nature should excite their ridicule only" (PJ 5:470, 3/5/53), and who considered the work on which he embarked at the start of the 1850s to be without precedent, indeed without definite boundaries and aims: "I do not know where to find in any literature whether ancient or modern–any adequate account of that Nature with which I am acquainted" (PJ 4:50–51, 9/7/51). As John Hildebidle argues in *Thoreau: A Naturalist's Liberty*, those who complain about Thoreau's shortcomings as a naturalist or scientist—in particular, about his failure to write an American version of Gilbert White's ever-popular *The Natural History of Selborne*—forget "how little Thoreau wanted to write a book *like* anyone else's."[83]

Although it is a truism to say that Thoreau and Dickinson were complex figures who, in Whitman's phrase, contained multitudes, recent scholarship seems increasingly one-sided in its depiction of the two writers. Versions of Thoreau and of Dickinson that an earlier generation of critics worked hard to reveal are ill-served by this bias: The Dickinson who "choos[es] not choosing," and so leaves her life's work in a state of permanent indeterminacy, its meanings always coming up against the limits of meaning (and of genre). The Thoreau who exchanges the vast ambitions of his fellow transcendentalists not for the equally vast ambitions of his scientifically-minded contemporaries, but for a kind of ambitionless writing which seems so assured of its own, immediate significance as to have no need of an audience, let alone an overarching goal. The Dickinson to whom "All men say 'What'" (L271), and in whose letters one finds not just evidence of passionate involvement in other people's lives, but also passages that are "the equivalent of shutting a door in the reader's face."[84] The Thoreau whose beau idéal is "sauntering," a kind of walking, thinking, and writing that by being landless (*sans terre*) reaches the Holy Land (*Sainte Terre*).[85] In reexamining these strange figures whose strangeness has become all-too familiar, the present study aspires to effect some modest version of what Stanley Cavell describes as the uncanny return of the familiar. Cavell's assertion that "what returns after skepticism"—in this case, skepticism about these author's profound, even disturbing originality—"is never (just) the same," gives me hope that such a "return" will be illuminating rather than irritating.[86] In particular, I think that a study which takes as its chief point of departure not the historicist approach of recent critics, but the language-centered approach of writers like Cameron, Cavell, Porter, and Howe, who attend to the mysteriously open-ended, deviant nature of Dickinson's and Thoreau's language rather than to its dialogic involvement in contemporary discourse, is likely to generate new insights into *how* these authors' texts mean, as opposed to *what* they meant to contemporary readers and therefore should mean (or so the argument goes) to us.

Howe's claim that Dickinson sought access to "an order beyond gender," for instance, while potentially antithetical to much of feminist criticism, is one that Dickinson critics still stand to learn from.[87] Her insight about Dickinson "being eternally on intellectual borders"[88] is weakened by subsequent claims that she was on the contrary in the thick of an alternative, less exclusionary tradition, whether this tradition is called epistolary verse, "versifying and verse-reading culture,"[89] "spasmodic" poetry,[90] "the counter-Sublime,"[91] or even simply "women's writing." Consider, for example, how Miller's deft survey of Dickinson's versatile and inventive language use yields, at an introductory chapter's end, a surprisingly reductive notion of what Dickinson was using her language, and the "linguistic and psychological freedom" it provided, for:

> Multiplicity, indeterminacy, and a fluctuating tone provide the poet with the linguistic and psychological freedom she needs to express, or inscribe, herself. Dickinson sees her place in the world primarily in terms of contrasting and shifting polarities. She—as daughter, woman, person uninvolved in the public sphere, female poet—has relatively little power, strength, or independence. In this capacity she speaks either defiantly and defensively or with longing. She resents her position, and she desires the enabling approval of the withheld love and power (in the drama of her poems, at least metaphorically male). Yet at the same time—again as daughter, woman, poet—she knows the responsibility of her daily tasks and the power of her voice. She speaks with authority, in pure essence, or else carefully, with the "infirm Delight" or outright suspicion of her audience in mind.[92]

The twin questions "Why does Dickinson write?" and "Why does she write as she does?" are answered too easily here, because there is a preexisting (though, in the nineteenth century, still nascent) tradition of female self-expression, "defian[ce]," and "resent[ment]" by which her writing can be framed. Against this vision of continuity between Dickinson's writing and her gender-specific positions ("daughter, woman, person uninvolved in the public sphere, female poet") and attitudes ("defian[t]," "defensiv[e]," "longing," "resent[ful]"; "authorit[ative]," "carefu[l]," "suspicio[us]"), Howe, two years earlier, writes:

> Yes, gender difference does affect our use of language, and we constantly confront issues of difference, distance, and absence, when we write. That doesn't mean I can relegate women to what we "should" or "must" be doing. Orders suggest hierarchy and category. Categories and hierarchies suggest property. My voice formed from my life belongs to no one else. What I put into words is no longer my possession. Possibility has opened. The future will forget, erase, or recollect and deconstruct every poem. There is a mystic separation between poetic vision and ordinary living. The conditions for poetry rest outside each life at a miraculous reach indifferent to worldly chronology.[93]

Whether or not one shares Howe's theory of "a mystic separation" between poetry and ordinary life, in practice this way of thinking permits readers a much greater degree of open-mindedness about the values and frames of reference of Dickinson's poems. For a critic such as Howe, Dickinson's words are allowed to mean much more, as well as much less, than they appear to mean for a critic such as Miller.

Porter's *Dickinson: The Modern Idiom* is one of the very few works of scholarship to receive approving mention in *My Emily Dickinson* (a fact that alone should make us question the common misconception that Porter's assessment of Dickinson's poetry is a negative one). Porter's decision to align Dickinson with poets who would not arrive till long after her death rather than with her contemporaries, and so to emphasize her indefinite place in any tradition (Howe's "worldly chronology") available to her, is a useful counterbalance to the current conception of Dickinson. As we've seen, today she is typically represented by critics as a writer steeped in nineteenth-century literary culture, answering its call for sociability, for an epistolary poetics, and/or for a "wilding," sound-oriented poetics, rather than refusing its demands for communication, cogency, and closure. While this new representation is justified to some extent by the historical and biographical evidence, the textual evidence more plainly justifies Porter's emphasis on what Harold Bloom calls Dickinson's "cognitive originality."[94] This Dickinson creates "strangely abstracted images" that can't be imagined.[95] She allows linguistic oddities—"Hostiler"; "passiver"; "opon"—to "begin the tilt into an alien world where old meanings do not apply, and the old consciousness must be super alert."[96] In her poetry "meaning, if such a word is even applicable here . . . lies almost completely within the enclosure of language."[97] This language-centric Dickinson—a performer, in Porter's phrase, of "language pyrotechnics"—is not quite the poet I see, as subsequent chapters will clarify.[98] But it provides a starting point from which to develop the argument I have to make about Dickinson. Her language experiments do indeed cause a "tilt" away from "old meanings," or what she calls "Ordinary Meanings" (F446), "into an alien world," but this movement is recursive rather than final; it is accompanied by a movement back to the ordinary, which as Cavell suggests is never quite the same upon return. Even the coinages Porter singles out, "Hostiler" and "passiver," are not so strange as to deflect attention entirely from what they obviously mean, namely, "more hostile" and "more passive." Such words, combined with Dickinson's inimitable syntax, point in two different directions: back (or inward) to their alien origins in a mind closed to us, and forward (or outward) to the familiar world. I will try to show that these two functions of Dickinson's language are often hard to distinguish from one another. The simplest assertions and references have something "tilt[ed]" or "slant" about them (F1263); indeed, their very simplicity makes us wonder what they are doing in the pages of this least simple of poets, punctuated (both literally and figuratively) by subtle signs of weirdness. "The Birds begun at Four o'clock" almost sounds like how a poem by Henry Wadsworth Longfellow might have opened, except that one cannot help but stumble over the solecism of "The Birds *begun*" (F504). Another nineteenth-century poet might start a poem by noting (without the hyphens, of course) that "The Mountains – grow unnoticed" (F768), but probably one would not suspect him or her, as one does Dickinson, of a paradoxical double entendre. Does the line mean simply that the mountains become unnoticed, or does it also claim, paradoxically, that the mountains become greater and more significant—*grow*, in the intransitive sense—the more we ignore them? These are not examples of a poet bracketing or sidestepping reality in order to perform "language pyrotechnics." Rather, the linguistic oddities serve to call attention—a slant, uneasy, puzzling attention—to reality, especially its "unnoticed" aspects: things like mountains and birdsong, which by their very obviousness tend to escape detection by the mind, if not by the senses. If in Dickinson one is uncertain "if such a word [as 'meaning'] is even applicable," it is not because her poetry is anti-mimetic, but on the contrary because it speaks of a world that produces the same uncertainty: is meaning applicable or extraneous, a more or less accurate interpretation, or an imposition?

Finally, the major contribution of Cameron's *Writing Nature* was to articulate a vision of the Journal as occupying, or trying to occupy, a different plane than that of all other literary texts, indeed than that of all other cultural enterprises. It not only raises but "redefin[es]" fundamental questions about the function and purpose of literature and the tripartite relationship between author, subject, and audience. "The Journal," she writes, "seems single-mindedly to be redefining not only the idea of a vocation or the function of journal-writing, but the following contingent questions: How am I to understand my subject (my relation to nature) when it is unmediated by a social context? If I were truly separate from mankind, and could consider nature in isolation, to whom would I be speaking?"[99] Yet this vision has been succeeded by a number of arguments that more or less ignore the difficulty—at least, the artistic aspect of the difficulty—that Thoreau faced, namely, how to put nature into a book without either manipulating nature or making the book totally unreadable, inaccessible to an audience. Instead, these arguments cast the Journal as a well-functioning tool and/or product of Thoreau's scientific investigations—or, as Peck would have it, of his aesthetic and epistemological endeavor to create a complete "picture of the world" by, as it were, taking and cross-referencing an endless series of snapshots.[100] The alternately boring, disorienting, and thrilling effect this text can have on readers, given its author's persistent sense of nature as resistant to interpretation and to incorporation within narrative, rhetorical, and epistemological structures, has been largely overlooked by recent critics, who celebrate instead the Journal's—and, by extension, nature's—usefulness for Thoreau as a writer, a scientist, and a thinker. In response to and anticipation of this teleological interpretation of the Journal, Cameron writes:

> One of the difficulties of regarding the *Journal* as draft material for *Walden* or for Thoreau's other writings (this is the way it is customarily considered) is that such a view fails to see the ways in which, though used for the published writings, the *Journal* is not, in fact, a version of the same enterprise, either inferior or superior to it, but attempts something different. . . . it seeks to discover alternative orders of significance.[101]

That "something different," those "alternative orders of significance," have much to do with the category of writing and experience that I call non-teleological: writing and experience that falls through the cracks, so to speak, of our genres and concepts, our traditions and careers.

What Howe, Porter, and Cameron have still to teach us, then, is not just the strangeness of Dickinson and Thoreau, but also their strong non-teleological bent, which is to say, their aversion to goals, to programs, to traditions—in short, to the available "orders of significance"—and their attraction to the astounding absence of such things in the natural world. Discussion of this last feature, however, is largely absent from these critics' studies of Dickinson, whose fascination with nature has been more closely examined by critics such as Joanna Feit Deihl, Anne-Lise François, and Paul Fry. In the following chapters I contend that both Dickinson and Thoreau recognize nature's alienness as a problem for humans in general and for writers in particular, but that instead of trying to solve or avoid this problem they foreground it, making the most, as it were, of what they don't know—in Thoreau's phrase, making of that insufficiency "a novel & grand surprise" (PJ 3:198, 2/27/51). Nature's resistance to meaning is therefore both their subject and their model, as the remarks quoted at the start of this chapter indicate. Thoreau says he wants to "attai[n] to" the obscurity of Walden Pond, whose ice when cut up for sale was undervalued because of its peculiar color (W 18:581). And Dickinson says that "Nature is a Haunted House – but Art – a House that tries to be haunted" (L459a). Thoreau and Dickinson try to make meaningful both nature's refusal to mean (at least in any way we're prepared to recognize: "Nature puts no question and answers none which we mortals ask" [W 16:547]) and their own refusal or inability to interpret nature.

CHAPTER 2

"Distance – be her only Motion"
Dickinson's Poetics

Nowadays it is not only my habit, it is also to my taste—a malicious taste, perhaps?—no longer to write anything which does not reduce to despair every sort of man who is 'in a hurry'. For philology is that venerable art which demands of its votaries one thing above all: to go aside, to take time, to become still, to become slow—it is a goldsmith's art and connoisseurship of the *word* which has nothing but delicate, cautious work to do and achieves nothing if it does not achieve it *lento*.

—Friedrich Nietzsche, *Daybreak*

Every word is a bias or inclination, Nietzsche said, and so every word, as a prejudgment, is already a slant, even as all truth should be told slant, according to Dickinson.

—Harold Bloom, *The Western Canon*

A "WORD-CENTERED" POETRY

Critics have long noticed a tension between the disjunctive, elliptical, and fragmentary quality of Emily Dickinson's language—what David Porter aptly describes as its "word-centered" quality[1]—and the poet's accustomed tone of seriousness, heightened emotion, and rhetorical urgency. Dickinson wants to let language speak for itself as much as possible—to leave the words of her poems to their own devices, as it were—but also marshals her strangely independent, centrifugal words to greatest rhetorical effect. The poet's object is to "Distil[l] amazing sense / From Ordinary Meanings" (F446). The poet's method is to isolate and foreground the units of sense, rather than to combine them in such a way as to make the units themselves—the linguistic instrument—transparent. This ambivalent combination of grandeur and fragmentation is Dickinson's version of the non-teleological mode. It is a poetics without a destination, which nonetheless is forever arriving, because in the absence of a telos, a hoped-for revelation or semantic achievement, each of the individual lines (in some cases, of the individual words) comprising Dickinson's poems are almost equally open to being read as revelatory, climactic, "amazing."

"Non-teleological" characterizes Dickinson's thinking about nature as well as her language use. Like Thoreau, Dickinson applies a special kind of pressure to ordinary objects and phenomena. Her poems would have us believe that this pressure or tension is intrinsic to ordinary things, as if they were straining to express themselves, yet also determined to stay concealed, unspent. In the poem beginning "The Tint I cannot take – is best" (F696), she describes this ambiguous impression:

> The eager look – on Landscapes –
> As if they just repressed
> Some secret – that was pushing
> Like Chariots – in the Vest –

It can hardly be a coincidence that in describing the landscape's "secret" Dickinson should use such a bizarre metonymical construction as "pushing / Like Chariots – in the Vest." Why "Vest" and not (since the point is presumably to compare the tension and pressure in the secretive landscape to the tension and pressure of a fast-beating heart) "Breast"? And why would Dickinson describe chariots as "pushing" when she knows that chariots are pulled? The language trips you up just as the poem's point is becoming clear. And this turns out to be itself the point, or part of it: if Dickinson's poems have strong arguments to make, they are at least equally committed to making us stumble over the words from which the arguments are made. We stumble over the word "pushing," for example, which Dickinson insists on applying to an object—chariots—without agency or volition. And we stumble over "Vest":

why did Dickinson choose this potentially bathetic term instead of the readily available rhyme-words *Breast* and *Chest*? Perhaps she was attracted to *Vest* because its closeness to *West* appropriately blurs the line between internal and external, the landscape of the self and the natural landscape. (She may also have wanted to evoke the word *veldt*.) There is an aptness, too, in Dickinson's using clothing as a metonym for the body and the soul. The landscape should be a point of arrival for the eye, yielding up what nature has to offer; but this is no more the case, Dickinson hints, than it is the case that the body once stripped of its clothing, or the mind and heart once freed from societal constraints, yield the contents of the self. The breast is just another kind of vest.

Cristanne Miller, at the start of *Emily Dickinson: A Poet's Grammar*, identifies the same tension in Dickinson's poetry that I have begun to describe. "One of the primary difficulties for the modern reader of Dickinson's poetry," she writes,

> is to understand [the] tension between the poet's partially articulated desire to speak to an audience, to move her reader, and her largely unarticulated decision to write the riddling, elliptical poetry she does. This tension, however, is at the root of the peculiar urgency in Dickinson's poems. Dickinson writes as she does because of a combination of factors: her belief in the extraordinary power of language, her responses to the language she reads in mid-nineteenth-century America, and her sense of herself as woman and poet.[2]

Setting aside the second and third factors Miller mentions, I will be focusing here on the first factor: Dickinson's "belief in the extraordinary power of language," even or especially language deprived of a context and of a conventional grammatical structure. Indeed, for Dickinson, it seems, the power of language was such that certain words repelled context, shaking off the organizing constraints imposed by narrative, logic, and grammar. Miller quotes a fascinating remark from the poet's correspondence (transcribed by her childhood friend Joseph Lyman): "We used to think, Joseph, when I was an unsifted girl and you so scholarly that words were cheap & weak. Now I dont know of anything so mighty. There are [those] to which I lift my hat when I see them sitting princelike among their peers on the page. Sometimes I write one, and look at his outlines till he glows as no sapphire."[3] A poet holding such a view of language is likely to write in a way that will baffle readers who do not entertain such a view, or who are not willing to try. Argument and narrative may be compromised in his or her texts, as we saw happen in the lines from "The Tint I cannot take," by what we might call *aura*: the "glow" of a word's or a phrase's associations; its "outlines." The surrounding words and phrases may build upon these associations (or build the scaffolding by means of which the "princelike" word is erected), or they may glance off of the associations as they project a separate aura of their own. "Chariots," for instance, naturally resists being yoked to "Vest"; on one level, that kind of resistance may be what Dickinson is referring to when she describes the chariots as "pushing." As Harold Bloom suggests in the epigraph above, words, like natural objects and phenomena, seem to have wills of their own, that clash with and even at times domineer over our ideas of what they should mean.

Non-teleological writing is writing that is alert to, and receptive to, this recalcitrant power in words. Stanley Cavell describes such writing when he speculates, "A book of philosophy suitable to what Thoreau envisions as 'students' would be written with next to no forward motion, one that culminates in each one of its sentences."[4] For the main unit of meaning in this kind of text would be, not the argument or story, the stanza or paragraph, but the word and the sentence, or sentence fragment. The building blocks of the text, rather than any larger overarching structure they might be thought to be in the service of, would be the focus of attention. Words would not be used so much as invoked, enunciated, like names.

The poem beginning "Sweet Mountains – Ye tell Me no lie" (F745), for example, like most of the poems I discuss in this chapter, puts an inordinate amount of emphasis on a single word. The speaker does not merely utter the word "Mountains"; she rediscovers it. A sudden insight into the meaning of a natural object generates an insight into the latent signifying power of an ordinary word, and vice versa:

> Sweet Mountains – Ye tell Me no lie –
> Never deny Me – Never fly –
> Those same unvarying Eyes
> Turn on Me – When I fail – or feign,
> Or take the Royal names in vain –
> Their far – slow – Violet Gaze –
>
> My Strong Madonnas – Cherish still –
> The Wayward Nun – beneath the Hill –

> Whose service – is to You –
> Her latest Worship – When the Day
> Fades from the Firmament away –
> To lift Her Brows on You – (F745)

Like so many of Dickinson's poems, this one boils down to an act of naming and invoking. Consequently, the second stanza, which ventures beyond that act into a gesture of supplication or prayer, might be seen as detracting from the blunt effect of the first. There is a sense in which development, forward movement, is neither possible nor desirable here. The poet is trying as it were to adjust her pace to the mountains' "far – slow – Violet Gaze"; to linger alongside their simplicity and negativity, or we might say, their intransitivity or lack of an object (their gaze is not directed at anything, which is why the speaker can pretend as though it is "Turn[ed]" on her). She does not want to leave behind the insight of the poem's first line, which is simply the intuition that the line is worth writing at all: that the mountains' silence and inaction, their blind gaze, are worth talking about, are "Sweet" even; that their non-signifying is significant.

A different approach to this poem—one emphasizing its subtle narrative elements—might discover in the second stanza an affecting attempt at intimacy with the non-human. What interests me, however, is the way in which the poem's first stanza does without story, and, in turn, does without the consolation of intimacy, of relation. Whereas the first stanza vaguely personifies the mountains but leaves open the question of whether their "Eyes" register the speaker's presence, the second pleads for the mountains' solicitation. Whereas the first stanza accepts as sufficient the mountains' "far – slow – Violet Gaze," the second normalizes the anomalous, open-ended relationship between the human and the non-human gaze by drawing an analogy between it and a nun's relationship with the Virgin Mary (though Dickinson defamiliarizes the religious trope by pluralizing "Madonna"). And, lastly, whereas in the first stanza Dickinson trusted in the power of the ordinary word "Mountains," in the second stanza the phrase "My Strong Madonnas" both claims possession of and rather heavy-handedly renames the subject of the poem. (It might be argued, however, that "Madonnas" trips the reader up much as "Vest" does in "The Tint I cannot take," and that by this means Dickinson achieves the desired effect of slowing the reader's gaze, attuning it to the presence of strangeness in the ordinary.)

In fact, the speaker of the first stanza does rename her subject, but subtly. We do not at first notice how the simple adjective "Sweet" shapes our reception of the succeeding lines, which tell, with a slant, the truth about the mountains' impassiveness: that they don't speak, don't judge, don't move, and don't change. Each of these negations is counterintuitively presented as an affirmation of meaning and value: the mountains don't lie, don't reject, don't abandon, and don't discriminate; and crucial to this presentation is the poem's first word, which unambiguously stamps the poem as affirmative in tone and spirit. To recall again Bloom's observation, the word "sweet" is itself a slant, which tries to counteract the prejudgment built into the word "Mountains." It might even be said that "Sweet Mountains" conveys the whole gist of the poem, for the gentle shock delivered by these incongruous words expresses, as it were silently and without comment, the crucial tension between nature and humans, desirelessness and the strange desire that that absence can give rise to. In this reading, the drama of a fantasized relation with the honest and loyal mountains does not get played out, because it doesn't need to. The drama, both inception and denouement, is implicit in the poem's first two words, which (with the aid of the rest of the poem of course) simultaneously suggest relation ("Sweet") and negate its possibility ("Mountains").

In poems such as this, sentences are subordinated to words, rather than vice versa. More technically put, predication, or the act of making propositions about an object, serves chiefly to bring out more fully the potential in mere indication—that is, mere naming, or, at an even more basic level, mere pointing. To apply to Dickinson the language of a key passage in Paul Fry's *A Defense of Poetry*, this poet brings to the fore the "grammatical form of indication":[5] that gesture of "saying that something just is" which Fry locates at the very heart of literary expression.[6] She shows indication "lurk[ing] within predication as a suspension of semantic closure, not an avoidance of reference."[7] When Dickinson follows up "Sweet Mountains" with "Ye tell Me no lie," for example, she is not really describing the mountains, but, seeing that muteness is already implied in the word "Mountains," unpacking the significance of the mere word, as well as of the mere thing; she is saying, with the crucial difference or "slant" that literature brings, "that something"—in this case, a mountain range—"just is."

"A suspension of semantic closure, not an avoidance of reference": Fry's phrase betrays his immersion in the poetry not only of Dickinson (an important figure in *A Defense of Poetry*) but also and especially of William

Wordsworth. Wordsworth is relevant here because of the way in which suspension, "a moment of arrest . . . a separation of the traveler-poet from familiar nature . . . a feeling of solitude or loss or separation," is, as Geoffrey Hartman influentially argued, a central phenomenon in his writing, even as his poems remain firmly grounded in natural description—in reference.[8] In Wordsworth, as in the Dickinson poem we've considered, the poet's "apocalyptic self-consciousness," or awareness of the mind's separation from the world of things, is softened, "mellow[ed]," "naturalized,"[9] as he or she attributes to a natural object the very cognitive powers that enabled him or her to see meaning and value in that object. Hartman writes: "The poem here is on the side of 'nature' and against the 'imagination' which fathered it; it hides the intense and even apocalyptic self-consciousness from which it took its rise; it is generically a veiling of its source."[10] If the poem is "generically a veiling of its source," to read it properly is to see through its more conventional elements (the personification and deification of mountains, for example) to its source in an experience of suspended sense, in which the poet has an insight into the imagination's strangeness and freedom from natural, logical constraints. What complicates this insight, however, and accounts for much of the tension in both Dickinson's and Wordsworth's poetry, is that, according to the poets at least, the insight is paradoxically brought about by a raw—Fry would say, "preconceptual," nonverbal—encounter with an ordinary natural object. The poet's glimpse of his or her imaginative and linguistic autonomy seems to depend on his or her glimpse of an equal and opposite autonomy and alterity in the natural world. "Nature is a Haunted House – but Art – a House that tries to be haunted" (L459a): art's strangeness or hauntedness, in other words, is not spontaneous, not native to art or to the artist. Rather, it is an imitation of, or a response to, the strangeness and hauntedness of nature.

Talking earlier about the subtle surprise produced by the phrase "Sweet Mountains," I said that the words delivered a "gentle shock" because of their pairing of human desire with non-human desirelessness: imagination and the impassive canvas on which imagination plays. Though unintentional, this echoing of Wordsworth's phrase "a gentle shock of mild surprise" was not coincidental.[11] Wordsworth's phrase, according to Hartman, exemplifies how Wordsworth seeks to soften the blow of his realization that the mind must achieve independence of nature as part of its development.[12] The "gentle shock" comes when the boy, who has been mimicking owl calls and eliciting their own calls by that means, is suddenly met with silence: nature ceases to echo art. Wordsworth's word for this independence, this solitude—somewhat surprisingly, Hartman notes—is "Imagination."[13]

Perhaps even more vigorously than Wordsworth, Dickinson resists the discovery, or the allegation, that the value and meaning she sees and feels in nature is largely a projection, or an echo, of her own imaginative powers—that she is alone, in short. "The Tint I cannot take," or imitate, internalize, "is best," she says (F696). Yet, however inaccessible and strange, that tint or shade or ghost of meaning arguably belongs more to her—or perhaps, to her poems—than to nature.

If Dickinson's is a poetics of naming—of establishing lines of connection between the poet and the world—it is also, as Bloom has written, a poetics of "unnaming": of severing those ties, or making them almost unbearably tenuous. "Literary originality achieves scandalous dimensions in Dickinson," Bloom argues, "and its principal component is the way she thinks through her poems. She begins before she begins, by the implicit act of unnaming she performs upon the Miltonic-Coleridgean-Emersonian blank [i.e., upon the trope of blindness explored by all three writers], with her hidden Shakespearean substitution."[14] She begins, that is, before deciding on the linguistic, discursive means by which she will bring the poem into existence, and without resorting to her precursors' device of adopting as their subject their own struggle to depict a world they cannot see aright, whether literally or figuratively. According to this view, Dickinson's word usage is as strange as it is because she begins not with words but with a kind of autonomous act of cognition. What Dickinson unnames is not just her subject, then, because in a sense she begins without a subject. Rather, unnaming is something she "performs upon the Miltonic-Coleridgean-Emersonian blank"—upon the very fact of the visionary poet's blindness, her separation from the visible world, her lack of a subject—"with her hidden Shakespearean substitution." It is as though writing a poem were a matter of "throwing away the lights and definitions,"[15] even those that reveal the shape of what one doesn't know: the shape of one's blindness, one's version of "blank." What remains is a "substitution," as of something for nothing, of poetry for despair. "I cannot think of any writer who has expressed desperation as powerfully and as constantly as Dickinson," Bloom writes,[16] yet neither can he think of any writer who is more "Shakespearean," more worthy of comparison with that ultimate figure of mysterious, almost miraculous creative power.

Bloom's allusions to both Dickinson's immense creative powers and her "desperation" run parallel with my own remarks about her Wordsworthian combination of apocalyptic self-consciousness and allegiance to an ultimately inaccessible natural world. Dickinson tells us, on the one hand, that her imagination and language are fiercely independent of the world: she describes herself in one poem as having "touched the Universe," then gone "out opon Circumference – / Beyond the Dip of Bell" (F633), and in other poems as having, in a sense at least, survived her own death. But she also tells us, on the other hand, that she is unable to represent the world in all its glorious strangeness: she cannot decode, much less translate, the "secret" in the landscape, nor can she "take" the "Tint" in nature that she likes "best" (F696). Her non-teleological approach to writing betrays a sense both of words' power and of their futility, a futility which necessitates beginning without them: unnaming, "taking away the lights and definitions." And yet, to recall Fry's terms, if Dickinson avoids semantic closure she does not therefore avoid reference. Despite her strong, almost nihilistic-seeming attraction to blindness and namelessness, the purpose of Dickinson's disjunctive, elliptical style of writing is not to undermine referential content, or simply to remove it from the poems, so that neither what a poem indicates (its subject) nor what it predicates (its statement) can be clearly discerned. It would be more accurate to say that in Dickinson, language, the system and practice of reference, is the referent. She wants us to look at words, to perceive the power they grant us, if only temporarily, both to acknowledge and to counter our blindness, our all-but total ignorance of the world.

Dickinson's non-teleological poetics—her practice of restoring to words their disorienting power by removing or distancing them from our functional but fragile systems of meaning—seems much grimmer when described in theoretical terms than when observed in action. In fact, Dickinson's seriousness is sometimes indistinguishable from archness, playfulness. Often the way her poems confront us with our blindness is by engaging us in games we can't win because we don't know the rules or the objective. John Michael compares Dickinson's peculiar manner of writing poetry to the telling of a "shaggy dog story"—a tale that pointedly lacks a point. "Dickinson's verses," he writes,

> often lure the reader along from line to line and from image to image to come to the end without being able to say exactly what it all amounts to and where the trip arrives, except that it has entailed a pleasurable immersion in the poem's slants of language that tease and seduce the susceptible reader in nearly every line, leading her or him to expect a meaning the poem never quite delivers.[17]

One of Dickinson's best-known poems is just such a "teas[ing]," "seduc[tive]" "trip" through the "slants of language" discovered or engineered by Dickinson. It is a poem which disappoints the reader who awaits, in Michael's phrase, "a meaning," but which makes that disappointment itself meaningful, and even strangely satisfying:

> A narrow Fellow in the Grass
> Occasionally rides –
> You may have met him? Did you not
> His notice instant is –
>
> The Grass divides as with a Comb –
> A spotted Shaft is seen,
> And then it closes at your Feet
> And opens further on –
>
> He likes a Boggy Acre –
> A Floor too cool for Corn –
> But when a Boy and Barefoot
> I more than once at Noon
>
> Have passed I thought a Whip Lash
> Unbraiding in the Sun
> When stooping to secure it
> It wrinkled And was gone –
>
> Several of Nature's People
> I know and they know me
> I feel for them a transport
> Of Cordiality
>
> But never met this Fellow
> Attended or alone
> Without a tighter Breathing
> And Zero at the Bone. (F1096C)

As in "Sweet Mountains," here we have a poem where a story seems to be lurking in the background without ever getting told. The poem's words are, like its rhymes, slightly off. They send the mind off on tangents, instead of moving it forward along a narrative, descriptive, or argumentative track. To start with, the snake is a "Fellow," despite his emphasized foreignness and unfriendliness. Since the latter qualities are already hinted at in the strange qualifier "narrow," the poem's first three words produce, as "Sweet Mountains" did, a gentle shock, which the next three words, "in the Grass," do not so much cushion as camouflage. "Occasionally rides" repeats the effect but in reverse: the first word is casual, reassuring; the second disconcerting. In or on what does the snake ride? The attribution of this human action to the inhuman snake recalls another famous second line of Dickinson's: "He [Death] kindly stopped for me" (F479).

In stanza 2, "Grass" is implicitly compared to hair parted "with a Comb," a striking metaphor, yet before we've taken it in and registered that the snake is what's combing the grass (and that *comb* also means *search*), "he" is described again as "A spotted Shaft." These three words, "A spotted shaft," are the only direct description of the snake's appearance in the poem. It's an oddly dehumanizing description, considering that the animal is referred to before and after as a fellow, one capable of riding and combing. Indeed, the reader is liable to think that "Shaft" refers not to the snake but to the gap in the grass, especially as this gap is the antecedent of the next pronoun: "And then it closes at your Feet / And opens further on." The quick paratactic shifts of this stanza suppress language's tendency to subordinate its parts to a central subject (in this case, the snake). Combined with the pronominal confusion just noted, these shifts impress us with the closeness of what is central and what is marginal or insignificant: the snake and the grass, the extraordinary and the ordinary.

The center/margin binary is further undermined in the third stanza, in which the snake's habitat is rendered nearly as extraordinary as the snake: "He likes a Boggy Acre – / A Floor too cool for Corn." The poet's attention seems to wander here, not just from her main referent, but from the work of reference altogether. Susan Stewart, noting the experimental quality of this poem's language, infers that its words were chosen in large part for their surface features.[18] In the lines just quoted, for instance, the double circles of *gg* and *oo* and the straight vertical lines of *l* and *t* suggest the movement of the "cylindrical" creature through the upright blades of grass.[19] Stewart's inference is plausible because here as in so many of Dickinson's poems the rationale behind her diction eludes ordinary interpretive methods (what semantic justification is there for "A Floor too cool for Corn"?), rewarding instead the almost morbid fascination with words for their own sake that Nietzsche described as a "connoisseurship of the *word*."[20] Thus it is not just the thematically marginal elements of the poem (the grass/bog/"Floor") that get foregrounded, but also its formally marginal elements: the letters which make up its words, and the words which make up its fragmentary sentences.

Study of the word seems to be an end in itself, whereas discoveries about the poem's meaning that such research yields are a means to that end. Or, in any case, means and ends are confused. The bizarre line "A Floor too cool for Corn," whose meaning is quite simple once it has been decoded, is a case in point. Many readers will initially, and in some cases ultimately, take the line as literally referring to a floor, perhaps the floor of a barn (somewhere corn might indeed be stored). In fact, the line is a riddle whose solution is hidden in plain sight in the previous line: the "Floor" is simply "a Boggy Acre"—a kind of land unsuitable for growing corn. Yet perhaps the poem is richer for those who have not solved the riddle, which is captivating in part because it echoes (though this turns out to be a sort of red herring) the lines of another famous poem about seeking and finding one of "Nature's People," namely, Keats's "To Autumn": "Who hath not seen thee oft amid thy store? / Sometimes whoever seeks abroad may find / Thee sitting careless on a granary floor."[21]

Dickinson's "Floor too cool for Corn" both echoes and inverts Keats's "granary floor," which is warm enough both to store grain and to comfortably seat the allegorical figure of Autumn. Certainly, the atmosphere of "A narrow Fellow in the Grass" is cooler, less humanized than that of "To Autumn." But Dickinson is following the example of Keats's ode when she identifies a subtle quality of mortality in nature that surfaces despite the circumstances of carefree, "Barefoot" boyhood and of "Noon." The snake's bite or venom, never mentioned but metonymically represented by the comparison of its body to a "Whip Lash," haunts the whole poem as winter and death haunt "To Autumn." The poem is not about the snake's danger exactly but about the nameless shadow it casts over the speaker's perception of nature, which Dickinson tries to imitate by casting a dangerous slant over all or most of her poem's words.[22] Just as, in the first line, the weirdness of the phrase "narrow Fellow" rubs off on the ordinary word "Grass," in the last line, "Zero at the Bone," the out-of-place, abstract word "Zero" hollows out the solid word "Bone." There's something "in" and "at" our familiar surroundings and selves, these lines insinuate, that is almost nothing—narrow, zero—but that this speaker, for one, cannot forget (though "he" may not have encountered it directly since his boyhood). Perhaps it is words, which can also seem to balance unnervingly between insignificance and significance, innocuousness and ominousness, that keep him from forgetting.

In place of (or, it may be, in addition to) story, description, and argument, Dickinson's poems confront us with, press our face up against, words. Despite their frequently tortuous syntax and riddling diction, their difficulty is not essentially a difficulty of understanding, of figuring out what any given line or stanza means. It is rather a difficulty of perspective. The reader must shrink his or her field of inquiry and frame of reference down to that of the philologist (Nietzsche's "connoiseu[r] of the *word*"), and seek drama in the lonely acts of signifying silently carried out by, or contained in latent form within, individual words: *narrow, fellow, grass, spotted, shaft, opens, closes, whip, lash, transport, zero, bone*. Listed in this way, the words seem harmless enough. Dickinson's genius lies in choreographing them so that they seem uncanny, appropriate and inappropriate at the same time. She does not make meaning out of them; she makes them mean. This process begins with simply selecting them, putting them in each other's suggestive, democratic company, as opposed to subordinating them all to a master concept or theme.

To recapitulate: Dickinson uses words almost as though they were names, invoking or enunciating them rather than using or deploying them for a purpose larger than themselves. She invokes words with a mysterious confidence that sustains the reader's interest despite the profound uncertainty engulfing her speech; despite, that is, the fact that her underlying subject is namelessness, and her underlying method, "unnaming." In this way she empowers words to signify independently of a grammatical and conceptual framework—independently of a system and tradition of meaning, in other words. Indication rather than predication is the dominant mode of Dickinson's writing, for if many of her speakers make assertions, the brevity, indefiniteness, disjunctiveness, and just plain weirdness of their language undermines those assertions' predicative force, aligning them more closely with the mute objects of the poet's speech—the things to which she points—than with a tradition of making propositions about those objects.

The distinctive motion of Dickinson's poetry, operating as it does at the circumference or outer reaches of the imagination—as far as words' digressive, centrifugal promptings will take one—is not like motion as we ordinarily think of it. It is not sequential, does not tend toward a destination or revelation, or bend to the sway of a telos. What Dickinson says of a dead loved one is as applicable to her poetry as it is to the departed: "Distance - be her only

Motion" (F759).²³ The tendency of her language is to preserve rather than to lessen the distance between itself and us (where "us" might include Dickinson herself). She seems to want it instead to measure that distance: to suggest, like a star, how much space had to be traversed for her words to reach us at all, beholden as they are to an object (in both senses of the word) that cannot be named. "If end I gained," Dickinson writes, "It ends beyond / Indefinite disclosed" (F484). This statement (if we choose to read it as the author's statement concerning her work) does not necessarily mean that her poems have transcendental meanings, nor that they have no meaning, but only that their meaning is always distant, always in motion. Dickinson's lyrics locate meaning in meaning's distance, and make of meaning's withdrawal an event.

"CONFIDENT DESPAIR"

In one of several depictions of more or less voluntary exile from human society, Dickinson, or at any rate her poem's speaker, describes herself thus:

> I saw no Way – The Heavens were stitched –
> I felt the Columns close –
> The Earth reversed her Hemispheres –
> I touched the Universe –
>
> And back it slid – and I alone –
> A speck opon a Ball –
> Went out opon Circumference –
> Beyond the Dip of Bell – (F633)

In her first book on Dickinson, Sharon Cameron aptly interprets this lyric as expressing the poet's resolution "to excavate the territory that lies past the range of all phenomenal sense," despite her dread of "the terrible space of the venture, as language is flung out into the reaches of the unknown in the apparent hope that it might civilize what it finds there."²⁴ Much of Dickinson's poetry is characterized by this ambivalent combination of resoluteness and dread. She delights in the unknown, it often seems, because she feels that the only alternative is to be annihilated by it. There is no authentic confidence in her world that is not complicated by the awareness of despair; that is not, as she calls it, "Confident Despair" (F634). The dialectical relationship between these two, which at times (as in the oxymoron just quoted) approaches the extreme of identification, is one of the few constants in Dickinson's poetry; it undergirds her "love" poems as well as her "nature" poems, her "religious" as well as her "philosophical" poems.

If scare quotes are necessary here, it is because knowing the ostensible subject matter or theme of Dickinson's poems is seldom enough; it does not usually tell us what a poem is truly about, what motivates or animates it. The kind of crisis Dickinson seems most interested in exploring is not specific to any of the categories of experience just named (love, nature, religion, philosophy); it is as likely to affect the baffled lover as the baffled nature-enthusiast, the aspiring devotee as the aspiring student. Take the poem beginning "Had I presumed to hope" (F634), which is the source of the phrase "Confident Despair." It is easy to say that this is a poem concerned with religious themes, but this would be to overlook all of the effort that has apparently gone into concealing or at least softening the poem's religiosity. Dickinson seems to have been determined to strip this poem, as she did so many others, of any telltale signs of its speaker's identity, situation, and beliefs. Although its general argument—that failure and loss may reflect greatness on the object sought—is clear enough, it never reveals what the specific object of the speaker's desire is. For it seeks a vocabulary and a grammar that will not only describe but also enact the fundamental drama of not knowing and never attaining, or as the poem puts it, of "Advancing on Celestial Lists – / With faint – Terrestrial power."

This essential ambiguity, which goes well beyond the undecidability of specific phrases, is what stands in the way even of such well-executed attempts at elucidation as Cameron's second book on Dickinson, *Choosing Not Choosing*. Cameron's revised reading of "I saw no Way," for example, which finds in the poem's fascicle context a partial solution to the mystery of its subject, is, to me, less persuasive than her reading of the poem in *Lyric Time*, quoted above. "For the first line of the previous poem," Cameron writes, referring to the ordering of Fascicle 31, "copied on the other side of the page of 'I saw no Way' is 'To lose one's faith—surpass/ The loss of an Estate—' (P 377), and this proximity, however loosely, establishes the poems in a relation to each other, suggesting that the cause of the disorientation might not be mysterious at all, but rather loss of faith."[25] This appears to assume that loss of faith is a more or less distinct experience or concept. Yet that is manifestly not the case here (as Cameron goes on to acknowledge, though without withdrawing her initial suggestion),[26] since Dickinson pointedly does not specify the object or nature of the faith referred to in "To lose One's faith," let alone the circumstances and consequences of its loss. Thus, the inferred connection between "I saw no Way" and "To lose One's faith" does not explain, and so does not lessen, the disorientation that is both the motif and the method of these two poems.

Cameron, again, acknowledges this, noting that "to establish a relation between and among poems is not yet to clarify it";[27] it simply raises a different set of questions than reading the texts as individual lyrics does. "There are relations among poems," Cameron observes, "that we cannot disregard and, as much to the point, that we do not precisely know how to comprehend."[28] But this is true whether or not we read the poems in the fascicle context. There are relations besides the ones that emerge when we use the fascicle groupings to try to identify the dramatic, rhetorical, or narrative situations out of which the poems arise—when, for example, Cameron speculates about both "To lose one's Faith" and "I saw no Way" being responses to "the lover's death" alluded to in "Me prove it now."[29]

More important than these thematic, intra-fascicle connections, I feel, are the connections that unite countless of Dickinson's poems, regardless of whether or not they share a fascicle, in that "fundamental drama of not knowing" I just mentioned. For this drama is what the writer and the reader have in common as both fall prey to the disorienting charm of words. When Dickinson says, in the poem beginning "I think I was enchanted" (F627), that "The Dark - felt beautiful," she is affirming her confidence in the value of experiences which rob her of all confidence. But she is also describing what it is like to read a poem—specifically, the poems of "that Foreign Lady" (probably Elizabeth Barrett Browning) which are the direct cause of her "enchant[ment]." What Dickinson describes—the peculiarly helpless feeling of being delighted by verse, or by anything that one does not understand—is also what her reader experiences. A similar argument might be made about the poem beginning "From Blank to Blank - / A Threadless Way / I pushed Mechanic feet" (F484). This lyric does not merely withhold the knowledge of its subject from us (who is the speaker and why does she feel this way?); it shares with us, by way of its own cryptic, destinationless lines (its last word is "Blind"), the experience of following "A Threadless Way," upon which "To stop - or perish - or advance - [are] / Alike indifferent." "If end I gained / It ends beyond / Indefinite disclosed": this is as much as to say that we readers are as well-positioned to judge what is the "end" (both purpose and extent or terminus is meant, I think) of Dickinson's utterances as she herself is.

What the fascicles reveal is already evident, if less clearly so, in the unsifted Dickinson corpus. Because Dickinson often obscures and makes abstract the subject matter of her poems—or better, because often obscurity and abstraction are themselves her subjects—poems that appear to be thematically diverse speak to each other, and to us, at the subtler level of verbal connotation and the indefinite, fugitive moods such connotation can be made to express. This is a kind of speaking-to or dialectic that operates independently of, on a different wavelength from, theme and purpose ("meaning" in the ordinary sense), indeed independently of all the familiar ways of organizing human experience. "For sense in its poetic significance," as Walter Benjamin argues in his influential essay "The Task of the Translator," "is not limited to meaning, but derives from the connotations conveyed by the word chosen to express it."[30]

Several of the poems found in Fascicle 38, for example, demonstrate how the confidence-despair dialectic identified above signifies in the absence of a clearly defined subject matter or narrative. In one of the poems, Dickinson speaks of "Despair's advantage" and "The Worthiness of Suffering," and compares "Affliction" to "Savors" (F854). In two others, she writes, "I play at Riches – to appease / The Clamoring for Gold," and, "On the Bleakness of my Lot / Bloom I strove to raise" (F856, F862B). In none of these poems is the source of either this despair or this confidence specified. The moods themselves, their mutability and the way in which the poet's supple language mimics that mutability, or perhaps enables it, are the point. Poetry is a kind of X factor, an unknown element, that transforms "Bleakness" into "Bloom," "Affliction" into "Savors," "Despair" into "Despair's advantage," and, perhaps most importantly, words into "princelike" figures. This transformation is not exactly the poems' subject, however, because subject matter is something that precedes and exists outside of a text, whereas this transformation coincides with and inheres within the process of the poems' composition. It also coincides with and inheres within the process of reading the poems, which means that after a reading is completed, the transformation is undone and the poem slips through one's fingers. Its words go back to seeming like objects of "faint – Terrestrial power," and one cannot say what the "Celestial Lists" were that they allowed the poet and reader to "Advanc[e] on."

THE LIMITS OF INTERPRETATION

We may sum up much of the argument of the preceding sections by saying that in Dickinson, the difference between presence and absence—whether of an object, event, or experience, or of hope, knowledge, or meaning—is indefinite ("narrow") to the point of seeming non-existent. Dickinson's frequently urgent and solemn tone, combined with her poems' abrupt openings, ubiquitous ellipses and ambiguities, jarring lexical transpositions, oddly concrete abstractions, and weird, hyperbolic diction, give one the impression that something of great moment has happened which, however, the poet appears unable to describe directly, or even to be sure that she has experienced. And this same unsettling feeling that something has happened or revealed itself to one, though one cannot be sure what if anything has happened or been revealed, is often all that a Dickinson poem gives to the reader. Understandably enough, critics are sometimes unsure whether to complain or to exalt.[31]

It is for approximately these reasons that Anne-Lise François includes Dickinson in her study of the "lyric of inconsequence" and the "literature of uncounted experience." In François's reading, Dickinson, along with Wordsworth and Thomas Hardy, is a poet for whom the difference between before and after is sometimes vanishingly small, not because in her poems nothing happens, but because often the poet (and in turn the reader) has no criterion by which to judge the significance or confirm the reality of what does happen. "The reception of experience in Dickinson," François writes, "often includes its own deflection, and contact recedes as informally, unceremoniously, as it occurs."[32] In "The Birds begun at Four o'clock," for example, Dickinson begins by announcing a "Miracle" (in fact, the everyday occurrence of birds singing before dawn), and ends by stating that the miracle was forgotten in the moment of its fulfillment:

> The Sun engrossed the East –
> The Day controlled the World –
> The Miracle that introduced
> Forgotten, as fulfilled. (F504B)

François coins such terms as "affirmative reticence" and "recessive action" to do justice to passages like this one, which is affirmative and negative at once, since it affirms, not so much a negativity, but a sameness. It insists on reporting an event which has changed nothing, not excepting the speaker. "But is it possible," François cautiously asks, "to define a lyric subgenre simply in terms of a temporal gesture of desistance, in the course of which one waits and then gives up waiting? In terms of a cadence of lapse or recessive progress that may occur in a single phrase as in Dickinson's 'Forgotten, as Fulfilled'?"[33] Evidently François believes it is possible, because two pages later she suggests that the "evacuation of telos" implicit in this sort of gesture is deliberate, and that it marks some of Dickinson's, Wordsworth's, and Hardy's poems as belonging to a "lyric subgenre—the lyric of inconsequence—variously worked out by three poets who . . . share a commitment to the possibilities of nonsequential connection opened up by lyric (as opposed to narrative) sequences or constellations."[34]

Where "The Birds begun" describes a quotidian event as though it were a singular "Miracle," the poem beginning "Conscious am I in my Chamber – / Of a shapeless friend" (F773B) describes what should be a singular, sublime occurrence—an encounter with "Immortality"—as though it were not an encounter but an ongoing, almost casual relationship. In both cases, what is transcendent is both eminently missable and eminently repeatable, which is to say, common: the birds' music is "numerous as space – / But neighboring as Noon"; immortality, though "shapeless," is as frequently available, at least in theory, as solitary thought. As Dickinson puts it at the start of another poem, "Drama's Vitallest Expression is the Common Day / That arise and set about Us" (F776). Nothing more important happens than what happens when we are not expecting anything to happen, or when we are not sure if anything at all has happened. Thoreau articulates approximately the same idea throughout *Walden*: "The morning wind forever blows, the poem of creation is uninterrupted; but few are the ears that hear it. Olympus is but the outside of the earth every where" (W 2:390).

To some, these two pronouncements ("Drama's Vitallest Expression is the Common Day" and "The morning wind forever blows") will seem unequivocally encouraging. Others, however, will hear in Dickinson's and Thoreau's aphorisms the note of resignation, and of implied negation: no heroic adventures, no otherworldly spaces, no greater mysteries to be investigated or obstacles to be overcome than those which reside in, or somewhere on the borders of, the self. Thus, the speaker of "Conscious am I in my Chamber" is not in fact the privileged recipient of a divine emissary but, if we read closely, a kind of student confronting the hard tasks of introspection and abstract, unconventional thought. She attempts a kind of thinking that would negate everything definite, tangible, public, and deal only with what is indefinite, unknowable, and private to the point of being hidden even from one's self. "Conscious am I" is an exemplary, if somewhat extreme, instance of what Bloom terms "the internalization of quest-romance":

> The movement of quest-romance, before its internalization by the High Romantics, was from nature to redeemed nature, the sanction of redemption being the gift of some external spiritual authority, sometimes magical. The Romantic movement is from nature to the imagination's freedom (sometimes a reluctant freedom), and the imagination's freedom is frequently purgatorial, redemptive in direction but destructive of the social self.[35]

"Every man supposes himself not to be fully understood," Emerson wrote. "The last chamber, the last closet, he must feel, was never opened. There is always a residuum unknown, unanalyzable. That is, every man believes that he has a greater possibility."[36] In this poem Dickinson hunts that residuum or possibility, fails, and, in the last word/line, honors her elusive game with the highest honorific she can think of:

> Conscious am I in my Chamber –
> Of a shapeless friend –
> He doth not attest by Posture –
> Nor confirm – by Word –
>
> Neither Place – need I present Him –
> Fitter Courtesy
> Hospitable intuition
> Of His Company –
>
> Presence – is His furthest license –
> Neither He to Me
> Nor Myself to Him – by Accent –
> Forfeit Probity –
>
> Weariness of Him, were quainter
> Than Monotony
> Knew a Particle – of Space's
> Vast Society –
>
> Neither if He visit Other –
> Do He dwell – or Nay – know I –

>   But Instinct esteem Him
>   Immortality – (F773B)

On the one hand the speaker is on intimate ("friend[ly]") terms with immortality: it impinges on her consciousness and is dimly recognized, even named, by her "Instinct"; and it pays her visits, or rather betrays its presence, when she is alone in her bedroom. On the other hand, the speaker's manner of receiving and honoring her friend is apparently to give no sign of having noticed him, since to do so would only show how far she is from understanding their relationship. (The meaning of the difficult fifth line seems to be that the speaker need not offer ["present"] her visitor a place to sit, or even acknowledge his presence as one would that of an ordinary visitor. The third stanza also appears difficult, but what its difficulty veils is a kind of joke: since the friend is a "he," it would be inappropriate for him to hold a private conversation with the speaker in her bedroom.) It is not a relationship between persons but between a person and an indefinable, "shapeless" property of her own existence, which of course is not a relationship at all but a sort of mood—what Dickinson might have called an "angle" or simply a "light" (or "Slant of light" [F320]). The speaker confronts the difficulty Emerson alludes to in "Circles," namely, that "Our moods do not believe in each other."[37] She is credulous and incredulous of immortality at once, and strains to speak of her subject without either affirming or denying its existence. This is almost a matter of straining to be two people at once, to fit into a single statement experiences or moods or conceptual frameworks (secular and Judeo-Christian) that would seem to cancel each other out but that nevertheless can, the poem attests, coinhabit a single person's consciousness.

The strain of doubleness is most keenly felt in the penultimate stanza, whose meaning is thrown into doubt by the apparent personification of "Monotony." This word at first seems to be the object of the sentence (weariness of immortality is quainter than monotony) until, in the stanza's third line, the sentence changes direction and "Monotony" seems to become a subject in its own right. It is a figure, perhaps, for consciousness deprived of the thought of absolute otherness, for which the only "others" are "Particle[s]" of matter. (The pejorative inflection on the word "Particle" would be in keeping with William Blake's use of the term in "Mock on Mock on Voltaire Rousseau": "The Atoms of Democritus / And Newtons Particles of Light / Are sands upon the Red Sea shore / Where Israels tents do shine so bright.")[38] This supposition cannot be confirmed, however, because whereas the first half of the stanza makes grammatical sense, the second half (taking "Monotony" to be the subject of "Knew") doesn't. For the thought to be complete, one must assume an implied "if" after "Than": "Weariness of immortality is quainter than *if* monotony knew a particle of space's vast society," or in other words, waiting indefinitely for the unknown is more interesting than knowing what little can be known.

"Weariness . . . were quainter." *Quaint*, Dickinson very probably realized, carries not just the suggestion of novelty and strangeness, but also the trace of the word *acquaint*; it derives from the Old French *cointe*, which in turn derives from the Latin root *cogn*: know. Weariness and boredom, Dickinson therefore seems to be saying, may be unexpected points of cognitive access to the transcendent or wholly other. Paradoxically, to be aware of one's limitations may be the only way one can be aware of (the possibility of) one's immortality, that is, one's limitlessness. For Dickinson as for Emerson (from whose "Circles" Dickinson may have borrowed), the most fitting image of the self peering beyond its limits is that of a circle on whose outer edge one perches: "and I alone – / A Speck opon a Ball – / Went out opon Circumference" (F633). This image, like the poem we've just considered and like Emerson's essay, is not about directly confronting the sublime and feeling an answering greatness in oneself; it is about turning from the self and from solid reality when there is as yet no apparent alternative to either, and no assurance that one is equipped to perceive an alternative should it present itself. "Every man *believes* that he has a greater possibility," Emerson says in "Circles"; he does not say every man realizes that potential, or receives definite confirmation of his belief.

An unlikely companion piece to "Conscious am I" is the earthier but no less indefinite poem of difficult witnessing that begins, "Bloom upon the Mountain – stated." If the previous poem imagined an alternative to egotism or cognitive "Monotony"—an alternative to knowing and understanding that is not simply ignorance—this poem seems to imagine an alternative to egotistical, monologic writing: the practice of stamping "a name" on one's creations, assigning them each a meaning, a title, a role within a career.

> Bloom opon the Mountain stated –
> Blameless of a name –
> Efflorescence of a Sunset –
> Reproduced – the same –
>
> Seed had I, my Purple Sowing
> Should address the Day –

Not – a Tropic of a Twilight –
Show itself away –

Who for tilling – to the Mountain
Come – and disappear –
Whose be her Renown – or fading –
Witness is not here –

While I state – the Solemn Petals –
Far as North – and East –
Far as South – and West expanding –
Culminate – in Rest –

And the Mountain to the Evening
Fit His Countenance –
Indicating by no Muscle
His Experience – (F787C)

I will focus on the poem's first two stanzas, which are its most challenging. The first verb, "stated," has no definite agent; it is not even clear whether it is in active or in passive voice. The absence of any other subject to which the predicate "stated" can be joined forces us into the supposition that the statement's maker is "Bloom" itself. It is just possible that Dickinson had in mind the passage from Exodus 3:2 in which a burning bush on Mount Horeb speaks to Moses on behalf of, or in the voice of, God. Alternatively, one could read this line as saying, by way of two ellipses, "Bloom opon the Mountain – [if that phenomenon were] stated – / [is] Blameless of a Name," but such a reading puts too many words in the poet's mouth to be convincing. Later this puzzle makes more sense, since in stanza 3 the source or creator of "Bloom" (evidently the poem's makeshift word for the expanding and contracting play of light and color on the mountain) is said to be, like its proper name, unknown. The speaker cannot definitely say either that bloom stated itself or that some other party stated it. The uncertainty here is not accidental, cannot be cleared up by diligent reading, but is intrinsic to the speaker's own statement and to her understanding of what she has seen "opon the Mountain."

More troubling still are lines 3 and 4: "Efflorescence of a Sunset – / Reproduced – the same." The lines seem to introduce a new subject: a different kind of bloom (though a "Reproduc[tion]"), transpiring in the sunset rather than on the mountain. But this doesn't make sense, as the bloom is referred to as a single thing throughout the rest of the poem, and no further mention is made of sunlight besides the metaphorical description of its flower-like expansion and contraction as reflected on the mountain's surface. The only reasonable inference, I believe, is that this flowering, the "Efflorescence" of line 3, is identical to the "Bloom" of line 1. One is misled into thinking that the light of the sun and the light on the mountains are two different things by the poem's conceit that the imprint or "state[ment]" of the setting sun's light on the mountains is not simply light but the flowering or efflorescence of light. Though it is "the same" light "Reproduced" on the surface of the mountains, a third entity emerges from this meeting of light and earth, which is not really an entity but a commingling of entities: the poem calls it "Bloom." This commingling is necessarily ephemeral; in this respect bloom differs from what the poet anticipates her own "Sowing" would be, hypothetical though that is: "Seed had I, my Purple Sowing / Should address the Day – / Not – a Tropic of a Twilight – / Show itself away." In other words, if I had the power that is evidently invested in nature, I would not make my greatest effects so transient.

But this of course is wishful thinking on the poet's part, as the subjunctive tense of lines 5–8 makes clear. If the language at her disposal is less ephemeral than the light of sunset, it is also less fruitful; it is not, properly speaking, seed-language. As a rule, language, unlike light and earth, is too much itself to flower into something wholly other. That is the challenge the poet faces: to transform the material she handles, or better, to create the conditions in which it will, like a seed, transform itself. This strange objective, romantically ambitious yet calling for a hands-off, non-teleological presentation of language (since to impose a telos on the words would interfere with the hoped-for emergence of a mysterious, innate meaningfulness in the words) partly explains the prevalence of poems about the life cycle of flowers in the Dickinson corpus. It also explains, ironically, the labored, almost mangled feeling of some of her stanzas, as well as the abundance of variants found in the manuscripts of poems such as the present one. In attending more carefully to the placement of the "Seed" or word than to the creation of a "Bloom" or statement—in trusting that bloom will somehow state itself, though no speaker or "till[er]" appear on the scene—Dickinson risks the awkwardness of fragmentation, as well as the bafflement of her reader.

That words might aspire to the condition of seeds, to be strategically placed on the page rather than enlisted in an argument, story, or even sentence, is the kind of notion that Theo Davis might classify as belonging to "Ornamental Aesthetics." In a recent book of that title, Davis argues that "there is a distinctive, non-hermeneutic mode of relationship to phenomena (including language) in Martin Heidegger, as well as in Thoreau, Dickinson, and Walt Whitman."[39] Her name for this mode is "ornamentation," which she describes as "a practice of relational notice. Such relational notice is involved with a way of understanding the relationship of mind to world that diverges from the representational model through which a subject knows a world of objects other to himself."[40] Approaching the same feature of Dickinson's poetry from a different angle, I have tried to show how nearly impossible a "non-hermeneutic," non-representational relation to phenomena is, judging from Dickinson's experiments in this direction. Though a diverse group, "Bloom opon the Mountain," "Conscious am I in my Chamber," "A narrow Fellow in the grass," and "Sweet Mountains – Ye tell Me no lie" are all about the difficulty of relation (except perhaps in the most abstract or figurative sense) in the absence of knowledge—in the absence, that is, of an established set of terms, concepts, narratives, and even grammatical conventions by which the other can be handled or (to use one of Davis's preferred terms) approached. One might say, in fact, that these poems are about the presence of distance—the presence of that which cannot be approached, and which therefore is as much an absence as a presence.

Between separate orders of existence there can be no relation, Dickinson argues again and again, only "Circumference," the strange circumlocutions of poetic language. "Their Graspless manners – mock us," she writes at the end of "The Tint I cannot take – is best," allowing "Their" to refer broadly to all things non-human, whether "Squirrels" or "Snow" or "Color": "Until the Cheated Eye / Shuts arrogantly – in the Grave – / Another way – to see" (F696). As in the poem beginning "From Blank to Blank – / A Threadless Way / I pushed Mechanic feet" (F484), the poet's power is in her ability to persevere through blindness: to speak without the knowledge that sensory perception is supposed to bestow, and without the narrative, conceptual, and grammatical "Thread[s]" that we use to orient and anchor our speech to an alien world. Perhaps more than any other, this is the strength—the visionary strength of doing without—that sets Dickinson apart and that we value her for. It is a strength that she imparts to the words she uses, which so often her poems seem to enlarge and set free.

"CIRCUMFERENCE BETWEEN"

Whether one emphasizes, as Davis does, Dickinson's "non-hermeneutic mode of relationship to phenomena" or, as I do, the harrowing distance from phenomena that Dickinson's avoidance of familiar hermeneutic procedures causes, Davis's juxtapositions of the poet with Thoreau and with the philosophy of Heidegger open up new and fruitful lines of thinking. The poems discussed in this chapter, which treat as central experiences that cannot be incorporated either into a coherent narrative or into a coherent body of thought, anticipate especially passages of Heidegger's *What is Called Thinking?* In this series of late lectures, Heidegger warns against overvaluing "what is actual" (or more precisely, "what we like to regard as constitutive of the actuality of the actual") and undervaluing what cannot be known or even encountered directly. Things belonging to the latter category cannot be made present to the mind, Heidegger suggests, not because they are not actual, but because their presence is, paradoxically, defined by "the event of withdrawal":

> But—withdrawing is not nothing. Withdrawal is an event. In fact, what withdraws may even concern and claim man more essentially than anything present that strikes and touches him. Being struck by actuality is what we like to regard as constitutive of the actuality of the actual. However, in being struck by what is actual, man may be debarred precisely from what concerns and touches him—touches him in the surely mysterious way of escaping him by its withdrawal. The event of withdrawal could be what is most present in all our present, and so infinitely exceed the actuality of everything actual.[41]

Reading in the light of this passage, we may better appreciate Dickinson's lyric beginning "At Half past Three, a single Bird"—a poem whose last two lines Yvor Winters deemed nonsensical.[42]

> At Half past Three, a single Bird
> Unto a silent Sky
> Propounded but a single term
> Of cautious Melody.
>
> At Half past Four, experiment
> Had subjugated test

And lo, her silver Principle
Supplanted all the rest –

At Half past Seven, element
Nor implement – be seen
And Place, was where the Presence was
Circumference between – (F1099)

"Presence," here as in "Bloom opon the Mountain" and "Conscious am I in my Chamber," is opposed to "Place" because, contrary to the everyday sense of the word, it is not tangible, indeed is scarcely different from absence. As Douglas Anderson puts it in "Presence and Place in Emily Dickinson's Poetry," presence's "opposite condition—the silence that precedes and follows—is not (as common sense might suggest) 'absence' but 'place,' not a condition of emptiness but a setting into which the bird's song has already once introduced itself and where it may yet again at any time."[43] It is likely, after all, that the bird has only been heard, not seen; and even its "melody" is "cautious," unforthcoming: it consists of "but a single term." When that term comes to seem like a "silver Principle / Supplant[ing] all the rest," it is evidently not because of any discernible development in the bird's song but because, first, the pale light of dawn suggests to the poet the ambiguous gray-white tint of silver; second, the song's very slightness, combined with the absence of other sounds, narrows the speaker's attention and sharpens her perceptions; and, third and most important, the song's disappearance retroactively enhances its value. As Heidegger puts it, "what is most present in all our present" may be the very instability of things: their capacity for flight, for disappearance. The sense of things as stable, solid, consistent, may be an illusion that absents us from all but the surface of the scene—"debar[s] [us] precisely from what concerns and touches [us]." For often our own satisfaction with things, our sense of them as confirming our ideas and expectations of them, rather than things themselves, is what we experience. (As Thoreau puts it, "The dinner even is only the parable of a dinner, commonly" [W 13:517].) Conversely, our experiences of loss, of a meaningful object's or phenomenon's withdrawal from perceptual access, can bridge the gap between things and ideas, though in a counterintuitive way. As a thing recedes into the distance, the poems we've considered suggest, so too do our ideas about it. As a thing's identity becomes indistinguishable from its inaccessibility, the distance between the thing and ideas about the thing lessens. "But are not all Facts Dreams as soon as we put them behind us?" Dickinson writes in a late prose fragment (L, prose fragment 22). The thing and its meaning—facts and dreams—become one, but only because both are too distant to be discerned; both are equally like dreams.

Working on this chapter, I kept thinking of a stray comment Laura Dassow Walls makes in a recent essay on the "Anthropocene." "The birdsong one can call up on a schoolroom computer," she writes, "lacks the dimension of meaning."[44] Meaning, then, like poetry, is what gets lost in translation, not only from one medium to another, but from one moment to another—from "Half past Four" to "Half past Seven," for instance. A "term" (the word deliberately links the bird's note with the poet's word) that in one moment seems like a "silver Principle / Supplanting all the rest," and therefore worthy of being "Propounded" rather than simply sounded, may in the next moment grate on the ear. Nothing actual—say, a bird feather, a photograph or audio recording, or even a narrative or logical description of what happened—can bridge the gap between such moments, because each of these media provides only a partial replica of the encountered object. They give the meaningful object *place*, as the speaker of "Conscious am I" pointedly refrains from doing ("Neither Place – need I present Him"), and so inadvertently rob it of *presence*, which is not so much meaning as "the dimension of meaning."

In contrast, "Circumference," Dickinson's word for the curved line of creative language and thought, stretches "between" presence and place; it is an alternative space or mode in which the poet is not obligated either to mourn the departed presence or to seek consolation in presence-substitutes. In fact, she is not obligated to do anything—a freedom Dickinson exercises to an extent that perhaps no other poet of the nineteenth century did. The freedom or curvature of poetic language, its refusal to travel in a straight line from subject matter to representation or interpretive comment, gives it a body and even a presence of its own, a quality at once of perpetual "Motion" and of irreducible "Distance" which aligns it with the natural objects that are so often Dickinson's subject. Dickinson did not invent this non-teleological dimension of literature all by herself; she also discovered it in the writers whom she read. But she exploited this feature or rather possibility of language with unprecedented consistency and self-awareness. Granting that non-teleological writing is far from being an isolated phenomenon, we may say that Dickinson is a non-teleological writer par excellence.

If Dickinson's overriding thematic concern is the distance of presence, her overriding formal strategy is to make words embody an alternative presence:

the presence of distance. Her non-instrumental, hands-off use of the word "Circumference" at the end of "At Half past Three," like her use of "Immortality" and "Mountains" elsewhere, registers an implicit claim about what words can do on their own, as well as about what words cannot do no matter how hard we try to make them bearers of our meaning. For a word that stands on its own is a reminder that words bear their own meaning; are each, as Bloom and Nietzsche attest, "a bias or inclination." The extraordinary trust that Dickinson places in words, the way that she makes them, rather than stories or arguments, ideas or descriptions, carry whole poems, is what saves her poetry, preoccupied as it is with bafflement, disappointment, aftermath, and withdrawing, from being merely melancholy. Thus, Anderson hears in "Circumference" both silence and exaltation: "Dickinson's exultant 'circumference' in the last line suggests a special amplitude in the silence that follows the song. Presence yields to Place, but the outcome of the exchange is fullness rather than deprivation."[45] The poem's last line, like the bird's call, and like a great many of Dickinson's lines, makes a kind of "cautious melody"—or, in Anderson's metaphor, an ample silence—by "Propound[ing] but a single term."

Anderson's hopeful reading notwithstanding, for Dickinson fullness and deprivation, presence and absence, are not easily separated; "At Half past Three" is as much about disappointment as it is about exhilaration. This paradox, and the ambiguities it produces in Dickinson's poetry, are two of my book's underlying subjects of discussion. They are, along with the paradoxes and ambiguities of Thoreau's dryly factual yet enthusiastic, even lyrical Journal, what the concept of non-teleological writing—writing at the limits of interpretation and of the self—is designed to help us understand. Chapter 3 will consider how such contradictions form the basis of the Journal's unique claim to the status of literature, and even of poetry.

CHAPTER 3

"Between Poetry and Natural Fact"
Thoreau's Journal

> You must be aware that *no thing* is what you have taken it to be. In what book is this world and its beauty described?
>
> —Henry David Thoreau, October 4, 1859

THREE CONTRADICTIONS

"Give me . . . the smallest share of all things but poetic perception" (PJ 4:17, 8/28/51), Thoreau wrote in his Journal in 1851—a decade before Dickinson's observation that "Perception of an object costs / Precise the Object's loss" (F1103). At two million words, Thoreau's Journal is a huge text which nevertheless aims not at accumulation and accomplishment but at loss and forgetting. Its ideal is not scientific or pedagogic but poetic, visionary. The writer wants simply to see things, which for him would mean to "ge[t] rid" of "knowledge and culture" (J 9:160, 12/5/56), "forget all our learning. . . . [and] approach [the natural object] as something totally strange" (J 12:371, 10/4/59):

> If you would make acquaintance with the ferns you must forget your botany. You must get rid of what is commonly called *knowledge* of them. Not a single scientific term or distinction is the least to the purpose, for you would fain perceive something, and you must approach the object totally unprejudiced. You must be aware that *no thing* is what you have

taken it to be.... You have got to be in a different state from common. Your greatest success will be simply to perceive that such things are, and you will have no communication to make to the Royal Society. (J 12:371, 10/4/59)

The Journal itself seems always to be "about to disintegrate," as François Specq has boldly observed.[1] Yet its subject, nature (the word derives, Specq notes, "from the Latin verb *nasci, natus*"),[2] is always just being born; each of its instantiations are "original and poetic ... not mere repetitions of the past" (J 10:241, 1/7/58). This is the vibrant yet ephemeral scaffolding against which the massive Journal rests; out of such "original and poetic" instants ("you have got to be in a different state from common") its prosaic bulk is cobbled.

Thoreau said of his "journalizing" that "it will allow nothing to be predicated of it" (PJ 1:237, 1/29/41). It is true that most predications about the Journal require qualification. It is exceedingly long, first of all—over seven thousand pages in the first, 1906 edition, which remains the only complete, or near-complete, edition—yet is composed almost entirely of short fragments. In the vast majority of entries, each paragraph, and often each sentence, records a new observation or insight, describes or responds to a different natural object or phenomenon.

Along with this first contradiction goes another, more complicated one. Although the Journal seems to be an attempt to comprehensively represent and catalog the flora, fauna, and natural phenomena of Concord, Massachusetts and its environs, it does not, in fact, provide such a catalog. Because there is no organizing principle to the Journal besides that of time and the seasons, its representations of nature are piecemeal. It gives glimpses of things rather than a natural history of things. Thoreau could easily have devoted some weeks or months to the study of a particular plant, animal, or phenomenon; if he had, the Journal would have become a series of exercises in natural history, on a par with his late essays in that discipline. He chose instead a peripatetic, paratactic mode of writing, such that the Journal never settles down on a topic or arranges topics in order of importance, but moves freely, apparently randomly, among its seemingly endless number of subjects: plants, animals, weather, light, water, clouds, fog, ice, snow, driftwood, sap, sound, local history, and so on. The book ends up feeling less like a study of these things than like a study of perception and interpretation, of how the mind relates to things and derives a kind of meaning from them despite having only the slightest connection with them. Thoreau's fragmentary observations are just that: evanescent connections with things which are otherwise alien and beneath notice. Thus, Theo Davis writes that, *pace* ecocritical interpretations of his work, Thoreau is most interested in "the precise experience not of place, or environment, but of the ongoing contacts made between mind and phenomena."[3]

Yet this fragmentary and evanescent quality is not a sign of lack of ambition, but quite the opposite:

> If it were required to know the position of the fruit-dots or the character of the indusium, nothing could be easier than to ascertain it; but if it is required that you be affected by ferns, that they amount to anything, signify anything, to you, that they be another sacred scripture and revelation to you, helping to redeem your life, this end is not so surely accomplished. (J 12:371–72, 10/4/59)

The "end" referred to here—"that you be affected by" natural objects, "that they . . . signify anything, to you"—is "not so surely accomplished," because it is not like ordinary ends; at least, it is not like the ends ordinarily attributed to writers. Thoreau wants simply to see things, and to be affected by them, rather than to know something about them and then put that knowledge to some more or less extraneous use. Practically any thing will do, which means that his subject is everything (i.e., nature) and his object, nothing (i.e., writing). Hence the odd but revealing statement, "My work is writing, and I do not hesitate, though I know that no subject is too trivial for me, tried by ordinary standards; for, ye fools, the theme is nothing, the life is everything" (J 9:121, 10/18/56).

Contradictory impulses are at play here. Thoreau aims simultaneously at self-consciousness (an intimacy with the self to whom trivial-seeming things "signify") and at selflessness or disinterestedness (a detachment from the self to whom they do not signify, for whom they could only be useful, in a scientific experiment for instance). Pursuing this vast, psychologically complex project interferes with the work of compiling, analyzing, and interpreting data about nature which the Journal is generally said to be performing. Its representations of nature, though painstaking at times, at other times can seem almost slipshod. Specq observes: "Many entries only offer suggestions of perception, sketchy notations, and minimal descriptions of the objects they mention."[4] "All nature is to be regarded as it concerns man," Thoreau says in a passage we'll return to (J 14:117, 10/13/60). And again: "man is all in all. Nature nothing, but as she draws him out and reflects him" (J 9:121, 10/18/56). This is not the self-effacing natural historian recent criticism has prepared us to expect. His aims are different than the scientist's: less concrete and communicable, and less modest as well. This may be a controversial claim today, but it was once taken for granted among Thoreau's detractors. Frank Egerton and Laura Dassow Walls provide a glimpse of these early critics' disapprobation of Thoreau as nature observer in their article, "Rethinking Thoreau and the History of American Ecology."[5] Of particular interest among the statements they quote from are John Burroughs's observation, "The scientific interpretation of things did not interest [Thoreau] at all. He was interested in things only so far as they related to Henry Thoreau. He interpreted Nature entirely in the light of his own idiosyncrasies,"[6] and Joseph Wood Krutch's even harsher judgment,

> The completely unsystematic, almost desperately pointless character of [Thoreau's] own quasi-scientific recordings is evidence enough that he did not really grasp what slight philosophical implications the vast enterprise of collecting and cataloguing did have; and it is quite obvious, from his various derogatory references to science, that in his mind it stood, not (as it might have) for an attempt to penetrate the secrets of life, but for the mere assembling of meaningless details.[7]

While Egerton and Walls are probably right in claiming that Burroughs and Krutch overlooked, as some prominent early ecologists did not, the useful contributions to science contained in the Journal and other of Thoreau's writings, Burroughs and Krutch were not entirely wrong either. The Journal may seem to aspire to comprehensiveness—to the "regularity and completeness" of "scientific notebooks [and] laboratory records," to borrow Walls's terms[8]—but in fact it aspires to a kind of visionary sensibility or "poetic perception," which disallows comprehensiveness and continuity.

Recent critical efforts to bolster the Journal's reputation as an artistically or (more often) scientifically significant document have emphasized the cohesiveness lent to its entries by Thoreau's preoccupation with tracking seasonal change, especially as reflected by the coming into blossom of perennial flowers. It is true that this subject keeps the Journal from feeling inordinately digressive, but it would be a mistake to say that charting seasonal change is the object of Thoreau's study. "The seasons and all their changes are in me," he writes. "I see not a dead eel or floating snake, or a gull, but it rounds my life and is like a line or accent in its poem" (J 10:127, 10/26/57). Thus, the Journal recurs to the subject of the seasons less because they are the object scrutinized than because they are the lens through which nature and the self can be viewed together, as complementary and even inseparable. Both nature and the self are seen to be constantly in flux, comprising an infinite number of minor phenomena, each of which plays a role, "like a line or accent in its poem." In other words, Thoreau writes about seasonal change because for him nature simply is seasonal change: it cannot be separated from the changes it is continually undergoing, any more than it can be abstracted from the myriad details that constitute it. Neither can Thoreau himself be separated from the fluctuating things he observes and writes about—the things which "dra[w] him out and reflec[t] him." Thoreau conceives of the self not as essential but as contingent, seasonal: a function of the seasons, and a seasonal phenomenon in its own right.

This is a difficult point, but one that is worth elaborating on, as will be seen when we arrive at the third and (from our perspective) central contradiction in the Journal, namely, the inseparability of poetry and natural fact in its pages. "Besides being nonhierarchical, Thoreau's Journal is also fundamentally nonteleological," Specq writes.[9] Because the Journal's subject is *just* nature, not any particular facet of nature but every and any facet, and because it views the self as inseparable from nature (the seasons are in the author; he encounters himself, his being, by way of his encounters with nature), none of the Journal's descriptions or reflections or flights of poetic imagination are specially privileged, given pride of place; no one of the writer's encounters is more likely than any of the rest to "amount to anything, to signify, to [him]" (J 12:371–72, 10/4/59). In the following passage, for example, every sentence does its work, is essential, because no one sentence or group of sentences conveys the "point" to which the others are subordinated. It is late March, the ground is slowly being laid bare of snow in a few spots, and "all the inhabitants of nature," Thoreau not excepted, are interested in whatever "bare and dry spot" they can find:

> P. M.—To Walden.
>
> The sugar maple sap flows, and for aught I know is as early as the red.
> I think I may say that the snow has been *not less than a foot deep on a level* in open land until to-day, since January 6th, about eleven weeks.

It probably begins to be less about this date. The bare ground begins to appear where the snow is worn in the street. It has been steadily melting since March 13th, the thermometer rising daily to 40 and 45 at noon, but no rain.

The east side of the Deep Cut is nearly bare, as is the railroad itself, and, on the driest part of the sandy slope, I go looking for *Cicindela*,—to see it run or fly amid the sere blackberry vines,—some life which the warmth of the dry sand under the spring sun has called forth; but I see none. I am reassured and reminded that I am the heir of eternal inheritances which are inalienable, when I feel the warmth reflected from this sunny bank, and see the yellow sand and the reddish subsoil, and hear some dried leaves rustle and the trickling of melting snow in some sluiceway. The eternity which I detect in Nature I predicate of myself also. How many springs I have had this same experience! I am encouraged, for I recognize this steady persistency and recovery of Nature as a quality of myself.

The first places which I observe to be bare now, though the snow is generally so deep still, are the steep hillsides facing the south, as the side of the Cut (though it looks not south exactly) and the slope of Heywood's Peak toward the pond, also under some trees in a meadow (there is less snow there on account of eddy, and apparently the tree absorbs heat), or a ridge in the same place. Almost the whole of the steep hillside on the north of Walden is now bare and dry and warm, though fenced in with ice and snow. It has attracted partridges, four of which whir away on my approach. There the early sedge is exposed, and, looking closer, I observe that it has been sheared off close down, when green, far and wide, and the fallen withered tops are little handfuls of hay by their sides, which have been covered by the snow and sometimes look as if they had served as nests for the mice,—for their green droppings are left in them abundantly,—yet not such plain nests as in the grain-field last spring,—probably the *Mus leucopus*,—and the wintergreen and the sere pennyroyal still retain some fragrance.

As I was returning on the railroad, at the crossing beyond the shanty, hearing a rustling, I saw a striped squirrel amid the sedge on the bare east bank, twenty feet distant. After observing me a few moments, as I stood perfectly still between the rails, he ran straight up to within three feet of me, out of curiosity; then, after a moment's pause, and looking up to my face, turned back and finally crossed the railroad. All the red was on his rump and hind quarters. When running he carried his tail erect, as he scratched up the snowy bank.

Now then the steep hillsides begin to be bare, and the early sedge and sere, but still fragrant, pennyroyal and rustling leaves are exposed, and you see where the mice have sheared off the sedge and also made nests of its top during the winter. There, too, the partridges resort, and perhaps you hear the bark of a striped squirrel, and see him scratch toward his hole, rustling the leaves. For all the inhabitants of nature are attracted by this bare and dry spot, as well as you. (J 8:222–24, 3/23/56)

Of particular interest in this passage is the fact that Thoreau effectively rewrote one of its paragraphs. The paragraph beginning "Now then the steep south hillsides begin to be bare," reprises the paragraph beginning "The first places which I observe to be bare now," switching from first- to third-person perspective, and removing place names and other details. On the one hand, this is evidence that Thoreau continued, in his late career, to use the Journal as a site for drafting passages that he might later use in published works. On the other hand, the repetition has an intrinsic value, for it helps to create a richer and more layered view of this scene, which is a picture not just of the earth exposing itself at the end of winter, but also of earth's inhabitants both exposing and (in the case of the mice) being exposed. The writer, too, exposes and is exposed: in the first-person paragraphs the reader accompanies him in his searching, and in the third-person paragraph the reader glimpses his mind at work (lightly) processing what he has found.

There is something pleasing about Thoreau's anticlimactic statement, "I go looking for *Cicindela*,—to see it run or fly amid the sere blackberry vines,—some life which the warmth of the dry sand under the spring sun has called forth; but I see none." Such sentences, from which the writer's thoughts are "seen by the reader not to be far fetched" but based on direct personal experience (PJ 4:296, 1/27/52), complete with all its disappointments and satisfactions, its boredom and excitement, are as crucial to the Journal's success as declarations along the lines of "The eternity which I detect in Nature I predicate of myself also." Likewise, the concise, third-person paragraph above, with its carefully constructed topic sentence and concluding sentence, is not to be preferred over the digressive, first-person, more detailed version. Their juxtaposition demonstrates the basis of poetry in the messiness of direct first-hand experience (mouse droppings and all). More than this, it shows poetry and fact to be interdependent, and so not really distinguishable. Without the details and circumstances of perception to anchor them, and without the punctuating digressions (the encounter with the squirrel, for instance) which are often all that an entry consists of, the Journal's eloquent general statements ("I am reassured and reminded that I am the heir of eternal inheritances which are inalienable"; "Now then the steep hillsides begin to be bare"; "For all the inhabitants of nature are attracted by this bare and dry spot, as well as you") would not seem poetic, because their eloquence would not, as it does here, seem hard-won, like a crystal in a cavern, as Thoreau once described the relation between his thoughts and their setting (PJ 4:296, 1/28/52).

This brings us to the third and most important contradiction characterizing the Journal. On the one hand the Journal is deliberately, even defiantly mundane in its outlook, and dwells with patience and pleasure on the minutest of subjects—subjects which show little promise of yielding poetic or philosophical insights. (Early commentators, who complained of the overwhelming proliferation of facts in the Journal, failed to recognize the deliberateness with which this seemingly "barren" subject matter had been chosen. A partial exception is Alfred Kazin, who acknowledged the self-consciousness of the Journal's ordinariness or dullness without pursuing the implications of this: "the Journal bogs down after the middle volumes into disjointed nature notes of whose barrenness even as scientific information [Thoreau] was well aware.")[10] On the other hand, in the midst of this resigned-seeming pursuit of the ordinary (which after all is not so much a destination as a refuge from destinations, a utopia or nowhere), the Journal evinces the author's conviction that he is tracking a profound mystery. "It is not natural for a man to write this well every day," Kazin said of the Journal.[11] The remark implies that not everything deserves to be written about, much less written about with the care and verve that Thoreau devotes indiscriminately to each of his myriad subjects. Even his friend and walking companion William Ellery Channing puzzled over the intensity of Thoreau's interest in the ordinary: "Why did he care so much about being a writer? . . . Why was he so much interested in the river and the woods and the sky, etc.? Something peculiar, I judge." So peculiar, in fact, that according to Channing "his journals should not be permitted to be read by any."[12]

We find in Thoreau a disillusioned or simply illusionless love of fact, combined with an equal love of language's fictive, evocative powers. It is perhaps this combination, this dual commitment to nature and to "being a writer," which Angus Fletcher picks up on when he cites the following phrase from *Walden* as an example of "the gnomic sentence": "I was determined to know beans" (W 7:451).[13] Like many of Fletcher's examples of the gnomic (which include *Hamlet*'s opening line, "Who's there?," and Keats's famous "Beauty is truth, truth beauty"), this line is more than a bit of word play but also more—by virtue of being less—than philosophy. It seems unclassifiable except, perhaps, as poetry. As Kenneth Gross suggests in some recent reflections on Fletcher's work, "the true gnome" tries to stand outside of or at least athwart discourse; it "is resistant to mere interpretation and also . . . to the appropriations of ideology. Inescapably an artifact of language, the gnome yet speaks its own silence, its own loss of sense, speaks of what language can only name or know by indirection, telling the truth 'slant,' as Emily Dickinson says one must."[14] Like the Journal, the gnome will allow nothing, or nothing definite, to be predicated of it. And like the standard Journal sentence, it will not lend itself to use in the construction of a larger linguistic artifact, but insists, instead, on its own inexplicable claim to the status of literature, of meaningfulness. But whereas the gnome tends toward abstraction, the Journal of course tends in the opposite direction, while retaining the allure of the intangible. We find a closer equivalent for its non-teleological, almost non-discursive poetics in Ezra Pound's explication of Imagism: "The image is itself the speech. The image is the word beyond formulated language."[15]

"Speak," Thoreau urges himself on December 25, 1851, "though your thought presupposes the non existence of your hearers.–thoughts that transcend life & death" (PJ 4:224, 12/25/51). Yet what such thoughts turn out to concern is not so much transcendent and unimaginable as simply unimagined—like Pound's "image," noticed by the eye, but never before by the imagination. They concern that which seems beneath notice. The day after forming the resolution above, Thoreau sees for the first time that tired oxen "behaved as a tired wood-chopper might. This was to me a new phase in the life of the laboring ox. It is painful to think how they may sometimes be overworked. I saw that even the ox could be weary with toil" (PJ 4:224, 12/26/51). And the day after that he discovers that preceding "the real sunset" there is another, "apparent" one, when "all the vales even to the horizon are full of a purple vapor–which half veils the distant *mts*–and the windows of undiscoverable farm houses– shine like an early candle or a fire" (PJ 4:224, 12/27/51). Equally exemplary of Thoreau's imaginative noticing, his (Gross might say) silent speaking or speaking silence, is the same entry's simple yet emphatic observation (it gets a paragraph all to itself), "It is remarkable that the sun rarely goes down without a cloud" (PJ 4:225, 12/27/51).

When a thaw sets in on the twenty-eighth, Thoreau writes, "The snow rapidly dissolving, in all hollows a pond forming–unfathomable water beneath the snow" (PJ 4:225, 12/28/51). As in the comparisons of the reflected sunlight to "an early candle or a fire," and of the ox to a tired laborer, the point of this sentence is not to bring the object closer, to humanize it, but rather to look farther into it, away from the human if need be. Thus, the ox becomes no longer just an ox, tool of man, but also something uncanny in its resemblance to a man, while the snow "rapidly dissolv[es]" and yields to something less definite and nameable: "unfathomable water beneath the snow." To see and report such things is close at once to poetry and to philosophy, though it also resembles science. It is a matter of knowing beans, of "be[ing] aware that *no thing* is what you have taken it to be" (J 12:371, 10/4/59), as when Thoreau looked across Walden Pond and "was reminded that this on which I dwelt was but *dry land*" (W 2:392).

Not in spite of but because of their unusual, almost gnomic starkness—the impression they give of leading nowhere, as if their significance were self-contained, immanent—observations such as those just cited are poetic. They suggest that there is, as Fletcher puts it, "an almost genetic connection between poetry and natural fact."[16] That connection is arguably the central concern of Thoreau's writing. His first book affirms that "We can never safely exceed the actual facts in our narratives. . . . A true account of the actual is the rarest poetry";[17] and the Journal, the only one of his books vast and formless enough to allow for "a true account of the actual," puts that hypothesis to the test. Making a true account of the actual, of things, is according to Thoreau not something science and philosophy have shown themselves capable of, or interested in: "In our science and philosophy, even, there is commonly no true and absolute account of things."[18] By a seeming paradox, expressing the plain sense of things, not ideas about the thing but the thing itself, is, as Wallace Stevens would have agreed, a task for a poet, not for a scientist or a philosopher. Because the poet's language is free to dispense with ideas, as we observed in the previous chapter, there is a kind of purity to his or her acts of naming and describing. "Beyond the bondage to institutions," Stanley Cavell writes in *The Senses of Walden*, "we have put nature in bondage, bound it to our uses and to our hurried capacities for sensing, rather than learning of its autonomy. And this means that an object named does not exist for us in its name."[19] Branka Arsić, seconding Cavell, calls this "Thoreau's central discovery."[20] It takes a poet to see that we don't know beans, and that therefore to tell the facts about beans, or simply to name them, is a task no less demanding than that of lyric or even epic poetry.

The Journal is the testing ground (Specq calls it "the workshop of being") for the hypothesis that there is a close connection between poetry and natural fact; that to accurately describe things, with no ulterior motive, no ideology, no telos, would be to write poetry. Borrowing one of Fletcher's key terms, we might call the Journal one long "environment-poem," a kind of descriptive writing in which "the most factual of relations to nature give rise to a new form of the transcendental, namely the gnomic expression of immanent transcendence."[21] There is a lightness or mere-ness of significance, even of transcendence, in the poets Fletcher's book discusses (John Clare, Walt Whitman, and John Ashbery), which recalls the tension, in the Journal sentences quoted above, between the sense that there is nothing more to say and the sense that nothing more needs saying: an impossible sense at once of barrenness and of pregnancy. "A book of philosophy suitable to what Thoreau envisions as 'students,'" writes Cavell, "would be written with next to no forward motion, one that culminates in each sentence."[22] As the example of the gnome demonstrated, what seems like failure to sustain a train of thought may be poetically, or philosophically, motivated.

Consider, as a specimen both of pregnant barrenness and of what I've described as the Journal's fluctuating scaffolding, the following passage:

> I do not know exactly what that sweet word is which the chickadee says when it hops near to me now in those ravines.
>
> > The chickadee
> > Hops near to me.
>
> When the air is thick and the sky overcast, we need not walk so far. We give our attention to nearer objects, being less distracted from them. I take occasion to explore some near wood which my walks commonly overshoot.
>
> What a difference it makes between two ravines in other respects exactly similar that in the one there is a stream which drains it, while the other is dry!
>
> I see nowadays in various places the scattered feathers of robins, etc., where some hawk or beast of prey has torn them to pieces.

I step over the slip-noose snares which some woodling has just set.
How long since men set snares for partridges and rabbits?

Ah, my friends, I know you better than you think, and love you better, too. The day after never, we will have an explanation. (J 10:171–72, 11/8/57)

The concluding sentence of this passage acknowledges the author's obligation to his audience once, and negates that obligation twice: first, by naming "the day after never" as the time at which this obligation will be fulfilled; and second, by recording this acknowledgment in his Journal, a text without a (contemporary) audience. When attempting to understand this enigmatic statement, two points are worth considering. First, when Thoreau says "My friends," it may be that he is referring not just to fellow human beings who might read his words—for instance, the men responsible for laying the "slip-noose snares"—but also to fellow creatures who could not read his words, whether they were published or not: for instance, the chickadee that hopped near to him, or even the dead birds whose remains he has just observed. This possibility opens up a second one: that when Thoreau says "we will have an explanation," he may be positioning himself not as the author—the figure of authority—responsible for providing, or at least for seeking, an explanation, but instead as a fellow reader, not of words but of events, phenomena, sensations, thoughts. "We will have," not "I will give," "an explanation." If this "we" is not exclusively human, then the kind of explanation that is envisioned here, and the unspecified hermeneutic problem which that explanation would presumably solve, are likewise not limited to human concerns and kinds of understanding; this would explain why Thoreau is not positioned to provide the explanation himself. As Cameron puts it, he "seeks to discover alternative orders of significance"; he does not pretend to hold the key to those mysterious "orders."

Thoreau in the Journal is more concerned about his relation to things and animals than he is about his relation to other humans. It is not surprising, then, that he does not harbor plans of publication for this text, does not compel his experiments and observations to yield results that might be useful or interesting or persuasive to scientific organizations, and does not cull the Journal for its more ostensibly literary passages in order to publish these elsewhere. The only goal he seems to entertain for this text is the exploration of and immersion in goals other than his own, indeed other than human. When he slips on the frozen river and spills a pail of sap he is bringing home to make syrup with (not, by the way, for the sake of the syrup so much as for the sake of seeing how it is made), he reflects that "when the river breaks up, it [the sap] will go down the Concord into the Merrimack, and down the Merrimack into the sea, and there get salted as well as diluted, part being boiled into sugar. It suggests, at any rate, what various liquors, beside those containing salt, find their way to the sea,—the sap of how many kinds of trees!" (J 8:209, 3/16/56). He is thinking (and writing) non-teleologically here, because he is deliberately opening his mind (and text) to purposes besides his own: purposes, like those of "various liquors . . . find[ing] their way to the sea," not detectable or explainable by scientists. Hence, "the day after never we will have an explanation": there is an explanation for how each event, no matter how accidental seeming, plays its role, fulfills its purpose, but (as Franz Kafka famously said of hope) it is not for us, at least not in this world, in this time.

Explanations are not what Thoreau traffics in, but mysteries, and the larger mystery of how each individual mystery interrelates:

> Why should just these sights & sounds accompany our life? Why should I hear the chattering of blackbirds–why smell the skunk each year? I would fain explore the mysterious relation between myself & these things. I would at least know what these things unavoidably are--make a chart of our life–know how its shores trend–that butterflies reappear & when–know why just this circle of creatures completes the world. (PJ 4:468, 4/18/52).

The selection of examples here is worth noting: the noise of birds, the smell of skunks, the lives of butterflies. The relevance of such things to human existence is real, but Thoreau chooses them for their apparent irrelevance. Not until "the day after never," that is to say, not until the human perspective is supplemented or supplanted by some kind of transcendent vision (one that, for instance, would not be governed by our conception of time), could it become possible to know "why just this circle of creatures" are our companions in this world. To "explore the mysterious relation between myself & these things" means living and thinking and writing at the margins of culture; it is to continually risk being irrelevant. Perhaps this is why Thoreau says he wishes to "know how its [our life's] shores trend." The shores are where "our life" ends and verges on other kinds of life, which cannot be explained to us so long as we are mortals, and which are therefore irrelevant insofar as relevance is a measure of what we can understand and, in turn, use. "Nature puts no question and answers none which we mortals ask" (W 16:547): it is full of answers, only not for us.

The text in which Thoreau concerns himself most directly with spiritual matters, namely, his correspondence with the ex-minister H. G. O. Blake, reveals a man of earnest spiritual aspirations, yet one who distrusted the forms that human spirituality takes. Even the word "God" is one that he uses only with a caveat, conscious that he is using a borrowed language which he cannot trust: "I say, God. I am not sure that that is the name. You will know whom I mean."[23] The point of this seems to be that, while God is real (Thoreau says in a previous letter, "I know that I am–I know that another is who knows more than I who takes interest in me, whose creature and yet whose kindred, in one sense, am I"),[24] the linguistic and conceptual equipment with which we approach Him is extremely faulty, even treacherous. Hence, "Let *God* alone if need be. Methinks, if I loved him more, I should keep him, I should keep myself rather, at a more respectful distance. It is not when I am going to meet him, but when I am just turning away and leaving him alone, that I discover that God is."[25] In keeping with this resolution, on the rare occasions when God is referred to in the Journal, it is either in a cryptic, riddling manner (as in a passage discussed below, where a fish is named "another image of God"), or indirectly, as when Thoreau alludes to the "Artist" responsible for nature's fantastic beauty and ingenuity. There is almost nothing in the way of explicit praise of God in the Journal, though indirectly the Journal does little else but praise God, by way of appreciating every nuance of His creation. ("I know that the enterprise is worthy–I know that things work well. I have heard no bad news.")[26]

The letters to Blake are characterized at once by the author's confidence in the worthiness of spiritual striving in general, and by his uncertainty about the success of his striving in particular. Thoreau seems to doubt, not the reality of what is strived for, but his (or anyone's) ability to define and know that object. The letters are full of acknowledgments of how far short the author falls of the ideal of which he receives vague but undeniable intimations. ("These things I say; other things I do," one letter concludes.)[27] Yet, rather than bemoan his failure to attain or even define his object, Thoreau almost seems to celebrate it. Quoting back to him Blake's complaint that "the serene hours in which

Friendship, Books, Nature, Thought, seem alone primary considerations, visit [him] but faintly," Thoreau responds by questioning the dichotomy between presence and absence, achievement and failure, realization and expectation: "Is not the attitude of expectation somewhat divine?–a sort of home-made divineness? Does it not compel a kind of sphere music to attend on it? And do not its satisfactions merge at length by insensible degrees in the enjoyment of the thing expected?"[28]

It may be that "the thing expected" to which Thoreau alludes here is precisely the "explanation" which he confidently declares "we shall have," but not until "the day after never." This perpetual deferment is, in Thoreau's eyes, both desirable and inevitable. It is desirable because "the attitude of expectation" is itself "somewhat divine," since "its satisfactions merge at length . . . in the enjoyment of the thing expected." And it is inevitable because what is expected is not in fact a "thing" like other things—the chickadee, the bird feathers, the animal traps—that could be simply perceived and described. It is, rather, something that can be experienced only by way of the "attitude of expectation" that one brings to such ordinary things when one is prepared to receive from them an intimation of the divine. This is the attitude in which the Journal was written. Thoreau dreams not of understanding ferns, but of being amazed by them, as if by "sacred . . . revelation": "If it is required that you be affected by ferns . . . that they be another sacred scripture and revelation to you, helping to redeem your life, this end is not so surely accomplished" (J 12:371–72, 10/4/59).

Thoreau's letters to Blake reveal a tension between his belief in an ultimate, overarching "thing" or "explanation," on the one hand, and his belief that such a thing or explanation is not available to us, at least not in this life, on the other. These two convictions explain the attitude of heightened, expectant, sustained attention directed at natural objects in the Journal, which is one of the text's defining characteristics. Each object suggests the presence of the divine, yet none is capable of more than suggesting; none can instantiate or represent or explain the divine. An explanation is believed in and even, in a sense, looked for, but it is not actively sought. Thus, when Thoreau says, "Why should just these sights & sounds accompany our life?" (PJ 4:468, 4/18/52), his desire for an answer is sincere, but he knows that that answer will not take the form of anything other than the sights and sounds themselves. Yet "the sights and sounds themselves" do not disappoint, for, as Thoreau says in another entry, "Mere facts & dates & names communicate more than we suspect" (PJ 4:296, 1/27/52). There is nothing modest, then, let alone defeatist, in Thoreau's statement of purpose, "Your greatest success will be simply to perceive that such things are" (J 12:371). It is, perhaps, a measure of the failure of human perception—or rather, of the failure of humans to take perception seriously—that it is so hard to accept that a writer of Thoreau's caliber should have adopted perception as his life's goal.

Consider once more the passage from Fletcher's *A New Theory for American Poetry* from which this chapter borrows its title:

> Besides recognizing the truths hidden in the long annals of natural history and natural science, we can recognize another truth, that poets seem quite unable to express what counts most for humans without invoking the merest things of nature and nature's various appearances. When I speak . . . of description, I am speaking about this almost genetic connection between poetry and natural fact.[29]

Especially interesting here is the word "merest," as well as the phrase "nature's various appearances." The subtle negativity of these words connects to the negativity implied in Fletcher's phrase "poets seem quite unable to express what counts most for humans." Note, though, how a superlative sneaks into this discussion of mereness, appearances, and the inability to express, for Fletcher apparently takes it for granted that the thing which poets seek to express, even when their ostensible subject matter is "the merest things of nature and nature's various appearances," is "what counts most for humans." The commingling here of negation and privation with affirmation and excess aligns Fletcher's statement with Thoreau's "Mere facts & dates & names communicate more than we suspect." "What counts most for humans," according to both Fletcher and Thoreau, is communicated to them, albeit cryptically, via nature; indeed, it cannot be communicated otherwise.

Fletcher echoes, as well, the Dickinson poem beginning "The Tint I cannot take—is best" (F696), which identifies in nature a "secret—that was pushing / Like Chariots," yet never quite able to escape, expose itself. What "counts most" for this speaker, what "is best," is what she cannot imitate or represent or express except, as Fletcher suggests, by "invoking the merest things of nature and nature's various appearances": "Color," "the sky," "Landscapes," "Summer," "Snow" (F696). What both Dickinson and Fletcher hint at is what

Pound phrases more programmatically when he says, "The image is itself the speech."[30] It is not an obscurantist impulse away from humanity and reason that motivates image-, appearance-, and thing-oriented poetry, but rather a commitment to precisely "what matters most to humans," even though this, paradoxically enough, seems to reside in the non-human: what we "cannot take," that is, absorb into our selves. (Dickinson alludes in this phrase to the dyeing of fabrics, which can "take" certain colors and not others.)[31] Thoreau's and Dickinson's reliance on images and things does not signal a rejection of ideas or of humanity, but is motivated by a commitment to ideas, or ideals, that perpetually elude and therefore perpetually fascinate humanity: ideals such as Thoreau hints at when he imagines a transformative "explanation" to be given "the day after never," and such as Dickinson hints at with her image of a "Color too remote / That I could show it in Bazaar—/ A Guinea at a sight" (F696).

"FORGOTTEN, AS FULFILLED"

Although keeping a journal was a common practice in mid-nineteenth-century New England, Thoreau's own journal-writing practice, which by the last decade of his life came to dwarf his other endeavors—namely, his composition of books and essays for publication, and of lectures for performance—was a source of bafflement for his contemporaries. Channing, as we've noted, felt that Thoreau's "journals should not be permitted to be read by any." He could never "understand what [Thoreau] meant by his life," such as it is recorded and, indeed, lived in the Journal: "Why did he care so much about being a writer? Why did he pay so much attention to his own thoughts? Why was he so dissatisfied with everyone else, etc.? Why was he so much interested in the river and the woods and the sky, etc.?"[32] And Emerson, in his eulogy for his former protégé, lamented: "I cannot help counting it a fault in him that he had no ambition. Wanting that, instead of engineering for all America, he was the captain of a huckleberry-party."[33] Emerson did not mention that those huckleberry parties were one of the myriad subjects of Thoreau's Journal, whose author, as Channing perceived, was more interested in huckleberries, and in the thoughts they gave rise to, than in readers, let alone in "engineering for all America." If writing enthusiastically yet indiscriminately about huckleberries, "his own thoughts," and "the river and the woods and the sky, etc.," counted as an ambition with Thoreau, it evidently did not with Emerson and Channing.

Taken at face value, the Journal is not problematic. It is, simply, a record—seven thousand pages long and twenty-four years in the making—of the author's daily hikes, observations, reflections, and experiments. What is problematic, as Channing's and Emerson's comments suggest, is that the author of *Walden* and of "Resistance to Civil Government," a writer and philosopher of great talent and ambition, seems to have devoted his last dozen years or so to the making of this modest-seeming record. I contend that Thoreau was aware of the problem—which we might loosely refer to as the pointlessness of the Journal, its lack of a telos—and that it was inseparable from the shift in thinking and writing that the Journal represented for him. His contemporaries as well as modern-day critics have failed to understand this shift, in large part because so few major writers before or since have undergone it. It is the shift toward disinterested writing: writing that lacks "ambition" in Emerson's sense; that is not for publication but for its own sake, or perhaps, for its subject matter's sake. As Thoreau put it, "A writer a man writing is the scribe of all nature–he is the corn & the grass & the atmosphere writing" (PJ 4:28, 9/2/1851).

How is one to read a text whose only goal is seeing, and whose author aspires to speak in a manner that "presupposes the non-existence" of his hearers? What interpretation can there be of a book of pregnant barrenness or "immanent transcendence," a book that seems both to begin and to end in each of its paragraphs—to culminate in a way that is indistinguishable from trailing off? I will argue that Thoreau is aware of these difficulties; that as a "reader" of nature he shares their burden; and that his own patient, negatively capable responses to natural objects and phenomena are meant to model the kind of attention we must bring to the reading of the Journal.

Think of the following passage as a lesson in seeing to see, or what we might call the reading of things. In it Thoreau first expresses interest in a natural object because of its association with something he has read, then feels depressed by an unfavorable comparison between his own "pursuit" and those he has read about, and finally feels renewed interest in the natural object, this time not because it has figured in another, more glamorous literary account, but because it has figured in the life of another creature—"*any* creature," never mind which.

These hot afternoons I go panting through the close sprout-lands and copses, as now from Cliff Brook to Wheeler meadow, and occasionally come to sandy places a few feet in diameter where the partridges have dusted themselves. Gérard, the lion-killer of Algiers, speaks of seeing similar spots when tracking or patiently waiting the lion there, and his truth in this particular is a confirmation of the rest of his story. But his pursuit dwarfs this fact and makes it seem trivial. Shall not my pursuit also contrast with the trivialness of the partridges' dusting? It is interesting to find that the same phenomena, however simple, occur in different parts of the globe. I have found an arrowhead or two in such places even. Far in warm, sandy woods in hot weather, when not a breath of air is stirring, I come upon these still sandier and warmer spots where the partridges have dusted themselves, now all still and deserted, and am not relieved, yet pleased to find that I have been preceded, by any creature. (J 8:421, 7/21/56)

The central sentence of this paragraph, "But his pursuit dwarfs this fact and makes it seem trivial," acts as a kind of litmus test, determining by its effect on the reader whether his or her outlook is or is not teleological. At first the sentence seems to exalt Gérard for having embarked on a life and work that make such simple natural phenomena "seem trivial" by comparison. But as the paragraph proceeds one starts to wonder if Thoreau did not mean to rebuke Gérard, or rather himself, for having belittled a natural fact. Under scrutiny, this passage, like many others of its kind, unearths a kind of poetry in facts: a mysterious value undetected by those who are impressed by lion killing and other "exciting" pursuits. Thoreau is here struggling—for our benefit as much as his own, it almost seems—to value a fact for its own sake rather than for its connection or contribution to a humanly constructed scheme. But it is not just the connection to Gérard's exploits that he struggles to forget, to lose his awe for; it is also the connection to his own text, which paradoxically becomes forgotten when it is most interesting, that is, when he is most interested in writing it. Perhaps this is why he lets the rhetorical question, "Shall not my pursuit also contrast with the trivialness of the partridges' dusting?" drop without answering it. In the moment of pure encounter, when he "find[s] that [he has] been preceded, by any creature," his "pursuit" becomes a matter of indifference, and the previously indifferent object becomes the sole focus of interest.

"It is interesting to find that the same phenomena, however simple, occur in different parts of the globe," Thoreau writes. The point is not to exoticize the ordinary, but to impress upon himself the reality of this seemingly simple fact, that partridges bathe themselves in dust. His aim is neither more nor less than "the perpetual instilling and drenching of the reality which surrounds us" (W 2:399). Elsewhere in the Journal, Thoreau considers conflicting accounts of how a seated partridge makes a loud "drumming" noise by beating its powerful wings. Does it "strik[e] its wings together behind its back, as a cock often does," or does it strike its own body or the object on which it is perched? (J 7:208, 2/22/55). Thoreau wants to get to the bottom of this matter for the same reason that he wants to measure the bottom of Walden Pond and is "determined to know beans." In another entry, he writes that their "drumming" is so "forcible" it is "as if it were a throbbing or fluttering in our veins or bones or the chambers of the ears & belonging to ourselves" (PJ 6:113, 5/11/53), and in yet another, "What singularly–space penetrating & filling sound–! why am I never nearer to its source!" (J 3:261, 6/13/51). As these sentences indicate, Thoreau is both more intimate with nature and more respectfully aware of its distance and difference than a scientist would allow him or herself to be. The last sentence of the passage above, for example, with its slow build-up, rather anti-climactic encounter, and oddly satisfied winding-down—"Far in warm, sandy woods in hot weather, when not a breath of air is stirring, I come upon these still sandier and warmer spots where the partridges have dusted themselves, now all still and deserted, and am not relieved, yet pleased to find that I have been preceded, by any creature"—sounds like a description of a strange sort of pilgrimage. Sites of pilgrimage are, after all, typically sites of absence: places where something holy once was, and where relics now are; hence, sites at once of disappointment and of mysterious, apparently causeless emotion.

I suspect that Thoreau, who was fond both of reading and of writing travel narratives, was aware of the pilgrim-like attitude adopted here and in other pages of the Journal; his disappointment and pleasure seem self-conscious, even deliberate. I also agree with Cavell that he was aware of the boredom and disappointment his style of writing could cause, and that indeed boredom is "part of his subject."[34] And surely he was aware of the connotations of dust, both in the Bible, where man is said to be originally, essentially dust, hence destined to return to being dust (Gen. 3:19), and in the popular imagination, where then as now dust suggested dullness, ugliness, discomfort, worthlessness, and even death and annihilation. If these assumptions are correct, it follows that the present passage, like significant portions of *Walden* and like many other, outwardly unassuming passages of the Journal, is not simply ignorant or careless of conventions, but defiant of them. For all its unsentimental matter-of-factness, it partakes of the romantic (especially Wordsworthian) tradition of valorizing and defamiliarizing the ordinary and despised. In the Journal things return to us slightly altered.

"Not relieved, yet pleased." Anxieties about "my pursuit" ("Shall not my pursuit also contrast with the trivialness of the partridges' dusting?") not resolved but momentarily tabled, forgotten. In a sense the object of Thoreau's pursuit is precisely such forgetfulness, as several of the statements quoted earlier suggest. But without a firm basis in self-interest, the writer's interest in his subject, and in turn the reader's interest in the text, has something phantom-like about it, reminding one of the disjunctive, short-lived reveries depicted in Keats's "Ode to a Nightingale," with its troubled last line, "Fled is that music:—do I wake or sleep?"[35] The paragraph immediately following the passage above, for example, does not pick up where the other left off, continuing its line of thought. It is just four words long, and lacks all but the slightest implication of a personal pronoun, an "I" to whom the reported fact matters and to whom the "I" of the previous paragraph is joined: "Grapes ready to stew" (J 8:421, 7/21/56). Absent here, however, is the feeling of disenchantment that concludes Keats's "Ode." For there is almost nothing in the Journal to bring the writer, as the word "Forlorn" brings Keats's speaker, "back from [nature] to [his] sole self."[36] This is one way of saying that there is no way of ending the poem, only countless ways of starting a new poem. If Keats had been Thoreau, his Ode would have gone right on to describe the sound of crickets or of frogs, or perhaps the sight of moonlight reflected in water, after the nightingale's music had fled. Or else it would have ended, but only to pick up again where it left off the next day.

The Journal is a book of losing and forgetting, of starting over, just as much as it is (in H. Daniel Peck's assessment) "a book of memory."[37] According to Specq, this text "possesses an indefiniteness, as if it were about to disintegrate, or rather refused ever to cohere."[38] In "Thoreau's Journal or The Workshop of Being," Specq argues that the Journal substitutes a non-linear for a linear time scale, of *kairos* for *chronos*.[39] This substitution is effectively a renunciation of telos: a renunciation, first, of a consistent goal, the gradual accomplishment of which meaningfully and hierarchically connects otherwise unrelated things and moments; and second, of a worldview according to which the value and meaning of a thing or moment is a function of its participation in a larger system, or of its demonstration of the law(s) governing that system.

Although Thoreau occasionally suggests that his writing has a destination, an end point—"and at last I may make wholes of parts" (PJ 4:277, 22 January 1852)—the Journal's overall structuring through mere juxtaposition and accretion means that there is no point where things come to a head: besides being nonhierarchical, Thoreau's Journal is also fundamentally nonteleological. This is deeply unsettling because it defies both the notion of artistic intent and the idea of practical purposefulness: the Journal is a huge achievement of virtually no practical use or value.[40]

The Journal "gained autonomy as a literary project as it moved away from repository or archive of discrete elements laid aside for their future flowering into truths, toward the realization of the intrinsic value of 'facts' and of the self's immersion in temporality," Specq writes.[41] As Thoreau sees it, if nature exists for humans and has meaning for them, it is only on a moment-to-moment basis. Knowledge about nature drawn from prior encounters, while indispensable, is of secondary value (not an end in itself, but a means of getting closer to nature), since it has been lifted from the uncontrived circumstances of its acquisition and incorporated into a humanly constructed system for making sense, and use, of nature. Thus, in an account of how he came to possess a detailed knowledge of botany, Thoreau reflects: "Still I never studied botany, and do not to-day systematically, the most natural system is still so artificial. I wanted to know my neighbors, if possible,—to get a little nearer to them" (J 9:157, 12/4/56). In the Journal, Thoreau at last finds a way of writing from the position of knowing ignorance, or of perpetually vanishing (yet perpetually recorded or "notch[ed]") knowledge, that in *Walden* he says he has been anxious to arrive at: "In any weather, at any hour of the day or night, I have been anxious to improve the nick of time, and notch it on my stick too; to stand on the meeting of two eternities, the past and future, which is precisely the present moment; to toe that line" (W 1:336).

At the end of a poem about the early morning singing of birds and its abrupt cessation, Dickinson writes: "The Miracle that introduced / Forgotten, as fulfilled" (F504B). The unselfconsciousness of the speaker's listening, which answers to the birds' unselfconsciousness, means that fulfillment and forgetting are simultaneous, inseparable. Such experiences, while they might seem meaningful, refuse to be contained by the mind long enough to be assigned a meaning. As Anne-Lise François, citing the lines above, puts it, "the reception of experience in Dickinson often includes its own deflection, and contact recedes as informally, unceremoniously, as it occurs."[42]

Thoreau would have appreciated the poem. Recalling a landscape viewed a day or two before, he writes, "I begin to see such an object when I cease to *understand* it–and see that I did not realize or appreciate it before–but I get no further than this" (PJ 3:148, 11/21/50). The sort of natural "Miracle" that troubles Dickinson and Thoreau can never be fully "realize[d] or appreciate[d]," either at the instant in which it is encountered or with the benefit of hindsight. Whatever the miracle "introduced" (Dickinson leaves it ambiguous whether she is using the verb transitively or intransitively) cannot be concluded or even continued; at most it can be partially reconstructed with the aid of memory, imagination, and language. Although in the same paragraph Thoreau marvels at "how adapted these forms & colors [are] to my eye," he appears to be struck above all by the difference between himself and them: "How adapted these forms & colors to my eye–a meadow & an island; what are these things? Yet the hawks & the ducks keep so aloof! and nature is so reserved!" (PJ 3:148). Evidently, knowing and understanding "what are these things" is in Thoreau's view beyond human ability. Humans' natural role, instead, is to love what they look upon: "I am made to love the pond & the meadow as the wind is made to ripple the water" (PJ 3:148).

Failure and success are not separable here. Thoreau says that "to see" something is to see that one has never really seen it before. Since one can "get no further than this," it is almost as if all one saw was one's own all-but permanent blindness, or one's permanent separation from what one sees.

In *Natural Life: Thoreau's Worldly Transcendentalism*, David M. Robinson quotes one of the first Journal entries, titled "Discipline," in which Thoreau writes: "I yet lack discernment to distinguish the whole lesson of to-day; but it is not lost–it will come to me at last" (PJ 1:11, 11/12/1837). And in the next day's entry, Robinson finds the related remark, "Truth is ever returning into herself. I glimpse one feature to-day–another to-morrow–and the next day they are blended" (PJ 1:11, 11/13/1837). On the basis of such statements Robinson draws the conclusion that Thoreau "is committed less to a sudden revelation than to a work of patient and disciplined attention in which knowledge emerges in measured stages from a process of many steps."[43]

Robinson is right that this passage envisages, with youthful optimism, a gradual accumulation of knowledge culminating in a final unveiling of truth. But these early statements, in particular "Truth is ever returning into herself," also contain the seeds of Thoreau's later, less sanguine conception of truth (which in this context is virtually synonymous with nature). For the writer of the mature Journal, truth/nature is something that can only be apprehended piecemeal, never entire. Any "blending" of its features would be conjectural, and so not to be preferred over direct perception however partial, or over "disciplined attention," however fruitless. This is the perspective from which, as Thoreau says in a later entry, "Mere facts & dates & names communicate more than we suspect" (PJ 4:296, 1/27/52). The "more" here is qualitative rather than quantitative; it echoes the "more" of Shakespeare's line (a favorite of Thoreau's), "There are more things in heaven and earth, Horatio, / Than are dreamt of in your philosophy."[44] Released from the task and the hope of compelling facts, dates, and names to blend together and yield "feature[s]" of the truth, let alone the truth itself, the mind is able to glimpse in them a value independent of significance, or at least of all familiar "orders of significance," to recall Cameron's phrase. It perceives a kind of meaning intrinsic to the "mere" things themselves, and therefore *extrinsic* to "your philosophy."

This "released" mood is the one Thoreau is in when he discovers what he takes to be a new species of bream in Walden Pond. The fact that this fish has swum in his cherished pond for years, perhaps for centuries, without his knowing of its existence impresses Thoreau with a sense of nature's self-sufficiency, its utter separation from the lives we lead: "The bream, appreciated, floats in the pond as the centre of the system, another image of God" (J 11:359, 11/30/58). The bream is so new and unexpected that for the moment Thoreau can do no more than wonder at the sheer fact that it exists. In itself this wondering is not so remarkable (we find it in Charles Darwin's writings, for example, and in Gilbert White's), but it is clear that Thoreau values his sense of "the miracle of [the fish's] existence," and the astonishment which this sense produces, more than any subsequent discoveries he might make (and indeed does make)[45] about the fish.[46] "It is the poetry of fishes which is their chief use; their flesh is their lowest use," he goes on to say, and this denigration of using the fish's "flesh" applies equally to "fisherman or . . . ichthyologist" (J 11:360). For himself, Thoreau prefers to linger in the moment of initial discovery, of pure encounter: "But in my account of this bream I cannot go a hair's breadth beyond the mere statement that it exists,—the miracle of its existence, my contemporary and neighbor, yet so different from me! I can only poise my thought there by its side and try to think like a bream for a moment" (J 11:358–59). "Think[ing] like a bream" is a very different thing, evidently, from thinking *about* a bream, for in the next sentence he writes, "I can only think of precious jewels, of music, poetry, beauty, and the mystery of life" (J 11:359).

Despite his appearance of being stymied by this encounter, Thoreau is here describing a middle way between the extremes of writing poetry and keeping silent. He envisions a kind of writing that is factual, that (in Wordsworth's phrase) "look[s] steadily at [its] subject,"[47] but that is nonetheless imaginative, because of the writer's efforts to think "like" nature: to "poise [his] thought there by its side," without ulterior motive, if only "for a moment" at a time. The difficulty of proceeding (for how can one think "like a bream," let alone put such thoughts in writing?) has the potential to raise this writing to the level of art; this explains the logical leap from discussing a fish to discussing jewelry, poetry, music. The writer is forced to be forever on his toes, making his writing, ironically, unnaturally artful—hence Kazin's remark, "It is not natural for a man to write this well every day."[48]

The subtle negativity or negative capability expressed in the phrase "I can only think of precious jewels, of music, poetry, beauty, and the mystery of life" operates on at least two levels. First, thinking "like a bream" evidently forces the writer to "only" deal with a certain kind of subject matter: jewelry, poetry, music, beauty, and the mystery of life. What these disparate topics have in common is an association with aesthetics, which, as Immanuel Kant argues in his *Critique of Judgment*, is a category of experience that disallows or at least discourages definite, objective statements: statements premised on the established meaning or purpose (the concept or use) of things. It is a category of experience in which the boundaries separating subject and object, imagination and sensation, break down.

The second level of negativity or negative capability in the passage is still more striking. Not only must the amazed fisherman-writer confine himself to such unusual subjects (so far removed from the subjects one would expect to be associated with fish), he must also refrain from writing about these subjects: he "can only think" of them. A strange, self-denying, and even apparently art-denying discipline, reminiscent of what one reads about "the way of haiku,"[49] is being proposed here, however tentatively and perhaps half-humorously.

What Thoreau calls "the mystery of life" and the mystery of humans' feelings about and toward life—any life, whether a fish's or a tree's or their own—become in the Journal one and the same mystery. In a late entry that declares his preference for "the poetic or lively description" over "the scientific" one, Thoreau writes: "Unconsidered expressions of our delight which any natural object draws from us are something complete and final in themselves, since all nature is to be regarded as it concerns man; and who knows how close to absolute truth such unconscious affirmations may come" (J 14:117, 10/13/60). The sentence comes as a surprise, for two reasons. First, Thoreau is claiming for his own writing the uncanny power which he attributes to nature, of seeming "complete and final" in every one of its parts ("*any* natural object"), its end, in both senses of the word, contained in every one of its beginnings. This is the rationale, now (in 1860) fully worked out, behind the younger author's modestly stated plan to try and make a work of literature out of fragments: "I do not know but thoughts written down thus in a journal might be printed in the same form with greater advantage than if the related ones were brought together into separate essays. They are now allied to life—& are seen by the reader not to be far fetched" (PJ 4:296, 1/27/52).

Second, the claim that "all nature is to be regarded as it concerns man" seems to be belied by the Journal's self-effacing, non-anthropocentric mode of description. But it is also obviously true, like the answer to a trick question: Thoreau bothers to render these descriptions at all because he is concerned by, feels himself somehow implicated in, what he describes. Crucially, however, just how nature "concerns man" is left entirely mysterious in the Journal. The origin and import of "our delight" in natural objects remains unstated, since the delight is deemed by the author "something complete and final" in itself, as well as something best suited to "unconsidered expressions," "unconscious affirmations." Indeed, Thoreau's expressions and affirmations are often not just unconscious, but silent as well. Typically his delight in an object is implicit in the care with which he describes it, and in his evident satisfaction with just a description, "as if," to quote Sharon Cameron, "the significance of the description of a tree were the description of that tree."[50] What Cameron says of two lyrics by Dickinson can equally be said of the Journal: "Meaning . . . resists knowledge and asserts itself, if at all, only at the level of intimation."[51]

Yet whereas Theo Davis sees Thoreau (along with Dickinson, Whitman, and Martin Heidegger) as seeking "a distinctive, non-hermeneutic mode of relationship to phenomena (including language)"[52]—a relation that privileges the work of "ornamentation" over the work of interpretation and representation—I see him as stubbornly, if cautiously, indeed almost secretly, seeking the meaning of things. The Journal seldom fails to cast things in an interrogative light; the author's hunger for "poetic perception" lends to everything he describes the potential to mean. Thoreau's great ambitions as a poet and philosopher do not, as many earlier readers believed, simply peter out in his later career, nor does this aspirational energy get transferred entirely to his efforts in natural history, as many contemporary scholars have argued. Rather, it subtends the entire Journal, betraying itself in the intensity of the observations and the meticulous honesty of the prose: its seriousness and psychological acuteness; its total lack of stock phrases and rhetorical filler.

Once awakened to Thoreau's deep emotional involvement in his subject—his conviction that the things he writes about have the potential to "be another sacred scripture and revelation . . . helping to redeem [his] life" (J 12:371–72, 10/4/59)—the reader is continually surprised by the writer's powers of restraint: what Keats would have called his "Negative Capability," or capacity for "being in uncertainties, Mysteries, doubts, without any irritable reaching after fact and reason."[53] Restraint comes to seem like extravagance, a paradox that Thoreau finds emblematized in natural objects and phenomena. In a fungus whose underside is bright red while the side visible to casual observers is dull, he seems to find a symbol for his own enterprise: "This intense vermilion (?) face, which would be known to every boy in the town if it were turned upward, faces the earth and is discovered only by the curious naturalist. Its ear is turned down, listening to the honest praises of the earth" (J 10:267, 1/29/58). We know what it means for a poet to sing the earth's praises (we find such singing in abundance in Wordsworth's *The Prelude*, for instance), but what would it mean for a poet to listen to the earth's praises? What kind of poetry is it that refrains from speech? One answer to this question would proceed by way of discussing Dickinson's poetics of reticence, ellipsis, and impersonality. Another would proceed by quoting at random from Thoreau's Journal.

CHAPTER 4

Two Models of Disinterestedness, Part I
Thoreau

> In my experience nothing is so opposed to poetry–not crime–as business. It is a negation of life.
>
> —Henry David Thoreau, June 29, 1852

The titles of this chapter and of the next one owe their inspiration to Susan Howe's *My Emily Dickinson*, in particular to a sentence from chapter 1: "Most literary criticism is based on calculations of interest."[1] Clearly, Howe does not think of her own work as conforming to this standard. In the same passage she makes a claim that goes against the grain of "most literary criticism," and especially of recent Dickinson criticism, with its commitment to showing Dickinson's purposeful engagement with nineteenth-century American culture. Howe, by no means insensible to the socially and indeed politically engaged quality of Dickinson's verse, proposes nevertheless that the poet's "self-imposed exile, indoors, emancipated her from all representations of calculated human order."[2]

These two remarks, which (overlooking the word "indoors") I take to be as relevant to Thoreau as to Dickinson, raise the question of what alternative there is to self-interested writing: writing that is informed by "calculations of interest," and so remains engrossed in the business of humans. Such writing, Howe seems to say, does not transcend or challenge the "representations of calculated human order" made by the other branches of culture; it merely adds to them. How can a writer escape this cycle of what Thoreau more simply calls "get[ting] knowledge & culture"? ("While you are pleased to get knowledge & culture in many ways I am delighted to think that I am getting rid of them" [J 9:160, 12/5/56].) Thoreau and Dickinson provide us with two different, but in some ways complementary, models. I will talk in this chapter about Thoreau's model of disinterestedness, and then, in chapter 5, about Dickinson's.

THOREAU'S VOLATILE SUBJECT

> Song, as you teach it, is not desire, not
> a wooing of something that's finally attained;
> song is existence [*Dasein*].
>
> —Ranier Maria Rilke, *The Sonnets to Orpheus*

In *My Emily Dickinson*'s single-page introduction, Howe discusses another introduction: that of Thoreau's *A Week on the Concord and Merrimack Rivers*. She describes how Thoreau "liked to watch [the river's] current that was for him an emblem of all progress. Weeds under the surface bent gently downstream shaken by watery wind. Chips, sticks, logs, and even tree stems drifted past. There came a day at the end of the summer or the beginning of the autumn, when he resolved to launch a boat from shore and let the river carry him." Emily Dickinson, she then tells us, is her "emblematical Concord River"; following the current of Dickinson's poetry, she feels herself "heading toward certain discoveries."³

What Howe may alert us to here is the thing-like quality that Thoreau's and Dickinson's texts have in common; the way in which they launch us on a strange current rather than guide us through a step-by-step argument, narrative, or representation. While Dickinson declined to title her works altogether (though, interestingly, she once referred to the poem beginning "A narrow Fellow in the Grass" as "my Snake" [L316]), Thoreau gave to his books the names of the places and things among which he wrote them (*A Week on the Concord and Merrimack Rivers*, *Walden*, *The Maine Woods*, *Cape Cod*), as if he wanted them to communicate, like Concord River, by being rather than saying what they mean. Like a river or a landscape, his texts lead or point the way toward "*certain* discoveries" (which is to say, probably not the ones anticipated), rather than being discovered and decoded themselves. If Howe is able to draw an analogy between Concord River and Dickinson's poems, then, it is because Thoreau had been there before her, practicing a kind of writing whose "progress" would be more like a current than a program, forward-looking yet envisioning only "certain," unspecified destinations, not any particular one.

A few pages later, as we've seen, Howe makes a claim about the motivation behind Dickinson's avoidance of publication, of society, and even of tradition—a claim that may explain why Thoreau, and the landscape he decided to let make his decisions for him, is a larger presence in her book's introduction than is Dickinson herself. "To release those gestures of intention that make her poems great, she chose for some reason to shut herself inside her childhood family constellation. This self-imposed exile, indoors, emancipated her from all representations of calculated human order."[4] Immediately after making this claim, Howe accurately predicts that it will gain little traction among literary scholars, given that "most literary criticism is based on calculations of interest."

One of my goals in writing this book has been to avoid basing interpretation of Dickinson and Thoreau on calculations of interest. I have resisted the assumption (though not completely, since interpretation depends on this assumption) that the texts they produced have motives extraneous to themselves—motives that are any less mysterious and irreducible than the texts, the words, themselves. When I say that Dickinson and Thoreau practice a non-teleological poetics, I mean that they evince the intention Howe describes, of, so to speak, "let[ting] the river carry" them: letting something guide their choices that is neither self-interest nor the interests and criteria of a tradition, a discipline, a genre, an ideology, or a nation. (Thoreau, Cavell argues, sought in *Walden* "to alarm his culture by refusing it his voice."[5] Dickinson, by refusing to publish despite considerable encouragement to do so, and by alluding to the major national issues of her day, most notably slavery and the Civil War, only in the most cryptic manner, refused her culture her voice twice over.)[6]

The results of such an effort at disinterestedness, as Howe suggests, may not contribute significantly to our store of representations of life and nature. The effort yields something closer to "gestures of intention," evaluating which is more than usually difficult, since the intention is neither explicit nor fully realized. Yet this implicitness or spontaneity or simply absence of choice

(Cameron, in her second book on Dickinson, goes so far as to call it "choosing not choosing"), the way in which Thoreau's and Dickinson's ideas remain in a state of potentia, closer to a gesture than to what Thoreau calls a "residual statement" ("the volatile truth of our words should continually betray the inadequacy of the residual statement" [W 18:580–81]) is according to Howe's logic what "make[s] [their texts] great," since it releases the author's intentional energies, allowing them to range over the subject matter rather than compel it to yield "representations of calculated human order." The sense of possible discoveries, of being "on the verge of something, perched,"[7] is what non-teleological writing gives us, rather than the sense of accomplishment, the sense of an ending.

Thoreau, as we saw in chapter 3, comes dangerously close to seeming like something less than or different from a literary writer, dependent as his late work is on the brute facts and apparently unfiltered circumstances of his physical surroundings. It can seem, in short, that Thoreau's pen is directed by something purely external and incidental, rather than by the writer's autonomous imagination. The argument I have to make about Thoreau demands that I acknowledge and even emphasize this apparent lack of artistic intention in the Journal, because, through a paradox I will be elaborating, Thoreau achieves autonomy of the imagination by ceding authorial control, or at least a major part of it, to nature. The crux of the paradox is Thoreau's implicit contention, which I will be teasing out of his statements in both the Journal and *Walden*, that the mind on its own, divorced from or rather inattentive to sensory perception, is not at all autonomous, and that only through brief encounters with the ultimately inaccessible natural world does the mind make contact with its own depths—with what Martin Heidegger would call "Dasein," which literally means "there-being" but which Heidegger uses to mean something like "human being."[8]

For Thoreau, as Howe reminds us, Concord River, and the woods and fields of Concord and its environs, are some of those things besides self-interest that guide the writer's choices. They provide in lieu of "calculations of interest" and "representations of . . . order" an alternative direction, or rather an infinite web of directions, following which easily fills up Thoreau's short life as well as forty-seven journal volumes. Often Thoreau seems not only indifferent but positively averse to the prospect that any one of his encounters with nature might lead to profit, whether conceived of in literary, philosophical, or scientific terms. He bristles whenever it is suggested that the value of a thing is conditional on its usefulness. His aversion to this teleological, instrumental conception of value partly explains his abiding love for the humble shrub oak, with its "scanty garment of leaves" and its "lowly whispering" (J 9:146, 12/1/56): "A farmer once asked me what shrub oaks were made for, not knowing any use they served. But I can tell him that they do me good" (J 9:184, 12/17/56).

At issue here is a kind of "good" that is not "good for" something else; whose goodness is not that of an instrument.[9] Thoreau tries to see each natural phenomenon as belonging to a self-sufficient order of being, hence, as incapable of being lifted out of its context and into that of any humanly conceived and constructed order. "I love best to have each thing in its season only," he characteristically remarks (J 9:160, 12/5/56); and he reproves science for not distinguishing between "a dead specimen of an animal" and "a living one preserved in its native element" (J 11:360, 9/30/58). In contrast to his non-appropriative manner of dwelling in and with nature, "science," according to Thoreau's own definition, "applies a finite rule to the infinite–& is what you can weigh & measure and bring away" (PJ 3:44, 1/5/50).[10] As Laura Dassow Walls, commenting on this unflattering definition, nicely observes, Thoreau's goal is "not to render facts portable, severing their connections to bring them away from the field, but rather, to render facts in all their connections, making them, if anything, too big, too 'comprehensive,' to be mobilized in service to narrow national, economic, or ideological ends." It was this insistence on dwelling on and among the myriad details and circumstances of his subject matter, Walls continues, that "lengthened Thoreau's walks and fattened his Journal"—that, in other words, kept him from other business and other writing projects.[11]

The Journal, therefore, is founded on Thoreau's conjecture, which grows into a conviction, that "Perhaps I can never find so good a setting for my thoughts as I shall thus have taken them out of," that is, as the setting which is furnished by the Journal's undiscriminating record of each day's observed phenomena. (PJ 4:296, 1/28/52). (Prior to around 1851, taking sentences out of their original setting in the Journal—in some cases actually cutting out the pages—was common practice for Thoreau.) The entry of the previous day clarifies this insight. To extricate certain thoughts and bring "the related ones . . . together into separate essays," Thoreau writes there, would be redundant. Such efforts of rearrangement, selection, organization—in a word, instrumentalization—would presume to make good on an experience and a record that are already good, and that might be spoiled by tampering. The entry goes on: "They [my thoughts] are now allied to life—& and are seen by the reader not to be far fetched—It is more simple—less artful—I feel that in the other case I should have no proper frame for my sketches. Mere facts & dates & names communicate more than we suspect" (PJ 4:296, 1/27/52). But they will not thus communicate if, unsuspecting, the writer (or editor, or reader) takes them out of their "proper frame" and tries to make them communicate no more than what he wants them to.

"The crystal never sparkles more brightly than in the cavern," reads the sentence directly following "Perhaps I can never find so good a setting" (PJ 4:296, 1/28/52). This is an acknowledgment not of any inferiority in the Journal's day-to-day writing, but of the huge, hard-to-differentiate mass that it forms, swallowing, cavern-like, any gems we might detect within it. The Journal frame of meticulous yet unfocused natural description may be, and indeed often has been, an obstacle rather than an aid to appreciation of the Journal's intellectual and artistic content. This is because the Journal blurs the distinction between frame and content, arbitrary physical facts and intellectual or artistic content, in a truly unprecedented way. In the crucial pair of entries we've been considering, Thoreau is realizing that if he is to speak, as he puts it in *Walden*, "somewhere *without* bounds, like a man in a waking moment, to men in their waking moments," with an "extra-vagance" that locates his speech "beyond the narrow limits of my daily experience," it will not be in a vacuum that he speaks, but in the clearly delineated setting of the perceived natural world (W 18:580). But he also knows that no amount of clear delineation can remove from nature its disorienting mystery, that is, its resemblance to an unexplored "cavern" in whose mouth the journal writer's thoughts cast only a faint light. This is, in fact, to be desired: the faintness or slightness of thought in the Journal, the way in which (as I explain below) the poet must substitute natural description for introspection, notation of facts for notation of thoughts and moods, is what signals to us that the author has ventured "beyond the narrow limits of [his] daily experience." At this distance from ordinary discourse, Thoreau can write:

> Those sparrows, too, are thoughts I have. They come and go; they flit by quickly on their migrations, uttering only a faint *chip*, I know not whither or why exactly. One will not rest upon its twig for me to scrutinize it. The whole copse will be alive with my rambling thoughts, bewildering me by their very multitude, but they will be all gone directly without leaving me a feather. (J 10:128, 10/26/57)

Nature, as Cameron puts it, "has been as if driven into the mind," without any diminution of its strangeness.[12] The writer's thoughts, though animated and animating, are as unrevealing and indefinite ("they come and go . . . I know not whither or why exactly. . . . they will be all gone directly without leaving me a feather") as creatures wholly external to and independent of him. This insight suggests to Thoreau both the strangeness of his own thoughts and the intimacy—the sameness, even—of what is supposed to be alien: "Those sparrows . . . *are* thoughts I have," not just like thoughts I have. What is "escaping [a person] by its withdrawal" may be "precisely what concerns and touches him," Heidegger states in the passage discussed in chapter 2.[13] Thoreau suggests that this is because what touches a person most closely, what belongs to him, is what he can't get hold of and control, whether it's a thought or a bird; a thought about a bird or a bird that instigates thought. François Specq's observation, that "Thoreau's Journal precludes issues of self-expression: Thoreau was concerned not with the intricacies of individuality or subjectivity but with the mystery of the world," is therefore only half true.[14] The latter mystery is inseparable from the mystery of the self as Thoreau understood it, as the present quotation as well as some others we'll look at in this chapter clearly show.

"Perhaps I can never find so good a setting for my thoughts as I shall thus have taken them out of." Given Thoreau's actual practice (which in February of 1852 he had perhaps not yet fully committed to) of "driv[ing]" nature "into the mind," enmeshing all of his thoughts in the details of natural phenomena, this seems like an understatement. Most often the natural setting is the source and focus of the journalist's thoughts, not just their frame. Thoreau doesn't want to lift his "sketches" out of this framework because he is convinced of a mysterious relation between frame and content, contingency and artistry ("We are rained and snowed on with gems" [J 10:239, 1/6/58]), the alien and the meaningful. He must express simultaneously the sense of nature as marginal (a "frame") and the sense of it as central: the "*proper* frame" for his thoughts, by whose means the thoughts' "alli[ance] to life," their significance, is uncovered.

"Life" here is not the writer's life in particular (the Journal is not an autobiography); it is the life he lives in nature. In a remarkable passage from an 1856 entry, Thoreau emphasizes the interdependence of living and writing: in particular, of disinterested, "homely" living (living that happens chiefly in the "fields and woods . . . and . . . river") and disinterested, homely writing (writing that takes as its "theme" whatever happens in the fields and woods, etc.). The writer must try to ignore specious distinctions between "significant" and "insignificant" themes just as he tries to ignore distinctions between "joy and sorrow, success and failure, grandeur and meanness," the "elysi[an]" and the "homely":

> Men commonly exaggerate the theme. Some themes they think are significant and others insignificant. I feel that my life is very homely, my pleasures very cheap. Joy and sorrow, success and failure, grandeur and meanness, and indeed most words in the English language do not mean for me what they do for my neighbors. I see that my neighbors look with compassion on me, that they think it is a mean and unfortunate destiny which makes me to walk in these fields and woods so much and sail on this river alone. But so long as I find here the only real elysium, I cannot hesitate in my choice. My work is writing, and I do not hesitate, though I know that no subject is too trivial for me, tried by ordinary standards; for, ye fools, the theme is nothing, the life is everything. All that interests the reader is the depth and intensity of the life excited. We touch our subject but by a point which has no breadth, but the pyramid of our experience, or our interest in it, rests on us by a broader or narrower base. That is, man is all in all, Nature nothing, but as she draws him out and reflects him. Give me simple, cheap, and homely themes. (J 9:121, 10/18/56)

"We touch our subject but by a point which has no breadth, but the pyramid of our experience, or our interest in it, rests on us by a broader or narrower base." What we touch, we touch for just an instant, either because it eludes us or because it fails to sustain our interest, but that slight point of contact is like the tip of a pyramid which "rests on us by a broader or narrower base"; it is connected, in other words, to "the depth and intensity of the life" that things excite in us and "dra[w] . . . out" of us. The easiness, accessibility, and occasional brilliance of sense perception conceals a difficulty of interpretation, of genuine revelation, and of lasting contact which aligns it, in Thoreau's mind, with the task of thinking: "My loftiest thought is somewhat like an eagle that suddenly comes into the field of view, suggesting great things and thrilling the beholder, as if it were bound hitherward with a message for me; but it comes no nearer, but circles and soars away, growing dimmer, disappointing me, till it is lost behind a cliff or a cloud" (J 10:128–29, 10/26/57). To call this experience of "suggesti[on]," "thril[l]," and finally "disappoint[ment]" the "loftiest" achievement available to thought is implicitly to reject scientific models of thinking. Such a conception of thought is deeply non-teleological, and opens the door for a kind of writing in which natural description is not denigrated because it yields no final revelations and culminates, if at all, in practically every sentence, but on the contrary is raised to the level of poetry for this reason.

In one entry we read, "A new moon visible in the east–how unexpectedly it always appears! You easily lose it in the sky." A few more notes follow: "The whipporwill [sic] sings–but not so commonly as in spring. The bats are active." And then: "The poet is a man who lives at last by watching his moods. An old poet comes to watch his moods as narrowly as a cat does a mouse" (PJ 4:16, 8/28/51). The mention of "the poet" and "his moods" will of course seem to have come out of left field: what do elusive moons, infrequent whippoorwills, and active bats have to do with poetry and moods? If there is an answer to this question, it is perhaps that the poetic observer of such things (specifically, the "old poet," one chastened by experience) knows that he does not really have access to the things themselves, but only to the shifting moods they elicit in him, or that just happen to be occupying him as he observes the world around him. He can "watch his moods as narrowly as a cat does a mouse," but he exercises no such power over the phenomena that pass continually before him, out of reach and unpredictable. Yet the comparison of moods to an animal, like the comparison of thoughts to sparrows and eagles, hints that for Thoreau introspection (according to the present passage, the poet's main task) and natural description are very close to each other. Thoughts in a setting are also, inevitably, thoughts about a setting. Conversely, observations of details in a setting may provide insights, both to the reader and to the writer, into what is going on in the observer's mind. Natural facts are made to stand in for the missing facts about Thoreau's personal, emotional, and spiritual life, much as unusual words and phrases are made to do in Dickinson's poetry. "The use of the outer creation," Emerson had written in the chapter of *Nature* titled "Language," "[is] to give us language for the beings and changes of the inward creation."[15] Thoreau works on a similar principle, but is inclined to see nature as more inseparable from "the beings and changes" of the mind. He wants to believe that a sentence that describes an object and a sentence that describes a thought or feeling can be the same sentence.

The inaccessibility of nature, then, is for Thoreau not necessarily a dead end, because one of the things he seems most interested in is the subtle influence that natural phenomena have on him in spite of this inaccessibility. The poet must watch his moods so closely in part because the insignificance of his moods, their irrelevance to the larger setting in which they transpire, may be only apparent. What he feels when he watches an eagle appear and disappear, or notes that the whippoorwill is less common than before, or sees that the moon is gone from sight again and the bats are flitting about, may tell him more—or at least, something quite different but equally important—about such phenomena than the closest study could do. As we saw in chapter 3, Thoreau, like Heidegger, is interested less in "entities" than in their "being." Less, that is, in specific existing things than in the meaning of their existing as they do; and this is a quality, or rather a question, a questionableness, that they have in common with the human who observes and responds to them. "Why should just these sights & sounds accompany our life?" he asks. "Why should I hear the chattering of blackbirds–why smell the skunk each year? I would fain explore the mysterious relation between myself & these things" (PJ 4:468, 4/18/52). And again, in a famous passage of *The Maine Woods*: "Talk of mysteries!—Think of our life in nature,—daily to be shown matter, to come in contact with it,—rocks, trees, wind on our cheeks! the *solid* earth! the *actual* world! the *common sense! Contact! Contact! Who* are we? *where* are we?"[16] This passage is often misread, outside academia at least, as Thoreau's cowed reaction to the unanticipated wildness he encountered in the forests of Maine.[17] Such misreadings rely upon ignoring the part of the passage where Thoreau suggests that the strangeness of Mt. Katahdin is identical with the strangeness of his own body and of his everyday natural surroundings ("the *solid* earth! the *actual* world!"). When he writes, a few sentences before the ones I've quoted, "I stand in awe of my body, this matter to which I am bound has become so strange to me," he is not recording an insight first experienced on Mt. Katahdin; rather, he is recurring to a major theme of both *Walden* and the Journal, namely, the "mysterious relation between myself & these things."

Consider in this connection Thoreau's account, discussed in the previous chapter, of having discovered a new type of bream in Walden Pond (J 11:358–60, 11/30/58). It is here that he most forcefully articulates his wish to preserve the integrity and objective independence—what he calls "the mystery"—of what he studies. But this passage, along with those already quoted ("Those sparrows, too"; "My loftiest thought"; "A new moon visible in the east"), also shows how the passionate, "extravagant," egregiously subjective writing that he showcases in *Walden* persists in the generally more staid and factual Journal. The purpose of such writing, he says in the earlier book, is not self-indulgent linguistic experiment, but accuracy, adequacy, and truth:

> I fear chiefly lest my expression may not be *extra- vagant* enough, may not wander far enough beyond the narrow limits of my daily experience, so as to be adequate to the truth of which I have been convinced . . . for I am convinced that I cannot exaggerate enough even to lay the foundation of a true expression. . . . The volatile truth of our words should continually betray the inadequacy of the residual statement. (18:580–81)

Thus, in the bream passage, nature calls up a strange mood in Thoreau which must be pursued, expressed in volatile words, if the strangeness and volatility of nature, "the mystery of the bream," is to be pursued and expressed in its turn.

Not the body of the bream, which after all can be measured and analyzed, but "its life" is what fascinates Thoreau: the way it has of occupying its own "orbit," "float[ing] in the pond as the centre of the system, another image of God" (J 11:359). As in his briefer response to the "unexpectedly" appearing and "quickly . . . los[t]" new moon, he suddenly feels disoriented, as if newly awakened to the truth that his "system," his "image of God," are not the only compass to steer by. ("This [moon]light & this hour takes the civilization all out of the landscape," he writes elsewhere [PJ 4:47, 9/5/51].)[18] Accepting the incommensurability of the bream's "system" and his own, he nonetheless tries to position himself "by its side," not as an observer performing a familiar task with the observed, but as a novice thinker apprenticed to a retiring sage:

> But in my account of this bream I cannot go a hair's breadth beyond the mere statement that it exists,—the miracle of its existence, my contemporary and neighbor, yet so different from me! I can only poise my thought there by its side and try to think like a bream for a moment. I can only think of precious jewels, of music, poetry, beauty, and the mystery of life. (J 11:358–59)

This seems to be a rather elaborate way of saying that, under the influence of his astonishment at the bream's existence, he can do nothing but write a poem, make art—or else keep silent. Glimpsed in its raw alienness, nature can be disabling as well as inspiring; it does not lend itself to what Howe calls "representations of calculated human order," because its significance lies precisely in its lying outside of such orders. The writing such glimpses yield will not resemble science, or philosophy, or even what we call poetry. It will look more like Thoreau's extra-generic Journal, or perhaps like Dickinson's still-controversial texts.

Confronted by the radical strangeness of nature, and wanting to somehow "be adequate to the truth of which [he has] been convinced" during such confrontations, Thoreau turns to "music, poetry, beauty, and the mystery of life." These, in other words, are his subject as much as nature is; or rather, they are his means of approach to the nebulous subject of nature. But this is not the same as writing poems or philosophical essays about, or inspired by, nature. Let us take Thoreau literally and say that in the Journal he writes about nature, with the factual, self-effacing rigor that such writing demands, while "think[ing] of" music, poetry, beauty, and the mystery of life, and that the reader who follows Thoreau's cue reads about nature, with the patience and tolerance of boredom such reading demands, while thinking of these (supposedly) extraneous matters as well. "I feel as if I had been to a university," Thoreau writes after a spell in the woods, and his point is that the woods have more to teach us than facts about themselves: that they are not merely an object of study but a whole course of studies as it were, assuming we are listening for something besides, "by [the] side" of, facts, namely, music, poetry, etc. It follows that writing about the woods, no matter how factual, also has more to teach us than facts about the woods, though what it has to teach us cannot be conveyed except through notation of such facts—"as if the significance of a description of a tree were that description."[19] For it is not, ideally, the writer who teaches us, but the woods: "A writer a man writing is the scribe of all nature–he is the corn & the grass & the atmosphere writing" (PJ 4:28, 9/2/1851).

It is as if what we were reading were written by a poet who continues to think like a poet (who else would try to think like a fish, or even grant that this was a thing one could attempt?), but who has decided to refrain from poetic speech, except when he lets escape "unconsidered expressions of [his] delight," such as those elicited by the bream (J 14:117, 10/13/60). Ideally, as I said in chapter 3, such expressions would be not only unconsidered but unvoiced, so that the description itself, the sheer fact of the author's having bothered to record it, would express his delight, making commentary, adornment, and development superfluous. "My life has been the poem I would have writ," Thoreau wrote (back when he still wrote verse), "But I could not both live and utter it."[20] Of interest here is, of course, the notion that a life could be poetic, indeed could substitute for the poems the writer did not write. The couplet suggests that although Thoreau refrains from verse-writing in the Journal, he nonetheless hopes that the life he describes and writes out of will possess the same quality of beauty and inevitability that is often attributed to good verse.

"I see not a dead eel or floating snake, or a gull, but it rounds my life and is like a line or accent in its poem" (J 10:127, 10/26/57). An earlier statement alerts us to the bedrock of theism on which Thoreau's belief in the meaningfulness of stray phenomena is based: "My profession is to be always on the alert to find God in nature–to know his lurking places. To attend all the oratorios–the operas in nature" (PJ 4:55, 9/7/51). Thoreau's contribution to the theory and practice of poetry consists of his non-teleological endeavor (and the record he made of it in the Journal) to indiscriminately take in everything that crosses his path; to treat each passing, trivial phenomenon as though it were part of a poem written by God.

The bulk of the Journal, the passages on which any claim for its greatness rests, are thus almost beyond interpretation. They seem to render interpretation superfluous, because the author makes no explicit claim for the significance of what he sets down, except, again, insofar as he does set it down. The Journal's "meditations," as Cameron writes, "give the disconcerting double impression of commanding attention and of being random," and thereby "prohibi[t] the use of many interpretive procedures ordinarily taken for granted."[21] Either what the Journal sets down is random, or it is significant, we have been trained to assume. There must be a specific intention behind the writer's act of setting down, or else there is no significance or value, no reason to pay attention. This view prevented the Journal from being seen as art until 1985, when Cameron's book was published and it became apparent that the Journal writer's renunciation of intentionality, his act of (partially) ceding authorial control to nature, was itself an intentional, artistic, and philosophical act. As Wallace Stevens writes in a poem titled "The Plain Sense of Things," "The absence of the imagination had / Itself to be imagined."[22]

The Journal's ostensibly prosaic passages form, as Thoreau says, the "setting" for the poetic and philosophical "thoughts" of the Journal; but they are also the source on which the writer draws for his thoughts, and inseparable from them. He would not minutely describe the structure of snowflakes, for instance, did he not think of them as a "gems. . . . the product of *enthusiasm*, the children of an ecstasy, finished with the artist's utmost skill" (J 10:239–40, 1/6/58). The minute description expresses that thought more eloquently than the explicit statement does.

Most of the Journal's facts are not accompanied by such statements and therefore remain, so to speak, untranslated, uncommunicative. Yet their presence is indispensable for a number of reasons: they replicate the vast, chiefly opaque presence of nature; they form a counterpoint to the writer's abstract or extravagant thoughts, and so assure us of those thoughts' authenticity—that they are not "far fetched" but "allied to life," based on close personal observation and engagement (PJ 4:296, 1/27/52); and they serve as a substitute for narrative, giving the reader of this massive, unconventional prose poem something to do. Like the readers of an epic poem, we must work our way heroically through much prosaic information, never knowing when what seems a negligible detail will turn out to illuminate all the rest.

Reproduced below, for instance, is Thoreau's description, or part of it, of his adventures in syrup-making. The description encompasses details about nature itself as well as details about the nature-explorer's (Thoreau would say, the saunterer's) trade, including the tools of his trade; but the distinction between these two is not absolute, for the important point is that it is things, not ideas or feelings or stories, which he handles and describes, and represents wholesale, undistilled and uninterpreted.

> 10 A. M.—To my red maple sugar camp. Found that, after a pint and a half had run from a single tube after 3 P. M. yesterday, it had frozen about half an inch thick, and this morning a quarter of a pint more had run. Between 10.30 and 11.30 A. M. this forenoon, I caught two and three quarters pints more, from six tubes, at the same tree, though it is completely overcast and threatening rain. Four and one half pints in all. This sap is an agreeable drink, like iced water (by chance), with a pleasant but slight sweetish taste. I boiled it down in the afternoon, and it made an ounce and a half of sugar, without any molasses, which appears to be the average amount yielded by the sugar maple in similar situations, *viz.* south edge of a wood, a tree partly decayed, two feet [in] diameter.
>
> It is worth the while to know that there is all this sugar in our woods, much of which might be obtained by using the refuse wood lying about, without damage to the proprietors, who use neither the sugar nor the wood.
>
> I left home at ten and got back before twelve with two and three quarters pints of sap, in addition to the one and three quarters I found collected.
>
> I put in saleratus and a little milk while boiling, the former to neutralize the acid, and the latter to collect the impurities in a skum. After boiling it till I burned it a little, and my small quantity would not flow when cool, but was as hard as half-done candy, I put it on again, and in a minute it was softened and turned to sugar.

> While collecting sap, the little of yesterday's lodging snow that was left, dropping from the high pines in Trillium Wood and striking the brittle twigs in its descent, makes me think that the squirrels are running there.
>
> I noticed that my fingers were purpled, evidently from the sap on my auger.
>
> Had a dispute with Father about the *use* of my making this sugar when I knew it could be done and might have bought sugar cheaper at Holden's. He said it took me from my studies. I said I made it my study: I felt as if I had been to a university.
>
> It dropped from each tube about as fast as my pulse beat, and, as there were three tubes directed to each vessel, it flowed at the rate of about one hundred and eighty drops in a minute into it. One maple, standing immediately north of a thick white pine, scarcely flowed at all, while a smaller, farther in the wood, ran pretty well. The south side of a tree bleeds first in spring. I hung my pails on the tubes or a nail. Had two tin pails and a pitcher. Had a three-quarters-inch auger. Made a dozen spouts, five or six inches long, hole as large as a pencil, smoothed with a pencil. (J 8:216–18, 3/21/56)

It is easy for the reader of the Journal to worry that he or she, like this syrup-maker reproved by his father, has been wasting his or her time. What the Journal has to teach us, like the sugar yielded by trees, could be found more conveniently, because more condensed, in Thoreau's published writings, we may conclude. I have been suggesting, however, that it is precisely for what it does not have to teach us that we go to the Journal: for what it does not know about nature, cannot take out of nature, and must therefore leave embedded in (descriptions of) nature. Returning from an excursion into the Journal's disinterested, directionless—or rather, infinitely directed—pages is like returning from walking in the woods. Walls comments that the Journal "is messy as a forest floor, lines crossing and crisscrossing, interfering with each other, dead-ending, tangling the clarity that truth commands."[23] We feel "as if [we] had been to a university," not just to a single book. The sugar that remains after the sap has been boiled down is sweeter because we have retrieved the sap ourselves, following Thoreau almost step-by-step, it often feels, in his heroic confrontations with a daunting myriad of facts: both natural facts and facts pertaining to a human being's life in, or next to, nature. We find in the Journal more of the darkness of nature, of its opacity or thing-ness, than in almost any other text. Yet, for this same reason, we find—brighter, or at least fresher, more interesting for having penetrated the shade of large trees—the light that the human mind can cast on things. Such a light illumines Thoreau's observation, "It dropped from each tube about as fast as my pulse beat." Still more surprising, it seems to peak around the edges of Thoreau's words when, concluding the entry, he names the tools of his trade, as if he wanted to linger over these artificial objects still redolent of the natural work they have been doing: "Had two tin pails and a pitcher. Had a three-quarters-inch auger." To borrow from the epigraph of Marianne Moore's *Complete Poems* (a book that like Thoreau's takes as its chief material the trivia and arcana of nature), the omission of "I" from each of these sentences is not an accident.[24] Ironically but characteristically, we see the poet's handiwork in the very place where he has removed himself, or at least the conventional sign of the self.

Plainly, syrup-making was for Thoreau not a final purpose but an intermediate one: not a telos but a kind of anti-telos. Like his other minor projects (gathering driftwood, taking measurements, conducting unsophisticated experiments, collecting local lore), it was a means of avoiding the more conventional, grander purposes that his father and Emerson urged upon him. But this negative work of avoidance was part of a positive project of keeping himself open, "comprehensive," his energies and identity uncircumscribed. Whereas Emerson faulted him for lacking ambition and the drive to succeed on a grand scale, he faulted Emerson for lacking "a comprehensive character": for succeeding too much in one direction. "I doubt if Emerson could trundle a wheelbarrow through the streets," he wrote in the Journal, "because it would be out of character. One needs to have a comprehensive character" (J 9:250, 1/30/52). For Thoreau, to have a comprehensive character was to be at ease in the company of things no less than in the company of people: to be unashamed of the former's company when walking through the streets, and unencumbered by the latter's company—not so much their physical presence as the pressure of their expectations—when walking through the woods. "In my afternoon walk I would fain forget all my morning occupations and my obligations to society," he writes in "Walking": "But it sometimes happens that I cannot easily shake off the village."[25]

While I have quoted rather heavily from those passages in which Thoreau, working out the theoretical underpinnings of the Journal, discusses poetry more or less explicitly, it would be no exaggeration to say that this text's least poetic-seeming passages contain in fact the most poetry. In such entries as the one just quoted, Thoreau is at his freest ("absolutely free from all worldly engagements," as he puts it in "Walking"),[26] ranging with pleasure, or just mild interest, over the concrete details of his innumerable hobbies. The Journal, partly by means of its more theoretical passages, trains us to associate poetry with just such freedom and disinterested notation of facts. Thoreau achieves in the woods (and in his imaginative reliving, via the Journal, of the time he spent in the woods) a freedom similar to what Dickinson expresses in the poem beginning "I dwell in Possibility." For Dickinson's "Possibility" is a freedom not so much from society as from vulgar self-interest; from the "Occupation" of the self by a career or goal or responsibility not native to it:

> I dwell in Possibility –
> A fairer House than Prose –
> More numerous of Windows –
> Superior – for Doors –
>
> Of Chambers as the Cedars –
> Impregnable of eye –
> And for an everlasting Roof
> The Gambrels of the Sky –
>
> Of Visitors – the fairest –
> For Occupation – This –
> The spreading wide my narrow Hands
> To gather Paradise – (F466)

The opposite of "Prose," for Dickinson as for Thoreau, is, not poetry exactly, but possibility: an openness that is literally an openness of the "Hands," unoccupied and ungrasping. Thoreau, anticipating Dickinson's extreme metaphor, "Publication – is the Auction / Of the Mind of Man" (F788), puts it with equal severity: "In my experience nothing is so opposed to poetry–not crime–as business. It is a negation of life" (PJ 5:163, 6/29/52).

Although Thoreau's comments on writing, thinking, and poetry are vastly outnumbered by his comments on nature, the two are inseparable. For Thoreau, to confront the problem of how to write about nature is also to confront the problem of how nature means even though it lacks human intentionality. The goal of non-teleological writing, the writing of disinterestedness, is to write as nature would write if it could: "to incarnate its articulating will," as Cameron puts it.[27] Consider together the following two quotations:

> Mere facts & dates & names communicate more than we suspect. (PJ 4:296, 1/27/52)

> We sometimes experience a mere fulness of life, which does not find any channels to flow into. We are stimulated but to no obvious purpose. I feel myself uncommonly prepared for *some* literary work, but I can select no work. I am prepared not so much for contemplation, as for force-ful expression. I am braced both physically and intellectually. It is not so much the music–as the marching to the music that I feel. (PJ 4:50–51, 9/7/51)

In the first quotation, Thoreau attests both to the mere-ness and to the more-ness of nature: its being just what it is, and its being in excess of whatever is said or thought about it; in a word, its volatility. He senses that the opaque, self-enclosed quality of nature when viewed objectively conceals a potential for meaning which has never been realized. Analogously, in the second quotation, he is convinced that he, too, contains "a *mere* fulness of life"; that he, too, is amply, "uncommonly" prepared for "force-ful expression," yet lacks something definite to express. Or rather, he does not wish to express anything definite, since something definite would necessarily be less than the unchanneled, irreducible fullness he finds both in nature ("I felt as if I had been to a university," though I learned only a few facts) and in the experience of writing about nature without aim. "It is not so much the music-as the marching to the music that I feel." It is not just a matter of marching to "a different drummer," then (W 18:581), but of marching to no drummer, and so "walk[ing] on" unaccompanied "into futurity" (W 4:411)—Dickinson would say, into Possibility. He "can select no work" that does not pale in comparison with this.

Maurice Blanchot would have argued that, far from distinguishing the Journal from other literary texts, the quality of incompleteness, we might even say of un-begun-ness, stemming from the author's refusal or inability to "select a work" establishes the Journal as quintessentially, starkly literary. For Blanchot, "the work of literature" is to be distinguished from individual books, and from the entire, profit-oriented mechanism of literary production, which imposes on the work "a dénouement of pure constraint," born not of the work itself but of "circumstances—that is, history."[28] But this, he says, is only "the least problematic aspect" of the literary work's "infinite quality."[29] The problematic aspect has to do with the literary work's negativity, or what Blanchot calls its "solitude":

> However, the work—the work of art, the literary work—is neither finished nor unfinished: it is. What it says is exclusively this: that it is, and nothing more. Beyond that it is nothing. Whoever wants to make it express more finds nothing, finds that it expresses nothing. He whose life depends upon the work, either because he is a writer or because he is a reader, belongs to the solitude of that which expresses nothing except the word *being*: the word which language shelters by hiding it, or causes to appear when language itself disappears into the silent void of the work.[30]

I find parallels for this radical insistence on the value of mere being, and on defining literature's task as the task of expressing or instantiating such being, in Thoreau's comments on nature, and in his overall approach of describing glimpses of, brief encounters with, animals, objects, and phenomena, rather than conducting sustained, methodical inquiries about them. But I find even more striking parallels in his comments on his own negative capability as a writer: the fact that he "cannot go a hair's breadth beyond the mere statement that it exists"; that his "greatest success will be simply to perceive that such things *are*" (J 12:371, 10/4/59); that "unconsidered expressions of our delight which any natural object draws from us are something complete and final in themselves . . . and who knows how close to absolute truth such unconscious affirmations may come" (J 14:117, 10/13/60); that "higher knowledge amounts to [nothing] more definite than a novel & grand surprise on a sudden revelation of the insufficiency of all that we had called knowledge before" (PJ 3:198, 2/27/51), and that therefore the highest knowledge is "negative knowledge," but also, "Beautiful Knowledge."[31]

Thoreau adopts the Journal as his chief literary outlet because he comes to think of his impasse—being unable to select a work because of his consciousness of "a mere fulness of life, which does not find any channels to flow into" and so remains an unapproachable mystery to him—as a necessary condition of his imaginative life. It is the condition of disinterested, non-teleological writing: writing that is not "far fetched" and calculating but that takes its occasion freely, almost randomly, from "the seasons and all their changes." The Journal writer, as we have seen, can afford to be random, to select no particular path, because he is convinced that despite their mystery "the seasons and all their changes are in me" (J 10:127, 10/26/57). Because of this interpenetration of writer and subject (or at least, because of the author's belief in such interpenetration), description of the subject matter, no matter how ostensibly objective and factual, cannot fail to be relevant to the human writer and reader, though either may fail to perceive its relevance.

In the remainder of this chapter, I will discuss further, using some passages from *Walden* as illustration, Thoreau's notion that to engage nature is simultaneously to engage the self, and that therefore thought and perception such as Thoreau wishes to practice cannot be separated, but form a composite which he terms "poetic perception" (PJ 4:17, 8/28/51). I quote freely from *Walden* because this is a theoretical point that is acted upon throughout the Journal but is not exclusively articulated there. Elaborating the theory of the Journal is important for two reasons. First, unless we grasp the Journal's theoretical basis, our appreciation of its "poetry," no matter how well justified by Thoreau's beautiful prose descriptions, may seem merely willful: an accidental side-effect of the text, rather than its *raison*. Second, the theory, once grasped, is so clearly borne out by the majority of Journal entries that there is no need to provide numerous block quotations (such as the five-hundred-word quotation above) from the Journal's unmanageably vast bulk. Closing the gap between text and interpretation is therefore not as difficult as it is in the case of Dickinson. Open the Journal at random and you will not need to interpret what you find there in order to grasp my point, which is that the author boldly invested the creative energies of his late career in the supposition that whatever he did, perceived, and thought in relation to nature could be recorded wholesale and the result would not be dross but poetry, or perhaps, dross whose mysterious redolence would make most "poetry" seem trifling by comparison.

But of course, for this to be the case, Thoreau could not just do, perceive, and think *anything* in relation to nature. The Journal is the product of an intense self-discipline whose object was, again, that the author's life should be "the poem [he] would have writ" were not poetry and the business of writing verse mutually exclusive. Disinterestedness is the name I have given to this discipline, which is non-teleological because its aim is not any one thing or text but a way or process in which living and writing, perceiving and thinking, are interdependent and immediately, invisibly fruitful, rather than subordinated one to the other for the purpose of some imagined future good. As

Thoreau puts it in an 1850 letter, "not writing is the most like writing in my case of anything I know."³²

THOREAU'S MEDITATIONS

Thoreau's word for that irreducible quality which, though it is potentially shared between humans and nature, nonetheless exposes the incommensurability of natural and human orders of significance, is "bloom." Bloom is at once a concrete and an abstract quality for Thoreau. In the first place (this is more or less its dictionary definition), it is a kind of ephemeral powder coating unpicked fruit, such as the huckleberries which Thoreau warns cannot be tasted except by those who pick them, and even then, only if they are being picked for personal enjoyment rather than for profit. Like Dickinson's "Bloom opon the mountain" and "Tint I cannot take," the bloom on huckleberries cannot be transposed or repurposed:

> The fruits do not yield their true flavor to the purchaser of them, nor to him who raises them for the market. . . . A huckleberry never reaches Boston; they have not been known there since they grew on her three hills. The ambrosial and essential part of the fruit is lost with the bloom which is rubbed off in the market cart, and they become mere provender. (W 9:461)

Note here how the most ephemeral, seemingly superficial aspect of the fruit, the aspect that is easiest to lose and hardest to define, becomes for Thoreau its "essential" quality, without which it is not itself. "A huckleberry," in his sense of the word, "never reaches Boston," has simply never been encountered by the majority of people. Later in *Walden*, he again suggests that it is easy to mistake ideas about a thing for the thing itself: "The dinner even is only the parable of a dinner, commonly" (W 13:517). Both statements anticipate Heidegger's notion that the ease with which someone recognizes and grasps "what is actual" may be a deception that "debar[s]" him from what truly concerns and touches him ("touches him in the surely mysterious way of escaping him by its withdrawal"). "What is most present in all our present" may be what our preoccupation with the idea of "actuality"—with "what we like to regard as constitutive of . . . actuality"—is causing us to miss, Heidegger and Thoreau alike suggest.³³ Under such circumstances it makes sense that, as Thoreau says in *A Week on the Concord and Merrimack Rivers*, making "a true account of the actual" is no simple feat, indeed "is the rarest poetry, for common sense always takes a hasty and superficial view."[34]

"Shams and delusions are esteemed for soundest truths, while reality is fabulous," Thoreau says in *Walden*: "If men would steadily observe realities only, and not allow themselves to be deluded, life, to compare it with such things as we know, would be like a fairy tale and the Arabian Nights' Entertainments. If we respected only what is inevitable and has a right to be, music and poetry would resound along the streets" (2:398). The reality of the huckleberry, then, its "ambrosial and essential part," its bloom in short, has not yet been observed, because it is valued only for its role as "provender"; but were it to be "steadily observe[d]," it would contribute its part to the poetry of existence ("like a line or accent in its poem"). Again, Thoreau seems to envision an approach to the natural object that is not quite writing poetry about it, but instead *thinking* about poetry while at the same time looking steadily at—and, in this case, handling and eating—the object.

This brings us to the second meaning of "bloom," which Thoreau extrapolates from the first, more common meaning. Simply put, bloom is a feature of anything, even or especially time, that has not been spoiled by use. It is a kind of autonomy or mysterious possibility in the object, even so humble an object as a huckleberry. "There were times," Thoreau writes in *Walden*, "when I could not afford to sacrifice the bloom of the present moment to any work, whether of the head or hands" (4:411). In this sentence "bloom" seems to refer to that which, as Thoreau says of the new moon, you "easily lose" as it returns into nature: that which cannot be held in the hand or head. It is not the product of human labor, whether manual or mental, nor can one add to, embellish, or preserve it by such labor. To borrow once more from Howe's language, one perceives bloom, if at all, after a "self-imposed exile" and "emancipat[ion]" from the fields and disciplines in which humans work, as well as from the marketplaces in which they buy, sell, and estimate value. So, sitting in his doorway doing absolutely nothing for an entire morning, Thoreau nonetheless feels that he "grew in those seasons like corn in the night, and they were far better than any work of the hands would have been. They were not time subtracted from my life, but so much over and above my usual allowance. I realized what the Orientals mean by contemplation and the forsaking of works" (4:411).[35] Crucial here is the absence not just of work performed by the man but also of work performed by the writer—at least, of the work we usually demand of writers: storytelling, describing, persuading, explaining. Even the physical surroundings of the meditator are not described, for this too would be a kind of work, and moreover, a description of definite objects would distract from the real subject of this passage, which is the indescribable quality of "bloom" or invisible growth characterizing the entire, strangely sustained "moment." This moment is not time spent, "subtracted," but time gained. It is an image of what the successful writer does when he or she discovers, without exactly locating, meaning and value where there were none before, and so transforms a profitless hour into a "seaso[n]" not bound by time.

"Song . . . is not desire, not / a wooing of something that's finally attained," writes Rilke, "song is existence [*Dasein*]." And then: "Easy for a god. But / when do *we* exist?"[36] Thoreau seeks an answer to this philosophical question in the same way Rilke does: through "song," which for both writers is an activity inseparable from looking "out / into the Open." This "Open," like Dickinson's "Possibility" and "Circumference," is not exclusively nature's territory, but simply the direction in which nature is constantly tending:

> With all its eyes the natural world looks out
> into the Open. Only *our* eyes are turned
> backward, and surround plant, animal, child
> like traps, as they emerge into their freedom.[37]

This is the freedom of disinterestedness, of a vision that is open rather than narrowed on what it wants.

It will be evident from my reading of Thoreau's thoughts on the bream, the huckleberry, and "the bloom of the present moment" that I am in partial agreement with Alfred Tauber's claim, in *Henry David Thoreau and the Moral Agency of Knowing*, that Thoreau challenged the "Cartesian construction" according to which "*res cogitans* was a distinct domain, and while humans might *know* the world and act in it, the mind was not *part of* the world."[38] Tauber writes that "Thoreau hoped to demonstrate that there was, in fact, no final divide between man and nature, and that man and nature might be integrated." However, if this was Thoreau's goal, Tauber goes on to say, it was not finally achievable: "But this picture of man and nature as fundamentally unified remained a poetic or spiritual aspiration. Despite the cogency of his enterprise, Thoreau was caught in the web of his own self-consciousness."[39]

Tauber's terms—"final divide between man and nature," "man and nature might be integrated," "Thoreau's goal," "caught in the web of . . . self-consciousness"—are altogether too simplistic for a discussion of the Journal. They are signs that Tauber is trying to interpret a non-teleological writer using a teleological framework. Admittedly, this is something of a necessary evil when writing on Thoreau, of which the present study is by no means innocent. But where I particularly differ from Tauber is in my sense that part of what is "poetic or spiritual" in Thoreau's efforts to bridge the "divide between man and nature" is the self-consciousness of those efforts, which is also a consciousness of their inevitable failure. So long as there is a work of literature, even if that work's essential gesture is, as Blanchot says, to "expres[s] nothing except the word *being*," there can be no unity between human and nature, the writer and the being that he speaks. I see little evidence that Thoreau bemoans this necessity; at least, he never tries to get around it by stopping writing. One might even say that he speaks the word *being* in order to remind himself of, to put himself in a position to see, his distance from being, which is also his distance from himself, as Heidegger would perhaps have agreed. As I suggested in my reading of "Conscious am I in my Chamber" (F773), to see one's distance from the transcendent or absolutely other may be the only form of transcendence available to humans in this world. Self-consciousness is thus not a "web" in which Thoreau gets "caught" despite his best efforts to merge with nature. On the contrary, it is as much his "goal" as consciousness of nature is, since he knows that nature can be encountered only through the self ("since all nature is to be regarded as it concerns man" [J 14:117, 10/13/60]).

Stanley Cavell, discussing *Walden*'s ideas of "nextness" and "neighboring," distinguishes these from the idea of mystical union between humans and nature:

> Our relation to nature, at its best, would be that of neighboring it—knowing the grandest laws it is executing, while nevertheless "not wholly involved" in them.
>
>> . . . I experienced sometimes that the most sweet and tender, the most innocent and encouraging society may be found in any natural object. . . . I was suddenly sensible of such sweet and beneficent society in Nature . . . an infinite and unaccountable friendliness all at once like an atmosphere sustaining me, as made the fancied advantages of

human neighborhood insignificant, and I have never thought of them since. ([*Walden*] 5:4)

... You may call this mysticism, but it is a very particular view of the subject; it is not what the inexperienced may imagine as a claim to the union, or absorption in nature.[40]

In a lengthy footnote Cavell aligns Thoreau's position on this point with Kant's controversial idea that the "thing-in-itself" is "unavailable to knowledge" but somehow still a "thing"—something we can productively think and speak about (though perhaps only with the aid of art: an afterthought that gets at the inseparability of philosophy and literature for Cavell as for Thoreau). "A thing which we cannot know is not a thing," Cavell writes:

> Then why are we led to speak otherwise? What is the sense that something escapes the conditions of knowledge? It is, I think, the sense, or fact, that our primary relation to the world is not one of knowing it (understood as achieving certainty of it based upon the senses). This is the truth of skepticism. A Kantian "answer" to skepticism would be to accept its truth while denying the apparent implication that this is a *failure* of knowledge.[41]

A Thoreauvian answer to Cartesian dualism would be to accept the difference between mind and nature while denying the apparent implication that by distinguishing the two we have succeeded in learning anything definite about either. The Journal shows, as *Walden* does not, or does only occasionally, that the writer's inability to unite mind and nature, such that he must almost remove himself from his descriptions in order to let nature be seen, is what gives to nature its freedom, hence, its value and significance—what Kant would perhaps consider its claim to being termed a "thing-in-itself." In the Walden experiment, Thoreau had to exile himself in the woods in order to not just learn but also "experienc[e] . . . that" the mind, being stranger than our discourse admits, bears a mysterious relation to "natural object[s]," distinct though it is from them. In the Journal his starting place is not the mind's strangeness but nature's strangeness, one aspect of which is nature's boringness, its apparent unsuitability as a source of intellectual stimulation. But the discovery the Journal yields is the same as that which *Walden* yields, for the mind in its exile from nature (an exile which it experiences as boredom) realizes in spite of its loneliness twinges of connection, and learns to value most highly those connections which never materialize but remain in potentia, just as the author learns to value the Journal though his devotion to it means that he "can select no work." "My loftiest thought is somewhat like an eagle that suddenly comes into the field of view, suggesting great things and thrilling the beholder, as if it were bound hitherward with a message for me; but it comes no nearer, but circles and soars away, growing dimmer, disappointing me, till it is lost behind a cliff or a cloud" (J 10:128–29, 10/26/57). This is an apt image for the Journal itself, which is never really Thoreau's own—it doesn't answer to his call or yield to his shaping imagination—and which does not bear "a message for" either the writer or the reader, except insofar as its digressions and evasions take the place, for him and for us, of revelations.

CHAPTER 5

Two Models of Disinterestedness, Part 2
Dickinson

> Lacking all subtlety, she displays the heavy hand of one unaccustomed to fragile objects; her efforts at lightness are distressing. Occasionally, instead of endeavoring to treat the small subject in terms appropriate to it, she endeavors to treat it in terms appropriate to her own temperament, and we have what appears a deliberate excursion into obscurity, the subject being inadequate to the rhetoric.
>
> —Yvor Winters, "Emily Dickinson and the Limits of Judgment"

DICKINSON'S SMALL SUBJECT

Dickinson's alternative to what Susan Howe terms "calculations of interest" is more obscure and more oblique than the alternative path described and tread by Thoreau. The obscurity and obliqueness of purpose evident in the Dickinson corpus is not accidental, I will argue, but the result of a lifelong interrogation of concepts such as purpose, (self-)interest, value, and, especially, meaning: an interrogation that yielded not answers but poems. The poet's questioning of meaning, rather than a set of meaningful assertions, is the source of her poems' value.

In chapter 2 we saw that Dickinson was the type of writer who would "lift [her] hat" to a word; a writer who built her poetics upon words rather than sentences, and who therefore directs readers' attention to the building blocks of her texts, rather than to any overarching statement or structure in whose service those "blocks" have been enlisted. In this chapter, I will try to show that such a poetics was inspired by the writer's ethical stance on how to be in the world, as we've seen was also the case with Thoreau's version of non-teleological poetics. The Journal invites readers to perceive unsuspected value and meaning in isolated facts, as well as in "unconsidered expressions of . . . delight" in facts. Dickinson's poems invite readers to look much more closely and appreciatively, not to say reverently, at the components of our language, as well as much more closely and critically—*ir*reverently—at the ideas which those linguistic components are ordinarily made to articulate.

The poems I will discuss in this chapter feature a self that has been ruthlessly pared down: we learn almost nothing about either her experiences or her thoughts and beliefs. Yet the phenomenon of paring down—or ellipsis, to use the more technical term—is so central to these poems, so inextricably a part both of how they construct meaning and of the meaningful experiences that they depict, that the speaker's effacement, like the poems' brevity and disjunctiveness, seems like a deliberate, principled decision rather than just an idiosyncrasy. I will argue, in fact, that the apparent renunciation of self which is the poems' dominant ethical feature is inseparable from the renunciation of conventional language and signification which is their dominant aesthetic feature. "Renunciation – is the Choosing / Against itself – / Itself to justify / Unto itself," Dickinson writes (F782). How do her renunciatory choices justify themselves? What logical or ethical system do they appear to body forth? That is the central question I will be pursuing in this chapter.

The speaker of the poem beginning "I am alive – I guess – / The Branches on my Hand / Are full of Morning Glory" (F605) is so bizarrely embodied—Dickinson having evidently identified, rather than simply compared, the blue veins in her hand with a blue flower—that we wonder whether the speaker is the poem itself rather than a human being. In other words, we can more readily imagine a non-human, intangible entity, the poem, speaking on its own behalf than we can imagine someone whose primary reason for believing herself to be alive is that the "Branches" she bears ("on" her hand rather than "in" it) are in flower. It scarcely makes sense for a human being to say this of herself. This near failure of sense is not an accident. The poem is one which puzzles over—seeks and does not find, except insofar as its inconclusive seeking is itself a discovery, an uncovering—the meaning of being human:

I am alive – I guess –
The Branches on my Hand
Are full of Morning Glory –
And at my finger's end –

The Carmine – tingles warm –
And if I hold a Glass
Across my mouth – it blurs it –
Physician's – proof of Breath –

I am alive – because
I am not in a Room –
The Parlor – commonly – it is –
So Visitors may come –

And lean – and view it sidewise –
And add "How cold – it grew" –
And "Was it conscious – when it stepped
In Immortality"?

I am alive – because
I do not own a House –
Entitled to myself – precise –
And fitting no one else –

And marked my Girlhood's name –
So Visitors may know
Which Door is mine – and not mistake –
And try another Key –

How good – to be alive!
How infinite – to be
Alive – two-fold – The Birth I had –
And this – besides, in Thee! (F605)

For all their strangeness, these lines are typical of the effacement of self—we might say, the replacement of self by language—in Dickinson's poetry. In this lyric as in many others, the aliveness of the person speaking seems to depend on the liveliness or originality—the originating power—of her utterance, making the speaker seem coeval with the poem. She has renounced everything—"House," "name," self-knowledge ("I am alive – *I guess*")—leaving her with just the present utterance, vanishing and indefinite. She guesses she is alive, she goes on to say, because "if I hold a Glass / Across my Mouth – it blurs it – / Physician's – proof of Breath." I take this to be a canny metaphor for the act of writing a lyric poem, which is paradoxically an assertion and "proof" of self that effaces or "blurs" the self. The ability to breathe, to be alive, is for this speaker the ability to speak, and, by speaking, to blur the mirror that we hold up to nature and to ourselves.

This dependence of poet on poem, of life on speech, explains why the speaker describes herself as a hybrid creature possessing both hands and flowering branches, as if she were half-human, half-artwork, capable of both doing and (merely) being. It also explains why she says at the end of the poem, "How good – to be alive! / How infinite – to be / Alive – two-fold – The Birth I had – / And this – besides, in – Thee!" In the absence of a clear antecedent for "Thee," it makes sense to guess that what the speaker has been reborn into is poetry, that is, poetic language, which is the sole unequivocal presence in the poem. "Poetry . . . does not come to us," writes Henri Meschonnic, "unless language itself has become a form of life. That is why it is so unquiet."[1] Dickinson, writing a hundred years earlier, understood this capacity of language to come alive, indeed to be more alive than oneself. "Are you too deeply occupied to say if my Verse is alive?" begins her famous correspondence with Thomas Wentworth Higginson (L260). "The most curious thing about the letter," Higginson later wrote of this initial message, "was the total absence of a signature" ("Emily Dickinson's Letters").

The absence from the poem of all other presences besides language would seem solipsistic were it not for the key fact that a self, too, is lacking here. The only thing the speaker is confident about, and the only fact we are given concerning her, is her ability to make herself double ("two-fold"), and therefore free ("infinite"), by means of her "breath," that is, her speech. Her breath, as we've seen, does not empower her to express herself so much as to challenge all representations of herself, even that of a "Glass" or mirror. Language for her is not a tool for building and naming but a tool for dismantling and unnaming; it is for fleeing from what is set in stone, established, and, especially, human-sized. Thus, the less the speaker of "I am alive – I guess" knows about herself, the bolder and more original, not to say more defiant, is her self-portrait. She is most confident of her aliveness when she announces what she lacks, namely, "a House – / Entitled to myself – precise – / And fitting no one else," and a "name" given to her in "Girlhoo[d]" and retained ever since, "So Visitors may know / Which Door is mine – and not mistake." This tightly fitting "House" with its marked "Door" is a metaphor for a crypt or grave (so long as she is not there, she is alive), but it is also evidently how the speaker conceives of identity, which she proudly professes to lack. It is because she lacks it that she is, or guesses she is, alive.

As in much of modernist poetry, language is everything in Dickinson's texts; but this is because language is entrusted with the romantic task of bringing things (including the self) to life, freeing them from the crypt-like names and categories which the speaker above, like the more famous speakers of "I dwell in Possibility" (F466) and "They shut me up in Prose" (F445), repudiates. We might even say that not language but meaning is everything in Dickinson's texts, but it is meaning that is in the form of a question (what does it mean to be alive? the present poem asks), and language is how the author makes meaning a question—how she brings it to life, though she may appear to be killing it off.

In *Dickinson: The Modern Idiom*, David Porter convincingly characterizes Dickinson as a poet for whom language, and the infinite field that language provides for innovation and discovery, is everything, subject matter virtually nothing. "Of great consequence to the evolution of poetry in America," he writes, "the poems establish a new and divisive relationship to reality. The language pulls back from clarity, from specificity, and from discernible referential links to an outside reality."[2] Yet it takes only a minor shift in emphasis or attention to see Dickinson as a poet who is profoundly attracted to a *minimal* subject matter: a subject matter continually under the threat of elision or erasure; always approaching, but never equal to, nothing. Think of the "shapeless friend" in "Conscious am I in my Chamber"; of the nameless play of light and color in "Bloom upon the Mountains – stated," "The Tint I cannot take – is best," and "Of Bronze – and Blaze"; and of the birds, trees, and mountains of which so little is positively affirmed in "The Birds begun at Four o'clock," "At half past Three – a single Bird," "Four Trees – opon a solitary Acre," and "Sweet Mountains – Ye tell Me no lie." Think, too, of the vanishing self that we encounter throughout Dickinson's poetry, who can only guess about and search for herself through her elliptical, renunciatory language—that strikingly "modern idiom" which, as Porter says, "pulls back from clarity, from specificity, and from . . . an outside reality." I hope that my readings of some of the above-named poems have shown that the vanishing quality of Dickinson's subject matter, its simplicity or evanescence, is symptomatic not of a repudiation of content or meaning but of a special kind of asceticism. It's as if the poet were testing her (and our) powers of imagination by starving her (and our) appetite for spectacle and incident; for "news" ("The only news I know," she wryly announces, "is Bulletins all Day / From Immortality" [F820]); and for positive statement and definite meaning. Porter aptly describes the ambiguous results of this experiment in asceticism when he writes of the poems' "intensely wrought simplicity."[3] Dickinson is a poet in whom intensity and simplicity, or what we might term extravagance and poverty, meet.

The metaphor of poverty, as we'll see, is one that Dickinson makes use of fairly often.[4] Almost always, however—even in one of her darkest poems, "It would have starved a Gnat," to be discussed later in this chapter—the metaphor is interlaced with suggestions of the subtle gain the poet, or perhaps merely, the poem, derives from her privation. This tendency to find interest in things, experiences, and situations that do not in an economic sense interest (i.e., benefit) humans, to find value in what is inimical and/or to all appearances valueless, is something she shares with Thoreau, who writes with great fondness of the useless shrub oak (J 9:145–46, 12/1/56), of "November Eat-heart" when all of nature's stores of warmth and beauty seem to be shut up (J 10:202–04, 11/25/57), and even of his own lack of wealth and fame, not to say of success (J 9:160; 12/5/56). "Give me . . . the smallest share of all things but poetic perception," Thoreau declares: "Give me but the eyes to see the things which you possess" (PJ 4:17, 8/28/51). Like Dickinson, he views a sort of mild asceticism, an avoidance of obvious forms of self-interested behavior (which for a writer can mean obvious, tried-and-true rhetorical or aesthetic choices, as well as the obvious move of publishing what one has written), as an essential characteristic of the poet. "The poet needs to have more stomachs than the cow," he writes, "for for him no fodder is stored in barns–He relies upon his instinct which teaches him to paw away the snow to come at the withered grass" (PJ 4:182, 11/13/51).

For Dickinson, too, poetry and poverty are closely allied terms. She envisions the poet as someone whose voluntary (or not-so voluntary) poverty prompts and even necessitates insight. In the lyric beginning "Some – Work for Immortality – / The Chiefer part, for Time," she gives what may be a covert definition of the poet: "A Beggar – Here and There – / Is gifted to discern /

Beyond the Broker's insight" (F536). Another lyric more openly defines the poet as one who discovers value where others do not:

> This was a Poet –
> It is That
> Distills amazing sense
> From Ordinary Meanings –
> And Attar so immense
>
> From the familiar species
> That perished by the Door – (F446)

What needs our attention in this passage is the subtle relation that Dickinson traces between privation and gain, couched here in terms of the relation between the ordinary and the extraordinary, or, more broadly, the meaningless and the meaningful. Privation and gain become almost indistinguishable in many of Dickinson's lyrics, and the present poem, especially this passage of it, can help us to understand both why that is and how this paradox relates to the paradoxical closeness of meaning and non-meaning which is the central subject of this book.

The relation between the binary pairs gain/loss and meaning/non-meaning is especially close in the six lines just quoted. The object lost—lost from the start, perhaps unbeknownst to all but the poet—and somehow regained is precisely meaning, or at least, meaningfulness: the capacity to affect and even "amaz[e]" which "Ordinary Meanings" and "familiar species" lack, unless the poet "distills" their latent force. But the poet's way of redressing this lack seems to endanger meaning in its turn. Dickinson would have known that "amazing sense," if one remembers earlier meanings of the word "amaze" ("to bewilder, perplex"),[5] is something of an oxymoron. The affirmation of extraordinary significance in ordinary things and words which many of Dickinson's poems seem to make does not simply stretch the concept of significance to accommodate previously excluded "species." It is a confounding gesture, which challenges the very notion of "Ordinary Meanings," and prompts one to ask whether the perception or supposition of meaning can ever be ordinary, simple, clear-cut—whether it is ever less than an imaginative feat, a leap of faith.

Poetry happens, Dickinson seems to be saying, when an ordinary thing or word is made to mean something besides, in excess of, itself: think of

Dickinson's customary rendering of "upon" as "opon," for example. But this claim cannot quite be the one Dickinson is making, because it presupposes a binary opposition which she ultimately rejects, between "Ordinary Meanings" and "amazing sense," a familiar thing or word and the something extra which the poet "distills" from it. As we saw in chapter 2, that something extra, though practically inaccessible, is in Dickinson's poetry immanent in the ordinary thing or word, like a "just repressed . . . secret" (F696). That is why, for her as for Thoreau, the poet's task is an ethical as well as an aesthetic one: a work of perception no less than of articulation; and a work that, because the object of perception is essentially elusive, requires self-denial and perseverance.

I submit that the six-line passage I've quoted, despite its pretense of making a confident assertion, was written in full awareness of the caveat just described, and that it is designed to raise the question of whether there is such a thing as "Ordinary Meanings": things and words whose meaning has been satisfactorily established. Would that not be a case of meaning*less*ness, a world of "familiar species," including homo sapiens, which have been classified and established nearly to death—whose familiarity breeds contempt? "I am alive – because / I do not own a House – / Entitled to myself – precise – / And fitting no one else." To be housed and named "So Visitors may know" who or what one is, is to be dead. This deadly familiarity is what Dickinson's "Poet," tapping like a bee into the invisible depths of the ordinary, sets out to remedy; to save us from by showing it to be an illusion (as opposed to merely sugarcoating the truth about the boringness of things, making the best of a bad situation). If the poet seems to want a thing to mean more than just itself, it is because he has perceived the familiar "thing itself" to be an abstraction standing in for the real thing, like Thoreau's "parable of a dinner" (W 13:517). To call the thing's identity—and in turn, our cognitive possession of the thing—into question is the only way to bring it to life and make it, rather than an idea about it, perceptible to us. Thus, the lines above are not about turning the flower into something else, something more, any more than the poem beginning "I am alive—I guess" is about becoming another person. Rather, both poems are about restoring a sense of meaningfulness and mystery, of the unsuspected and uncontainable, to things and to the self, as well as to the language by means of which we approach things and the self. To be confounded by an object is the only way to grasp it and not some ersatz substitute.

Poetry, then (to revise my initial paraphrase of Dickinson's meaning in "This was a Poet"), happens when a word produces a "glo[w]" ("Sometimes

I write one, and look at his outlines till he glows as no sapphire"),[6] or a thing yields an "Attar," whose "immens[ity]" belies our assumption that we are familiar with that word or thing—that we know it. I think again of Thoreau's remark, discussed in chapter 3: "Unconsidered expressions of our delight which any natural object draws from us are something complete and final in themselves" (J 14:117, 10/13/60). The emphasis here as in Dickinson's poem is on the subjective response to an object, which might seem disproportionate to that object: an "Attar so immense" one might question its authenticity. But the response, rather than going beyond the object, stops with it. The "delight," or its spontaneous, "unconsidered" expression, is "something complete and final" in itself, rather than the first step in a cognitive and artistic process deemed more important than the object that initiated it. So, while the poet's attention shifts from object to subject, what he or she attends to is the subject's strange sense of being satisfied with the object, or perhaps, of being stymied by the object, amazed by it, to the point of having virtually nothing to say about it.

If the opening lines of "This was a Poet" seem, at least at first glance, confident and affirmative, the remainder of the poem presents the poet in a much more negative, nebulous light, though here too it is not easy to distinguish positive from negative, gain from loss:

> This was a Poet –
> It is That
> Distills amazing sense
> From Ordinary Meanings –
> And Attar so immense
>
> From the familiar species
> That perished by the Door –
> We wonder it was not Ourselves
> Arrested it – before –
>
> Of Pictures, the Discloser –
>
> The Poet – it is He –
>
> Entitles Us – by Contrast –
> To ceaseless Poverty –
>
> Of portion – so unconscious –
> The Robbing – could not harm –

> Himself – to Him – a Fortune –
> Exterior – to Time – (F446)

"We" readers may be delighted by poetry's revelations, but we are also perturbed that "it was not Ourselves" who saw the meaningfulness which, poetry alerts us, has been hidden in plain sight all along. Why did we not see what the poet sees, before? And why do we continue to struggle to see it, now? The poet is "Of Pictures, the Discloser": a poem bestows vision, but, like a flash of lightning, it illuminates a residing darkness as well as a fragment of what that darkness conceals. Since of course the poet cannot always accompany us (he cannot disclose the picture of every scene we encounter) we must resign ourselves to being blind to much of what life presents to us. Thus, poetry attests simultaneously to the existence of meaning in the world and to meaning's difficulty of access. It is the tension or "Contrast" between these two attestations, I think, that Dickinson alludes to when she says that the poet "Entitles Us – by Contrast – / To ceaseless Poverty." Poetry (a word whose resemblance to *poverty* would not have been lost on Dickinson) privileges us with knowing how deprived we are, because it affords glimpses of what we cannot have or even understand. What the poet has to give us is a sense of our own poverty as compared with his wealth, except that when we say "his" we must remember that this is not a person so much as an ideal to which a person may briefly attain when he or she writes a poem; hence the surprising pronouns in lines 1–2: "*This* was a Poet – / It is *That*. . . ."

The pronominal oddness in that first line, and the paradoxical notion that poetry entitles us to poverty, both reappear in exacerbated form in the puzzling last stanza. The poet is "a Fortune" unto himself, cut off from all economic systems, along with everything else that is under the sway of "Time." He is incapable of possession ("Of portion – so unconscious – / The Robbing – could not harm"), despite his ability to detect value in virtually anything, no matter how "Ordinary" or "familiar." I would argue, in fact, that it is precisely because he is attuned to the presence of the extraordinary within the ordinary that the poet's wealth entails "ceaseless Poverty" for both himself and his audience. Unless we notice this causal relation, the poem splits into two apparently unrelated halves, its first two stanzas describing poetry's investment in the ordinary, and the third and fourth stanzas describing the incommensurability of poetry's value with other forms of value. It is crucial, therefore, to see that in Dickinson's view poetry's incommensurability, its apparent uselessness or worthlessness, derives from the incommensurability of the value that she and other poets detect in, and distill from, ordinary objects and words. As I suggested above, to locate meaning in the thing itself or the word itself goes against all the unwritten rules of how we assign meaning; it is to make ordinary things and words the site of a mystery that is more a threat to the construction and consumption of meaning than an aid. (How does one *use* a word that emits a "glo[w]"?)

The Dickinsonian poet's talent for distilling amazement from things of established meaning does not simply give him or her access to all of the world's perceptual riches, making him or her an exceptionally happy person. This is because, first, that talent is intermittent (no one person is "a Poet" all the time: the poet is more a "That" than a "who"); and second, the poet's amazement at the ordinary obstructs his or her access to the "familiar species" that usually attract people's attention, and compels him or her to investigate instead the mysterious, inexplicably strong reactions (as to an "Attar" incommensurate with the flower one sees) that things and words sometimes trigger in the mind and body. This I think is the meaning of the lines "Himself – to Him – a Fortune – / Exterior to Time": the poet does not own what he sees, not even in the form of an idea; he only owns himself, that is, his power to see. Thoreau's prayer comes to mind: "Give me . . . the smallest share of all things but poetic perception." The poet's perception of a thing is not equal to possession of it, whether cognitive or material; in fact, it is incompatible with such possession, or at least with possession beyond "the smallest share." Poetic perception, the ability "to discern / Beyond the Broker's insight," as Dickinson puts it (F536), is all that the poet calls his or her own. It is the poet's only true subject, the mystery at the center of all of his or her investigations.

The poem beginning "It would have starved a Gnat – / To live so small as I" (F444) might be read as a further meditation on the poet's fortunate poverty or interested disinterestedness. The thing to which the speaker responds, and from which she almost recoils, is herself; and poetry, rather than a model of responding to the world, is figured as a compulsive activity keeping her in the world against her will. Anticipating Franz Kafka's story "The Hunger Artist," the poem externalizes a writer's love-hate relationship with her vocation:

> It would have starved a Gnat –
> To live so small as I –
> And yet, I was a living child –
> With Food's necessity

> Opon me – like a Claw –
> I could no more remove
> Than I could coax a Leech away –
> Or make a Dragon – move –
>
> Nor like the Gnat – had I –
> The privilege to fly
> And seek a Dinner for myself –
> How mightier He – than I!
>
> Nor like Himself – the Art
> Opon the Window Pane
> To gad my little Being out –
> And not begin – again – (F444)

This speaker emphasizes her own humanness in a way that almost makes us miss the fact that she is also a writer. She introduces herself, first, as phenomenally capable of doing without ("liv[ing] . . . small"), but immediately undercuts the positive, artistic associations that this self-denial has in other Dickinson poems: "And yet I was a living child – / With Food's necessity // Opon me – like a Claw." Why then should we assume that the speaker is a writer who has chosen her privation, for whom to "choos[e] / Against itself" is "to justify [itself] / Unto itself" (F782)?

First, there is the simple fact that we know the author to be a poet, so any self-referential utterance is bound to invite the speculation that the speaker, too, is a poet. Second, the fact that the speaker feels it necessary to say that she is a mortal being, "With Food's necessity // Opon" her, suggests that in the preceding lines she was, in contrast, describing an almost superhuman quality—the kind of thing we typically find in Dickinson's reverential descriptions of the poet. Third, because no external cause for the speaker's predicament is stated, it is reasonable to guess that the cause is internal to herself: a choice (one that the veiled boasting of lines 1–2 suggests she is proud of) rather than a curse. Fourth, the hyperbolic quality of the poem's language alerts us to the fictiveness of this self-portrait. It seems unlikely that the speaker's problem is literally that she cannot "seek a Dinner for [her]self" or "gad [her] little Being out" (i.e., obtain sufficient food or destroy herself, empty out her life force), so our attention is preoccupied by the odd phrasing of these claims. Is it that she can seek a dinner (or sustenance in a broader sense) only not "for [her]self"?

And what would that mean? Why refer to her vitality as "my little Being," with a capital "B"? Why figure life as a process of repeatedly "begin[ning] – again," which is closer to what the writer does? And why figure death (or is this a figure for life?) as a process of "gad[ding]" one's "Being out," in the manner of a gnat consuming its life force by flitting purposelessly about, even bashing itself against a window pane? Fifth and finally, the reference to "Art" in the last stanza hints that art is on the speaker's mind as well as life; that these two are for her subtly intertwined. Though art's lack is what the speaker blames for her dilemma (unlike the gnat, she lacks the art of ceasing to be), I will argue that it is actually art's nagging, insubstantial, gnat-like presence that stops her from dying, compelling her to live even though life has become an unwelcome burden, and even though art does not "remove" the pain of foregoing personal needs.

"Art" enters the poem on the wings of the gnat; it is what the gnat is said to possess and the speaker is said to lack:

> Nor like Himself – the Art
> Opon the Window Pane
> To gad my little Being out –
> And not begin – again –

Why does this artful speaker associate an insect with art while associating herself with art's absence? Like the fly of "I heard a Fly buzz – when I died" (F591), the gnat of this poem alerts the speaker to her own insignificance ("How mightier He – than I!"), and yet, so doing, prompts an effort of imagination that gives the poem its significance: namely, the effort to find meaning in this insolent creature's antics, its fatal "gad[ding]" about, which somehow becomes paired in the speaker's mind with her own living and dying. The gnat and the fly seem to inspire their respective poems to "gad" themselves out as well, recklessly expending their linguistic ingenuity on the ordinary, not to say the picayune. The poet's unaccountable interest in an insect despite its insignificance is thus related to her unaccountable compulsion to keep writing despite the "small[ness]" of her efforts: their brevity, their incompleteness or indefiniteness, their phenomenally delicate hold on meaning. For again, the incommensurability of Dickinson's poetry's value, the inexplicability of her devotion to her art (since if that art has no definite purpose what motivates its practitioner?), derives from the incommensurability of the ordinary's value, the inexplicability of ordinary objects' attraction or pull.

I suggest, then, that "It would have starved a Gnat" represents Dickinson's lifelong devotion to writing (in particular, her penchant for starting poem after poem only to leave it, even after laborious revisions, "at a threshold state of organization that can just barely be called a poetic event")[7] as a private "necessity" even more pressing, because more deeply-rooted and harder to satisfy, than food. It—the poetic, creative impulse—is like a gnat that will not die but continues to roam about in search of invisible sustenance; or, more precisely, continues to goad the poet to search on its behalf rather than "seek a Dinner for [her]self." The speaker's "little Being," which for all its littleness she has not the art to extinguish, would then be, along with the gnat, a figure for Dickinson's subject matter. Despite being trivial and/or intangible almost to the point of nothingness, Dickinson's small subjects—a fly, a gnat, a bird; a tint, a slant of light; a self unsure of its own existence—lay some mysterious claim on her, compelling her to write though what she writes brings sustenance neither to herself nor, so far as she knows, to anyone else. For poetry as she conceives of it in the end disseminates nothing more definite than a candle's light, and that, in all likelihood, only after the poet him or herself has "go[ne] out": "The Poets light but Lamps – / Themselves – go out" (F930). The present poem acknowledges the great personal cost this kind of devotion to the intangible involves.

Yvor Winters, in the passage quoted in this section's epigraph, writes of Dickinson:

> Her descriptive poems contain here and there brilliant strokes, but she had the hard and uncompromising approach to experience of the early New England Calvinists; lacking all subtlety, she displays the heavy hand of one unaccustomed to fragile objects; her efforts at lightness are distressing. Occasionally, instead of endeavoring to treat the small subject in terms appropriate to it, she endeavors to treat it in terms appropriate to her own temperament, and we have what appears a deliberate excursion into obscurity, the subject being inadequate to the rhetoric, as in the last stanza of the poem beginning, "At half-past three—a single bird."[8]

Winters's judgment, while harsh, is not merely cranky. Porter expresses a similar sentiment when he writes, "there is difficulty in understanding all of [Dickinson's] labors [of drafting and revision], for sometimes the effort seems unjustified, as in the second stanza of poem 1211, a slight piece on a sparrow taking flight."[9] The poem Porter refers to is, like "At half-past Three – a single

Bird" (the poem singled out by Winters), "A narrow fellow in the grass," "The Birds begun at Four o'clock," and the last stanza of "It would have starved a Gnat," about the nearness, in time as well as in ontological status, of an animal's appearance and disappearance. The impression that the animal makes on the observer's imagination is "forfeited" almost as soon as it's been made. The observer tries (again and again, as we shall see when we consider the poem's variants) to put this significant disappearance or disappearing significance into words:

> A Sparrow took a Slice of Twig
> And thought it very nice
> I think, because his empty Plate
> Was handed Nature twice –
>
> Invigorated, waded
> In all the deepest Sky
> Until his little Figure
> Was forfeited away – (F1257B)

The proximity of appearance and disappearance, beginning and ending, in poems such as this, and the fact that the speaker evidently knows nothing after the experience that she did not know before it, would seem to justify Winters and Porter in describing certain of Dickinson's nature poems as "slight" and certain of her subjects as "small": objects of "unjustified" effort; subjects demanding "lightness" of treatment. What these two critics seem to forget, however, is that slightness, evanescence, the lightness and uninstructiveness of being, are some of Dickinson's chief subjects of investigation. They are also concepts that she turns on their head by writing about them, as Winters complains, in a manner that "distressing[ly]" combines "efforts at lightness" with "the hard and uncompromising approach to experience of the early New England Calvinists." This effect, I will try to show in my reading of the above poem, is both more calculated and harder to diagnose than Winters assumes. In Dickinson's writing one frequently detects, beneath a thin layer of irony or levity, a grandeur and severity, a hardness and refusal to compromise with one's convictions no matter how indistinct and impracticable (how "light"). One detects this hardness where one would least expect it, as when she writes to Thomas Wentworth Higginson, who had requested a photograph, "I had no portrait, now, but am small, like the Wren, and my Hair is bold, like the Chestnut Bur–and my eyes, like the Sherry in the Glass, that the Guest leaves–Would this do just as well?" (L268). Here as well as in the gnat poem and in "I am alive – I guess," the claim to being small (or to "liv[ing] . . . small," or to being uncertain of oneself) is belied by the claim's boldness, a boldness that in all three texts consists in the speaker's refusing to present a picture or clear idea of herself and, in the ambiguous self-portrait she does offer, associating herself more with animals and plants than with her human audience (she identifies more with "the Sherry in the Glass" than with "the Guest" who drank from the glass), thereby eschewing the measurements and standards of judgment of the latter. What were the author's own standards of judgment, her criteria for measuring value and significance? What were the convictions that lent to her writing its hardness and boldness, its resolute nonconformity? Because of these latter qualities, Winters guesses that Dickinson's unconventional "approach to experience" derives from her Calvinist heritage; but the truth is that it seems to be peculiar to her, originating in some sort of private religion, and stated nowhere explicitly and summarily but instead implicitly and piecemeal throughout her poems and letters.

Susan Howe is a key figure in the history of Dickinson criticism because she identified, with unprecedented enthusiasm and conviction, the determined originality of Dickinson's writing and thinking, as opposed to the involuntary eccentricity that Winters perceived (and that Porter, himself a groundbreaking Dickinson critic, occasionally overemphasized as well). Wryly quoting John Ruskin's maxim, "*He* may pause but *he* must not hesitate" (italics Howe's), Howe writes of Dickinson as "a 'sheltered' woman audaciously invent[ing] a new grammar grounded in humility and hesitation."[10] Thus, on the one hand, Dickinson seems humbly conscious of how little she has to tell or give the reader. "Would this do just as well?" she demurely asks Higginson, and in "A Sparrow took a Slice of Twig" she follows up the already watered-down seeming claim, "A Sparrow . . . thought it very nice," with the qualification, "I think." On the other hand, she seems in both of these texts to be peculiarly unembarrassed, as though what she really wanted to share was just this rhetorical or pedagogical conundrum of having nothing definite or impressive to tell or give. The very existence of the poem, given this poverty on the speaker's part, is a kind of riddle. It's as though Dickinson wanted to enact, to dramatize, her own ambivalence about the poem she had undertaken to write, which she feels compelled to write, and to revise extensively, though it appears to lack a reason for being.

Dickinson's grammar of "humility and hesitation" is less the cause behind this poem's riddle than a means of coping with it, for the original riddle—the meaning of not meaning, the drama of uneventful events such as a sparrow's arrival and departure—is set by nature, not by art. The speaker, as we've noted, admits that she has little to say about what she saw, but she also makes the most of the incident by rendering it indistinct, hard to pin down and therefore potentially greater than it appears. She does this, first, by introducing a challenging metaphor (the sparrow as beggar and nature as benefactor), then by qualifying her testimony ("I think"), and finally by concluding the poem with an action word ("waded") as ambiguous as the one with which the poem began ("took"). In what does the sparrow's taking consist, seeing that the twig is not a comestible object? (It is not a cake one can take "a Slice of.") And does his wading in the sky precede a drowning (hence "forfeited away") or an ascension? The poet does not provide the answers to these questions because she is not in possession of them. If the poem is a riddle, she is on the reader's side of it: at the poem's circumference rather than at its concealed center.

The manuscript evidence of the trouble that Dickinson took with the poem's second stanza, which is what prompts Porter's uncharacteristically ungenerous remark about Dickinson's labors seeming wasteful, reinforces the textual evidence that she wasn't sure exactly what she wanted to say. The version of the poem I've quoted from (and that Porter comments on) is embedded in an 1872 letter to Susan Dickinson. An alternative version, also dated 1872 by R. W. Franklin, concludes, "Invigorated fully – sprang lightly to the sky / As an accustomed stirrup – / And boldly rode away," or alternatively (switching out the underscored line), "And rode Immensity," or again, "And rode deriding by" (F1257A). Nor is this "alternative version" of stanza 2 the only site of variants. The manuscript page of this version is fairly littered with other possibilities, proposed and never canceled by the author. While these revisions and variants reveal a surprising degree of authorial uncertainty about the semantic purpose of the poem—what it finally has to say about the bird; what the speaker actually saw and/or felt, or what the author imagined her to have seen and felt—they also suggest that the author was confident it was worth trying to say, whatever "it" was, at the expense of much time and labor. The author's hesitation over her statement, combined with her devotion to the craft of style (evidenced by her revisions as well as by the striking metaphors and diction described in the previous paragraph), point up her "audaciou[s]" determination to speak in the absence of definite knowledge and purpose; to make "a new grammar" out of her own uncertainty. The poem, especially when read in its manuscript context, expresses Dickinson's paradoxical confidence that the nearer something (a fly, a gnat, a sighting of a sparrow, a poem) is to being nothing, or to never having happened, or to being simply unknowable and unsayable, the more important it has the potential to be. As Howe suggests, this alternative value system called for an alternative poetics.

The speaker of "A Sparrow took a Slice of Twig" is evidently not in a position to know either what satisfaction the sparrow finds in its twig or what motivates its sudden flight, much less to state what these mean to her. Her ignorance mixes oddly with the sharpness of her perception of the bird's shape and movements (its "little Figure"), which is presumably what prompted the utterance. These two characteristics of the experience, uncertainty of meaning and clarity of perception, are not really opposed but on the contrary mutually reinforcing. A similar dialectic between uncertainty and simplicity, strain and pleasure, is experienced vicariously by the reader as he or she tries to handle this utterance that manages to be pleasingly simple, bold, and direct (like "A Bird came down the walk" [F359], it consists primarily of paratactically arranged verb clauses, whose vagueness and ambiguity are tempered by the verbs' outward simplicity ["took," "thought," "handed," "waded"]) while saying almost nothing definite, final.

This lyric bears comparison with another eight-line poem on a natural subject, in which again the speaker adopts an attitude of knowingness and clear-sightedness (for in this case she holds the answer to a riddle, though an easy one), ambivalently combined with an attitude of awe and uncertainty. As before, the two attitudes are inextricable; the first forces the poem abruptly into existence and the second forces it to abruptly end:

> Blazing in Gold and quenching in Purple
> Leaping like Leopards to the Sky
> Then at the feet of the old Horizon
> Laying her Spotted Face to die
> Stooping as low as the Otter's Window
> Touching the Roof and tinting the Barn
> Kissing her Bonnet to the Meadow
> And the Juggler of Day is gone (F321C)

Like the previous poem, this single-sentence lyric is not just about ending (here, the end of day; in the other poem, the end of an encounter) but is itself in the process of ending from the very first line. The gerunds with which it opens, rather than introducing and qualifying a central predicate, are themselves the main attraction, as we find out for certain when we read on and find that the gerunds keep coming until the very last line. This lack of subordination, of the structural hierarchy that telos always imposes, is a formal feature of the poem that doubles as an implicit argument about the unnamed subject, sunset, which doesn't seem to do or mean or intend anything besides the auxiliary-seeming effects captured by Dickinson's gerunds—unless one counts its final trick of disappearing ("is gone").

Given the poem's lack of a build-up to a final revelation of meaning, there is nothing to stop the first, inimitable line, "Blazing in Gold and quenching in Purple," from being the best in the poem; from encompassing in its seven words the whole "meaning" of the poem. If the poet begins in this way it is not necessarily because she has a plan and this opening enables the fulfillment of that plan. More probably, the poem starts thus because with this line Dickinson hit upon a perfectly balanced arrangement of contrasting meanings and sounds—two trochees, "Blazing" and "Quenching," the first characterized by a long "a" and followed by a monosyllable with a long "o" ("gold"), the second characterized by a short "e" and followed by a disyllable with a short "u" ("purple"), giving the line a feminine ending—that expresses in an instant the feeling of a particular natural phenomenon. The line, doing in seven words what the whole poem does in fifty-four, conveys the closeness, the near identity, of the sunset's triumphant beginning and gentle ending, as well as the impression the sunset gives of being a complex action (a series of do*ings*) rather than an object or a finite phenomenon.

In keeping with this opening, the final line, rather than concluding the preceding statement—or better, rather than undoing the preceding lines' determined avoidance of making a statement—insists on the incompleteness of the speaker's experience and description. For the series of actions witnessed and described by the speaker is never really completed. Finally, the sun, "the Juggler of Day," "is gone," but its juggling has not stopped; the viewer's allotment of vision has simply come to an end. The last line, then, is successful in that it brings the poem to an end without creating a superficial sense of closure, such as is sometimes achieved by pointing up the moral of a natural description. Since it makes clear that the experience ends not because the observer has learned something but simply because the object under observation "is gone," the line preserves the sense that the poem is a fragment, yet at the same time confirms the intentionality, the artfulness, of its fragmentation. There is no chance, here, of editors marking the poem "unfinished," as Franklin sometimes does. Thus, over and above what it actually says about sunset, the poem tacitly challenges the distinction between fragment and complete poem, as well as that between glimpse and whole vision.

"Capacity to terminate / Is a specific Grace" (F1238). It is a grace, a fearlessness in the face of incompleteness and indefiniteness, not to say of pointlessness, that Dickinson finds in the things of nature, and tries to cultivate in her verse. It is also a grace that her verses demand of us readers, who must again and again find meaningful ways of ending: of finding an ending, an endpoint, to texts that seem too short and too indefinite in meaning and purpose to have a beginning, middle, and end; texts that can almost literally be read in a single glance. We balance uneasily between the sense that the poems' brevity is itself meaningful and fraught with intention—a kind of riddle—and the sense that their brevity is a renunciation of meaning and of authorial control: a sign that the author is herself at the mercy of some awful riddle.

Winters, evidently, was disturbed by the latter sense: the sense that the author, instead of mastering her subject matter and handling it with the proper tools (a "rhetoric" appropriate to it), was herself mastered by her subject matter, and therefore compelled (in Howe's phrase again) to "inven[t] a new grammar grounded in humility and hesitation." He charges, with some truth, that Dickinson's grammar was "appropriate to her own temperament" rather than to "the small subject." In other words, we learn more about Dickinson from her poems on nature than we do about nature. But it is not merely temperament that compels Dickinson to describe the small subject as though it were a large subject; it is also her reasoned conviction that distinctions between small and large, trivial and important are often specious, and belied by some of our most intimate and affecting encounters, with nature as well as with literature. Likewise, her "excursion[s] into obscurity" are not spontaneous and random but, as Winters himself admits, "deliberate." If Dickinson's syntax and diction are cryptic, it is because they are designed to change how we see and experience her poems' subject matter, as well as their medium. In poem after poem, Dickinson seeks a plane or perspective from which what is small will not appear small, and what is obvious, like the meaning of a word or the meaninglessness (arbitrariness, irrelevance to human affairs) of a natural object, will no longer be obvious. Evidently, she would rather her reader not see her subject at all, not understand her meaning at all (as when she ends

"At half-past Three – a single Bird" with what Winters deems the nonsensical phrase "Circumference between") than that he or she should be on contemptuously familiar terms with her subject and with her poem. This, I propose, is the ethical underpinning, or at least a major component of the ethical underpinning, of Dickinson's seemingly amoral, apolitical, non-ideological poetics.

CODA ON DICKINSON AND MODERNISM

Dickinson's resistance to hierarchy—in particular, to the teleological prejudice against what is small and undeveloped, what is obscure and contains unrealized signifying potential—is expressed, not only in the syntax and diction of her poems, but also in their punctuation. As anyone knows who has read Higginson's and Mabel Loomis Todd's bowdlerized editions of the poems, which in addition to altering words and phrases replace many of her dashes with commas and other, less ambiguous punctuation marks, Dickinson's dashes tend to make the spareness of her poems less jarring, not more. The reader is trained by the dashes, as well as by the engrossing peculiarities of Dickinson's elided syntax, slant rhymes, solecistic verb tenses, and unconventional capitalization (most of which features are ostensibly lacking in semantic content), to dwell inside the lines rather than to proceed steadily to their potentially disappointing, and always imminent, conclusion. Paradoxically, the bigness of the poems, the wide-openness of the cognitive space they "wad[e]," manifests itself most clearly when our attention is engrossed by these small, seemingly meaningless or arbitrarily decided-upon details. For it is here that the poet makes contact with the weirdness of language and the mysteries of the unconscious creative mind, admitting into her well-wrought urn the hazards of chance, of randomness.

Toward the end of the nineteenth century, Stéphane Mallarmé would confront these hazards somewhat more recklessly, arguably succumbing to them altogether, in an influential though baffling text—a veritable haunted house of a poem—titled "Un coup de dés jamais n'abolira le hasard," or "A throw of the dice will never abolish chance." "The 'blanks' [between words, phrases, and lines] indeed take on importance," Mallarmé wrote in the poem's preface: "Everything happens, by ellipsis, as supposition; narrative is avoided."[11] Dickinson was there before him. In and from her poetry, we learn the lesson of modernism as Paul Valéry defined it: we learn "to conten[t] [ourselves] with little."[12] Little, that is, in the way of narrative, of sustained argument ("Everything happens, by ellipsis . . ."), of explicit, authoritative, non-hypothetical meaning.

Like Mallarmé's significant "'blanks,'" Dickinson's dashes alternately slow reading down and speed it up; they can ask us to go back to and linger with the previous word or words rather than move on to the next one(s), or else signal a shortcut away from the present, unfinished phrase and straight into a new one. Mallarmé could almost have been speaking of Dickinson when he wrote, "The literary value, if I am allowed to say so, of this print-less distance which mentally separates groups of words or words themselves, is to periodically accelerate or slow the movement, the scansion, the sequence even, given one's simultaneous sight of the page."[13] Often the words themselves perform the same ambiguous function, stopping or fast-forwarding (as if to an apparently unearned climax) the flow of communication, instead of easing or harnessing it. Even when dealing with her less elliptical, more narrative-like poems, interpretation is commonly halted by the absence of logical sequence or of a full narrative arc on the one hand, and the presence of highly charged, enigmatic phrases on the other hand.

In "I felt a Funeral, in my Brain" (F340), for example, Dickinson seems content to let her story and extended metaphor fall apart when it brings her to an image of extreme strangeness. It's as if the climax she had been pursuing was not a narrative or rhetorical climax but a linguistic and cognitive one—the point of maximum estrangement from ordinary modes of speech and thought:

> Then Space – began to toll,
>
> As all the Heavens were a Bell,
> And Being, but an Ear,
> And I, and Silence, some strange Race
> Wrecked, solitary, here – (F340)

The partial narrative that had been developing in the preceding stanzas collapses here, and is replaced by one of Dickinson's signature "images" that cannot be pictured or imagined. Thought—the speaker's as well as the reader's—is interrupted, indeed dead-ended, and more or less left to its own devices. The reader is free to make what she will of the bizarre arrangement of concrete abstractions ("Space," "Heavens," "Bell," "Being," "Ear," "Silence," "Race"); she is not compelled or persuaded to interpret them in any particular way, or even to credit them as being more than wordplay—more than nonsense, even. As Mallarmé would put it, everything happens here as hypothesis.

Cristanne Miller has persuasively argued that, when subjected to an "aurally focused reading"—the kind of reading, she claims, that was most common in Dickinson's time but is rare in ours—this poem is seen to climax in the penultimate stanza (the one I've just quoted).[14] The closing lines, therefore—"And then a Plank in Reason, broke, / And I dropped down, and down – / And hit a World, at every plunge, / And Finished knowing – then"—are in Miller's view "distinctly anti-climactic."[15] It is true that the poem's conclusion is a kind of non-conclusion, a privation that an "aurally focused" reader might be more willing to accept and move past than a reader avidly in search of meaning, who is likely to be baffled and disappointed by the poem's ending. But this disappointed reading is not to be dismissed. "Aurally, the poem does not ask us to linger on this inconclusive ending," Miller claims,[16] but the inconclusiveness of the ending is jarring nevertheless—and we may question whether this would really not have been the case for nineteenth-century readers, as Miller's broader argument implies. Modern readers are right, I think, to sense that the poem's willingness to trail off in the last stanza, without even indicating whether its final "then" is terminal or initial in function, is central to its meaning, that is, to the story it tells, or fails to tell, about some unspeakable psychic trauma. In the final stanza the speaker confronts her inability to finish her own story; pointedly, the only thing she has "Finished" is "knowing." Rather than locate the poem's climax elsewhere, it would be better to say that Dickinson's poetry as a whole, like Thoreau's Journal, is a poetry without climax, since in it meaning is never finished or finalized. But perhaps it would be better still to say that, again like the Journal, Dickinson's is a poetry that is all climax, poetry that is always finishing knowing and so, rather than communicating knowledge, is at every turn putting the burden of understanding, of finding or hypothesizing meaning, on the reader.

Conclusion

> Not to know how to express what is perceived may be not to know how its parts go together; what the parts are; or the frame that would make the whole legible, a state of affairs that does not attenuate the question of how to regard aspects of the world that can't be grasped and that may even leave us speechless, a question I take to be ethical.... What hangs in the balance in such a confrontation is how to respond—how to be in relation—to aspects of world with which we are not affiliated, but from which we are also not estranged, which call to us, the way voiceless things, or things that lack our voice, can be said to call to us to see them, unobstructed by the shadow of categories and ideas.
>
> —Sharon Cameron, *The Bond of the Furthest Apart*

"With all its eyes the natural world looks out / into the Open," Rainer Maria Rilke writes in a poem I discussed in chapter 4: "Only *our* eyes are turned / backward, and surround plant, animal, child / like traps, as they emerge into their freedom."[1] What, then, would it be like if a human being, or a human artifact, were to look out into the Open; if a writer or his or her text looked in the same direction—rather, the same non-direction or non-telos—as a plant, an animal, a child? In Emily Dickinson's terms, what would it mean for a piece of art to be as haunted by that openness, that absence of purpose, as nature is?

There is a passage in Rudyard Kipling's *The Jungle Book* that offers a glimpse of what it is like to experience what Rilke calls "The Open." It describes the daily activities of child buffalo herders as they look after the somnambulant animals placed in their keeping:

> They sleep and wake and sleep again, and weave little baskets of dried grass and put grasshoppers in them; or catch two praying-mantis and make them fight; or string a necklace of red and black Jungle-nuts; or watch a lizard basking on a rock, or a snake hunting a frog near the wallows. Then they sing long, long songs with odd native quavers at the end of them, and the day seems longer than most people's lives, and perhaps they make a mud castle with mud figures of men and horses and buffaloes, and put reeds into the men's hands, and pretend that they are kings and the figures are their armies, or that they are gods to be worshipped. Then evening comes, and the children call, and the buffaloes lumber up out of the sticky mud with noises like gunshots going off one after the other, and they all string across the grey plain back to the twinkling village lights.[2]

Then, too, the book goes back to its suspenseful narrative (Mowgli is just about to kill his enemy, the tiger Shere Khan, with the help of those same idling buffaloes), and the reader, perhaps, makes a mental note to return to this breathtaking swerve away from narrative and from the human altogether, which is breathtaking because it breathes differently, as it were, more slowly and more deeply, than the rest of the book and than the reader who eagerly thumbs the book's pages.

While Thoreau and Dickinson would probably have been impressed by the above passage, they would have been justified in thinking that their own writings look deeper and longer than Kipling's into that mysterious region where time ceases ("and the day seems longer than most people's lives") and one's own pursuits are dwarfed, indeed swept out of mind, by those of animals, even slumbering ones ("or watch a lizard basking on a rock"). "Where is the literature which gives expression to Nature?" asked Thoreau,[3] who presumably found similar isolated passages in the pages of the books he read—Wordsworth, Emerson, Darwin, Gilbert White—but no sustained body of writing, no thoroughgoing poetics of the non-teleological. That is the gap which the Journal tries to fill, while Dickinson's poems express more consistently than perhaps any other body of writing the awful "leisure" of the mind

"Without a thing to do," unless it is to look at nature and at itself (F683). Think of how many of her poems begin, and end, with such looking—that special Dickinsonian noticing that evinces a sense both of awe and of leisure: "A Bird came down the Walk – / He did not know I saw – / He bit an Angleworm in halves / And ate the fellow, raw" (F359B); "There's a certain Slant of light, / Winter Afternoons – / That oppresses, like the Heft / Of Cathedral Tunes" (F320); "Four Trees – opon a solitary Acre – / Without Design / Or Order, or Apparent Action – / Maintain" (F778).

A symptomatic assumption of contemporary western culture is that science is more capable than literature of such looking: of objectively, self-effacingly recording natural facts; of letting a tree just be a tree, as Heidegger put it; of not interfering with the intrinsic communicativeness of nature that Thoreau wrote about and tried to channel; of grappling with the philosophical and ethical question of "how to respond—how to be in relation—to aspects of world with which we are not affiliated, but from which we are also not estranged," as Cameron describes it in one of her recent books.[4] Implicitly I have meant to challenge this disciplinary bias. "The absence of the imagination had / Itself to be imagined," Wallace Stevens wrote.[5] According to this view, it is literature, ironically, that best recognizes the limitations of the imagination and of human beings more generally; hence it is literature that is most capable of gesturing to what there is beyond these, or at least to the possibility of looking beyond them. And because it is commonly in literature that the attempt to imagine imagination's absence is made, it is more often literature than science that confronts the difficulty of this endeavor—that confronts, in other words, the absolute difference of nature, the gap separating it from culture. Thus, Thoreau lacked the naiveté that underlies a good percentage of scientific writing; he wrote with surprising sophistication about the inseparability of subjectivity from "objective observation"; in fact, he denied the possibility of purely objective writing (PJ 8:98, 5/6/54). The nearest we can get to nature, Thoreau understood, was by way of our own imagining of it: "The poet is a man who lives at last by watching his moods" (PJ 4:16, 8/28/51).

This book began with the observation that scholars are exceptionally uncertain how to categorize Dickinson's and Thoreau's writings, and, consequently, how to evaluate and understand them. It has argued that the inability to assess value, or assign meaning, is precisely the dilemma which Dickinson as well as Thoreau want us to confront and celebrate and linger with. The most obvious form this dilemma takes is when we look at a natural object and recognize its incommensurability vis-à-vis human value systems. Dickinson wrote countless poems that dramatize that recognition; but whatever their subject matter, her poems themselves, I've argued, imitate the "hauntedness" of natural objects, in order to confront readers with the alienness that can occur even in human artifacts—even in our selves.

A few hours before I defended the dissertation from which this book arose, I happened to look out the window of my apartment and watch for a few seconds the movements of some sparrows. It helped, to a surprising extent, to remember that for these sparrows there was not, as there was for me at that moment, the excitement of an impinging public performance, nor was there the apprehension of the come-down that was sure to follow. In their world, as far as I could judge (but of course this was not very far), there were no pursuits such as I experienced them, no time such as I experienced it. What little there was—the littleness of what there was, or rather, of what I could perceive—seemed unimportant compared with these shocking, wonderfully refreshing absences.

And yet, as Thoreau writes in one entry, "Those sparrows, too, are thoughts I have" (J 10:128, 10/26/57). Their inaccessibility is like that of my self to itself; the fascinating blankness I experience when I watch the birds is the blankness of my best thinking. "My loftiest thought is somewhat like an eagle that suddenly comes into the field of view . . . but circles and soars away, growing dimmer, disappointing me" (J 10:128–29, 10/26/57). And Dickinson, in the poem beginning "I am alive – I guess" (F605), says that her hand does not hold but contains (is "full of") the bluish-purplish flower known as morning glory: this is her figuration for the veins pumping blue blood just beneath the skin of her wrists, proving, if anything can (she herself cannot) that she is alive. Dickinson would have appreciated the Qur'an verse which states that God is nearer to a person than his or her jugular vein (50:16). Closer, yet farther away; closer because farther away.

Notes

PREFACE

1. *The Journal of Henry David Thoreau*, ed. Bradford Torrey and Francis H. Allen, 14 vols. ([Boston: Houghton Mifflin, 1906] New York: Dover, 1962), 9:121, 10/18/56. Hereafter abbreviated J and cited by volume, page number, and date. Reference will be made to this edition when quoting from later volumes of the Journal. Where possible, reference will be made to the as-yet incomplete Princeton edition of the Journal, cited below.
2. *The Poems of Emily Dickinson: Variorum Edition*, ed. Ralph W. Franklin, 3 vols. (Cambridge, MA: Harvard University Press, 1998), poem 778. Hereafter abbreviated F and cited by poem number. Unless otherwise noted in the citation, quotations are from the "A" versions of the poems.
3. *Journal: The Writings of Henry D. Thoreau*, ed. Elizabeth Hall Witherell et al., 8 vols. to date (Princeton, NJ: Princeton University Press, 1981–), 4:182, 11/13/51. Hereafter abbreviated PJ and cited by volume, page number, and date.

INTRODUCTION

1. Thoreau, *Walden, or Life in the Woods*, in *A Week on the Concord and Merrimack Rivers, Walden, The Maine Woods, Cape Cod*, ed. Robert F. Sayre (New York: Library of America, 1985), 1:329. Hereafter abbreviated W and cited by chapter and page number.
2. Thoreau, "Life Without Principle," in *Collected Essays and Poems*, ed. Elizabeth Hall Witherell (New York: Library of America, 2001), 348–66.
3. Thoreau, "Walking," in Witherell, *Collected Essays and Poems*, 229.
4. Stanley Cavell, *In Quest of the Ordinary: Lines of Skepticism and Romanticism* (Chicago: University of Chicago Press, 1988), 18.
5. Quoted in Richard B. Sewall, "The Lyman Letters: New Light on Emily Dickinson and Her Family," *The Massachusetts Review* 6, no. 4 (Autumn 1965): 774.
6. Thoreau, "Walking," 225.
7. Branka Arsić, *Bird Relics: Grief and Vitalism in Thoreau* (Cambridge, MA: Harvard University Press, 2016); Jane Bennett, *Vibrant Matter: A Political Ecology of Things* (Durham, NC: Duke University Press, 2010); Mark Noble, *American Poetic Materialism from Whitman to Stevens* (Cambridge, UK: Cambridge University Press, 2015); Rochelle Johnson, "'This Enchantment is No Delusion': Henry David

Thoreau, the New Materialisms, and Ineffable Materiality," *Interdisciplinary Studies in Literature and Environment* 21, no. 3 (Summer 2014): 606–35.
8. Theo Davis, review of *American Poetic Materialism from Whitman to Stevens*, by Mark Noble, *ALH Online Review* IX (January 2017): 3.
9. Noble, *American Poetic Materialism*, 2.
10. Alfred Tauber, *Henry David Thoreau and the Moral Agency of Knowing* (Berkeley, CA: University of California Press, 2001), 4.
11. Maurice Blanchot, *The Space of Literature*, trans. Ann Smock (Lincoln: University of Nebraska Press, 1982).
12. Angus Fletcher, *A New Theory for American Poetry: Democracy, the Environment, and the Future of Imagination* (Cambridge: Harvard University Press, 2006), 22.
13. Thoreau, *A Week on the Concord and Merrimack Rivers*, in *A Week on the Concord and Merrimack Rivers, Walden, The Maine Woods, Cape Cod*, ed. Robert F. Sayre (New York: Library of America, 1985), 266.
14. Sharon Cameron, *Writing Nature: Henry Thoreau's* Journal (Oxford University Press, 1985; repr., University of Chicago Press, 1989), 5.
15. David Porter, *Dickinson: The Modern Idiom* (Cambridge, MA: Harvard University Press, 1981); Susan Howe, *My Emily Dickinson* (Berkeley, CA: North Atlantic Books, 1985), 21.
16. John Hildebidle, *Thoreau: A Naturalist's Liberty* (Cambridge, MA: Harvard University Press, 1983).
17. *The Letters of Emily Dickinson*, ed. Thomas H. Johnson and Theodora Ward, 3 vols. (Cambridge: Harvard University Press, 1958), letter 268. Hereafter abbreviated L and cited by letter or prose fragment number.

CHAPTER 1

1. Stanley Cavell, *The Senses of Walden: An Expanded Edition* (Chicago: University of Chicago Press, 1981), xv.
2. To Thomas Cholmondeley, February 7, 1855, in *The Correspondence of Henry David Thoreau: Volume 2: 1849–1856*, ed. Robert N. Hudspeth (Princeton, NJ: Princeton University Press, 2018), 371 (bracketed text added).
3. Ralph Waldo Emerson, "Thoreau," in *Essays and Poems*, ed. Joel Porte, Library of America College Editions (New York: Library of America, 1983), 1025.
4. Susan Howe, *My Emily Dickinson* (Berkeley, CA: North Atlantic Books, 1985), 13, 21.
5. Howe, *My Emily Dickinson*, 11.
6. Thomas Wentworth Higginson, "Letter to a Young Contributor," *Atlantic Monthly* 9, no. 54 (April 1862): 401–11.
7. David Porter, *Dickinson: The Modern Idiom* (Cambridge, MA: Harvard University Press, 1981), 143.
8. Laura Dassow Walls, *Henry David Thoreau: A Life* (Chicago: University of Chicago Press, 2017), 273.
9. Michael Granger, "Antimodern Thoreau," in *Thoreauvian Modernities: Conversations on an American Icon*, ed. François Specq, Laura Dassow Walls, and Michael Granger (Athens: University of Georgia Press, 2013), 48.

10. See Thoreau's letter To Spencer Fullerton Baird, December 19, 1853, in Hudspeth, *Correspondence*, 181–82.
11. François Speçq, "Thoreau's Journal or the Workshop of Being," *Criticism* 58, no. 3 (Summer 2016): 386.
12. Paul Celan, "Wet from the world," in *Glottal Stop: 101 Poems*, trans. Nikolai Popov and Heather McHugh (Middletown, CT: Wesleyan University Press, 2000), 60.
13. John Michael, *Secular Lyric: The Modernization of the Poem in Poe, Whitman, and Dickinson* (New York: Fordham University Press, 2018), 13.
14. Michael, *Secular Lyric*, 14.
15. Michael, *Secular Lyric*, 181.
16. Cavell, *The Senses of Walden*, 3, 60.
17. Before this Perry Miller, in *Consciousness in Concord: The Text of Thoreau's Hitherto "Lost Journal," 1840–1841* (Boston: Houghton Mifflin, 1958), published a long, rather scathing essay on Thoreau and the Journal, along with a newly discovered volume of its contents. And in 1983 William Howarth's biographical study *The Book of Concord: Thoreau's Life as a Writer* (New York: Viking, 1983), discussed the Journal at some length, acknowledging the major role it played in Thoreau's late career.
18. Sharon Cameron, *Writing Nature: Henry Thoreau's* Journal (Oxford University Press, 1985; repr., University of Chicago Press, 1989), 3.
19. Cameron, *Writing Nature*, 6.
20. Cameron, *Writing Nature*, 4.
21. J. V. Cunningham, "Sorting Out: The Case of Dickinson," in *The Collected Essays of J. V. Cunningham* (Chicago: Swallow Press, 1976), 354. Diagnosis of the problem or challenge facing Dickinson's readers is controversial, however. Virginia Jackson describes Cunningham's observation as "symptomatic of the century's ongoing attempt to construct the scope of Dickinson's work, to make out of the heterogeneous materials of her practice a literature 'to hold in mind' and to hand down—to sort her various pages into various poems, those various poems into a book." Jackson, *Dickinson's Misery: A Theory of Lyric Reading* (Princeton, NJ: Princeton University Press, 2005), 1.
22. Gary Lee Stonum, *The Dickinson Sublime* (Madison: University of Wisconsin Press, 1990), 3.
23. Porter, *Dickinson: The Modern Idiom*, 105.
24. Sharon Cameron, *Choosing Not Choosing: Dickinson's Fascicles* (Chicago: University of Chicago Press, 1992), 5–6.
25. Cameron, *Choosing Not Choosing*, 15.
26. My own experience at Amherst College's archives was mixed. Although I had originally been granted permission, by email, to view about forty of Dickinson's manuscripts, upon arrival in August of 2015 I was told that this had been an oversight, and that the recent digitization of the archive's holdings obviated the need to see the actual, very delicate documents. After some discussion I was allowed to see the manuscripts I had requested, though I was told that I would probably be the last to view them in private—an assertion that I took with a grain of salt.
27. Cameron, *Choosing Not Choosing*, 19.
28. Robin Peel, *Emily Dickinson and the Hill of Science* (Madison, NJ: Farleigh Dickinson University Press, 2010), 14.

29. Porter, *Dickinson: The Modern Idiom*, 5.
30. Jackson, *Dickinson's Misery*. This is how Jackson's question is phrased on the back of her book. In the text of the book itself it appears thus: "But how do we know that lyrics are what Dickinson wrote?" (17). It is interesting that Jackson's own publisher—presumably to grab potential readers' attention, and/or to avoid technical, discipline-specific terms—evidently makes the same conflation of poetry with lyric which her book sets out to critique.
31. Jackson, *Dickinson's Misery*, 3.
32. Jackson, *Dickinson's Misery*, 6–7.
33. Jackson, *Dickinson's Misery*, 6.
34. Jackson, *Dickinson's Misery*, 7.
35. Yvor Winters, "Emily Dickinson and the Limits of Judgment," in *Emily Dickinson: A Collection of Critical Essays*, ed. Richard B. Sewall (Englewood Cliffs, NJ: Prentice-Hall, 1963), 29, 40, 31.
36. R. P. Blackmur, "Emily Dickinson's Notation," in Sewall, *Emily Dickinson*, 87.
37. Winters, "Emily Dickinson," 29; R. P. Blackmur, "Emily Dickinson: Notes on Prejudice and Fact," *The Southern Review* 3, no. 2 (Autumn 1937): 336.
38. For example, she quotes Blackmur's complaint that Dickinson "never undertook the great profession of controlling the means of objective expression," and comments: "Blackmur wants Dickinson to be a professional because he wants literary critics to be professionals, which is to say that the intersubjective function of the poem for Blackmur is . . . to create academic culture." Jackson, *Dickinson's Misery*, 97.
39. Jackson, *Dickinson's Misery*, 95.
40. Winters, "Emily Dickinson," 36.
41. Jackson, *Dickinson's Misery*, 8.
42. Jackson, *Dickinson's Misery*, 97.
43. Jackson, *Dickinson's Misery*, 17.
44. Blackmur, "Emily Dickinson: Notes on Prejudice and Fact," 323.
45. Jackson, *Dickinson's Misery*, 92.
46. Jackson, *Dickinson's Misery*, 97.
47. Jackson, *Dickinson's Misery*, 100.
48. Jackson, *Dickinson's Misery*, 100.
49. Porter, *Dickinson: The Modern Idiom*, 6.
50. Timothy Morris, "The Development of Dickinson's Style," *American Literature* 60, no. 1 (March 1988): 40.
51. Porter, *Dickinson: The Modern Idiom*, 40.
52. Porter, *Dickinson: The Modern Idiom*, 27.
53. Porter, *Dickinson: The Modern Idiom*, 125.
54. Howe, *My Emily Dickinson*, 11.
55. Sharon Cameron, *Lyric Time: Emily Dickinson and the Limits of Genre* (Baltimore: Johns Hopkins University Press, 1979).
56. Michael, *Secular Lyric*, 14.
57. Michael, *Secular Lyric*, 16.
58. Michael, *Secular Lyric*, 15.
59. Michael, *Secular Lyric*, 161.

60. Cristanne Miller, *Reading in Time: Emily Dickinson in the Nineteenth Century* (Amherst: University of Massachusetts Press, 2012), 20.
61. Miller, *Reading in Time*, 9.
62. Laura Dassow Walls, *Seeing New Worlds: Henry David Thoreau and Nineteenth-Century Natural Science* (Madison: University of Wisconsin Press, 1995), 11.
63. Miller, *Reading in Time*, 9–10.
64. Walls, *Seeing New Worlds*, 4.
65. Michael, *Secular Lyric*, 15.
66. Samuel Beckett, *Three Dialogues with Georges Duthuit*, in *Proust and Three Dialogues with Georges Duthuit* (London: Calder and Boyars, 1965), 103.
67. William Rossi, "Thoreau's Transcendental Ecocentrism," in *Thoreau's Sense of Place: Essays in American Environmental Writing*, ed. Richard Schneider (Iowa City: University of Iowa Press, 2000), 32.
68. Bradley P. Dean, introduction to *Wild Fruits: Thoreau's Rediscovered Lost Manuscript*, ed. Bradley P. Dean (New York: W. W. Norton, 2000), x–xi.
69. Cameron, *Writing Nature*, 3.
70. Henrik Otterberg, "Character and Nature: Toward an Aristotelian Understanding of Thoreau's Literary Portraits and Environmental Poetics," in Specq et al., *Thoreauvian Modernities*, 131.
71. Kristen Case, "Thoreau's Radical Empiricism: The Kalendar, Pragmatism, and Science," in Specq et al., *Thoreauvian Modernities*, 194.
72. Kristen Case, "About the Kalendar," Thoreau's Kalendar: A Digital Archive of the Phenological Manuscripts of Henry David Thoreau, accessed May 11, 2024, thoreauskalendar.org/about.html.
73. Case, "Thoreau's Radical Empiricism," 194.
74. H. Daniel Peck, *Thoreau's Morning Work: Memory and Perception in "A Week on the Concord and Merrimack Rivers," the Journal, and "Walden"* (New Haven, CT: Yale University Press, 1990), 94.
75. Peck, *Thoreau's Morning Work*, 75.
76. Otterberg, "Character and Nature," 131.
77. Walls, *Seeing New Worlds*, 182.
78. Walls, *Seeing New Worlds*, 183.
79. Walls, *Henry David Thoreau*, 304.
80. Henry D. Thoreau, *Faith in a Seed: The Dispersion of Seeds and Other Late Natural History Writings*, ed. Bradley P. Dean (Washington, DC: Island Press, 1993).
81. John Hildebidle describes "The Succession of Forest Trees" as being, "in comparison with Thoreau's greater works, orderly in an unusually explicit way." Hildebidle, *Thoreau: A Naturalist's Liberty* (Cambridge, MA: Harvard, 1983), 62. But, he adds after a close consideration of the text, "whatever its virtues as science, the lecture as art is something of a disappointment; and it may well be a disappointment that Thoreau himself shared." Hildebidle, *Thoreau*, 68.
82. Jackson, *Dickinson's Misery*, 3.
83. Hildebidle, *Thoreau*, 26.
84. Susan Eilenberg, "Emily v. Mabel," *London Review of Books* 33, no. 13 (June 2011): 3.
85. Thoreau, "Walking," 225.

86. Cavell, *In Quest of the Ordinary: Lines of Skepticism and Romanticism* (Chicago: University of Chicago Press, 1988), 166.
87. Howe, *My Emily Dickinson*, 13.
88. Howe, *My Emily Dickinson*, 21.
89. Jackson, *Dickinson's Misery*, 99.
90. Miller, *Reading in Time*, 22.
91. See Joanna Feit Diehl, *Women Poets and the American Sublime* (Bloomington: Indiana University Press, 1990).
92. Miller, *Emily Dickinson: A Poet's Grammar* (Cambridge, MA: Harvard University Press, 1987), 18.
93. Howe, *My Emily Dickinson*, 13.
94. Harold Bloom, *The Western Canon: The Books and Schools of the Ages* (New York: Harcourt, 1994), 291.
95. "Strangely abstracted images," which serves Porter as a chapter title, is a phrase coined by Archibald MacLeish in "The Private World: Poems of Emily Dickinson," in Sewall, *Emily Dickinson: A Collection of Critical Essays*, 150.
96. Porter, *Dickinson: The Modern Idiom*, 21.
97. Porter, *Dickinson: The Modern Idiom*, 123.
98. Porter, *Dickinson: The Modern Idiom*, 192.
99. Cameron, *Writing Nature*, 26.
100. Peck, *Thoreau's Morning Work*, 62.
101. Cameron, *Writing Nature*, 6–7.

CHAPTER 2

1. David Porter, *Dickinson: The Modern Idiom* (Cambridge, MA: Harvard University Press, 1981), 6.
2. Cristanne Miller, *Emily Dickinson: A Poet's Grammar* (Cambridge, MA: Harvard University Press, 1987), 1.
3. Miller, *Emily Dickinson: A Poet's Grammar*, 6; quoted in Richard B. Sewall, "The Lyman Letters: New Light on Emily Dickinson and Her Family," *The Massachusetts Review* 6, no. 4 (Autumn 1965): 774.
4. Stanley Cavell, *In Quest of the Ordinary: Lines of Skepticism and Romanticism* (Chicago: University of Chicago Press, 1988), 18.
5. Paul H. Fry, *A Defense of Poetry: Reflections on the Occasion of Writing* (Stanford, CA: Stanford University Press, 1995), 54.
6. Fry, *A Defense of Poetry*, 55
7. Fry, *A Defense of Poetry*, 55.
8. Geoffrey H. Hartman, *Wordsworth's Poetry, 1787–1814* (New Haven: Yale University Press, 1964), 17–18.
9. Hartman, *Wordsworth's Poetry*, 18, 16.
10. Hartman, *Wordsworth's Poetry*, 17.
11. William Wordsworth, *The Prelude: 1799, 1805, 1850*, ed. Jonathan Wordsworth, M. H. Abrams, and Stephen Gill (New York: W. W. Norton, 1979).
12. Hartman, *Wordsworth's Poetry*, 18–19.

13. Hartman, *Wordsworth's Poetry*, 16–17.
14. Harold Bloom, *The Western Canon: The Books and Schools of the Ages* (New York: Harcourt, 1994), 295.
15. Bloom, *The Western Canon*, 295.
16. Bloom, *The Western Canon*, 295.
17. John Michael, *Secular Lyric: The Modernization of the Poem in Poe, Whitman, and Dickinson* (New York: Fordham University Press, 2018), 187.
18. Susan Stewart, *The Poet's Freedom: A Notebook on Making* (Chicago: University of Chicago Press, 2011), 159–60.
19. Stewart, *The Poet's Freedom*, 160.
20. Friederich Nietzsche, *Daybreak: Thoughts on the Prejudices of Morality*, ed. Maudmarie Clark and Brian Leiter, trans. R. J. Hollingdale (Cambridge: Cambridge University Press, 1997), 5.
21. John Keats, "To Autumn," in *The Poems of John Keats*, ed. Jack Stillinger (Cambridge, MA: The Belknap Press of Harvard University Press, 1978), 477.
22. Like other riddle poems, observes Christine Gerhardt, this one performs a "formulaic withholding of the object's identity," and so "intensifies the attention to an ostensibly minor spectacle," while "push[ing] against scientific nomenclature." But "instead of playfully leading readers closer to understanding what is meant," the poem proliferates misunderstandings, for instance by re-naming the "Fellow" snake "Whip Lash," and so "offer[ing] an unsettling solution in which the animal turns out to be potentially dangerous to the vulnerable, 'Barefoot' speaker." Gerhardt, *A Place for Humility: Whitman, Dickinson, and the Natural World* (Iowa City: Iowa University Press, 2014), 49.
23. Dickinson's variant for "Motion," in the manuscript of this poem, is "Signal," a word that suggests both signification—language—and mute gesturing, as from a place too far away to allow for conversation.
24. Sharon Cameron, *Lyric Time: Dickinson and the Limits of Genre* (Baltimore, MD: Johns Hopkins University Press, 1979), 9.
25. Sharon Cameron, *Choosing Not Choosing: Dickinson's Fascicles* (Chicago: University of Chicago Press, 1992), 31.
26. Cameron, *Choosing Not Choosing*, 32.
27. Cameron, *Choosing Not Choosing*, 31.
28. Cameron, *Choosing Not Choosing*, 32.
29. Cameron, *Choosing Not Choosing*, 32.
30. Walter Benjamin, "The Task of the Translator," in *Illuminations: Essays and Reflections*, ed. Hannah Arendt, trans. Harry Zohn (New York: Harcourt, 1968), 78.
31. And some, like David Porter, are misperceived as having complained when in fact they had set out to exalt. See the somewhat misleading representation of Porter's argument in Fred D. White, *Approaching Emily Dickinson: Critical Currents and Crosscurrents since 1960* (Cambridge: Cambridge University Press, 2008), 163–64; and in Gary Lee Stonum, *The Dickinson Sublime* (Madison: University of Wisconsin Press, 1990), 7–10.
32. Anne-Lise François, *Open Secrets: The Literature of Uncounted Experience* (Stanford, CA: Stanford University Press, 2008), 153.
33. François, *Open Secrets*, 153.

34. François, *Open Secrets*, 155.
35. Harold Bloom, "The Internalization of Quest-Romance," in *Romanticism and Consciousness: Essays in Criticism*, ed. Harold Bloom (New York: W. W. Norton, 1970), 5–6.
36. Ralph Waldo Emerson, "Circles," in *Emerson: Essays and Poems*, ed. Joel Porte, Library of America College Editions (New York: Library of America, 1983), 405–06.
37. Emerson, "Circles," 406.
38. William Blake, "Mock on Mock on Voltaire Rousseau," in *The Poetry and Prose of William Blake*, ed. David V. Erdman (New York: Doubleday-Anchor, 1970), 468.
39. Theo Davis, *Ornamental Aesthetics: The Poetry of Attending in Thoreau, Dickinson, and Whitman* (Oxford: Oxford University Press, 2016), 9.
40. Davis, *Ornamental Aesthetics*, 4–5.
41. Martin Heidegger, *What is Called Thinking?* trans. J. Glenn Gray (New York: Harper, 1968), 9. This lecture, and its relevance to Dickinson's poetry, was brought to my attention by my colleague, Nasheed Zaman.
42. Yvor Winters, "Emily Dickinson and the Limits of Judgment," in *Emily Dickinson: A Collection of Critical Essays*, ed. Richard B. Sewall (Englewood Cliffs, NJ: Prentice-Hall, 1963), 31.
43. Douglas Anderson, "Presence and Place in Emily Dickinson's Poetry," *The New England Quarterly* 57, no. 2 (June 1984): 210.
44. Laura Dassow Walls, "Natural History in the Anthropocene," in *A Global History of Literature and the Environment*, ed. John Parham and Louise Westling (Cambridge: Cambridge University Press, 2016), 188.
45. Anderson, "Presence and Place in Emily Dickinson's Poetry," 210.

CHAPTER 3

1. Françoise Specq, "Thoreau's Journal or the Workshop of Being," *Criticism* 58, no. 3 (Summer 2016): 385.
2. Specq, "Thoreau's Journal," 387.
3. Theo Davis, *Ornamental Aesthetics: The Poetry of Attending in Thoreau, Dickinson, and Whitman* (Oxford, UK: Oxford University Press, 2016), 88.
4. Specq, "Thoreau's Journal," 379.
5. Frank N. Egerton and Laura Dassow Walls, "Rethinking Thoreau and the History of American Ecology," *The Concord Saunterer*, New Series 5 (Fall 1997): 4–20.
6. John Burroughs, *The Last Harvest* (New York: W. H. Wise, 1924), 122.
7. Joseph Wood Krutch, *Henry David Thoreau* (New York: William Morrow, 1974), 182.
8. Laura Dassow Walls, *Henry David Thoreau: A Life* (Chicago: University of Chicago Press, 2017), 304.
9. Specq, "Thoreau's Journal," 385.
10. Alfred Kazin, "The Journal of Henry David Thoreau," in *The Inmost Leaf: A Selection of Essays* (New York: Noonday, 1959), 104.
11. Kazin, "The Journal of Henry David Thoreau," 104.
12. Quoted in William Howarth, *The Book of Concord: Thoreau's Life as a Writer* (New York: Viking, 1983), ix.

13. Angus Fletcher, *Colors of the Mind: Conjectures on Thinking in Literature* (Cambridge, MA: Harvard University Press, 1991), 102.
14. Kenneth Gross, "About Angus Fletcher," *The Spenser Review* 47, no. 2 (Spring-Summer 2017), https://www.english.cam.ac.uk/spenseronline/review/item/47.2.23/.
15. Ezra Pound, *Gaudier-Brzeska: A Memoir* (London: John Lane, 1916), 88. Cf. Pound's earlier statement, "the natural object is always the adequate symbol." "A Few Don'ts by an Imagiste," *Poetry* 1, no. 6 (March 1913), 201.
16. Angus Fletcher, *A New Theory for American Poetry: Democracy, the Environment, and the Future of Imagination* (Cambridge, MA: Harvard University Press, 2006), 22.
17. Thoreau, *A Week on the Concord and Merrimack Rivers*, in *A Week on the Concord and Merrimack Rivers, Walden, The Maine Woods, Cape Cod*, ed. Robert F. Sayre (New York: Library of America, 1985), 265–66.
18. Thoreau, "Life Without Principle," in *Collected Essays and Poems*, ed. Elizabeth Hall Witherell (New York: Library of Congress, 2001), 349.
19. Stanley Cavell, *The Senses of Walden: An Expanded Edition* (Chicago: University of Chicago Press, 1981), 64.
20. Branka Arsić, *Bird Relics: Grief and Vitalism in Thoreau* (Cambridge, MA: Harvard University Press, 2016), 6.
21. Fletcher, *A New Theory*, 119.
22. Stanley Cavell, *In Quest of the Ordinary: Lines of Skepticism and Romanticism* (Chicago: University of Chicago Press, 1988), 18.
23. To Harrison Gray Otis Blake, April 3, 1850, in *The Correspondence of Henry David Thoreau: Volume 2: 1849–1856*, ed. Robert N. Hudspeth (Princeton, NJ: Princeton University Press, 2018), 55.
24. To Harrison Gray Otis Blake, March 27, 1848, in *The Correspondence of Henry David Thoreau: Volume 1: 1834–1848*, ed. Robert N. Hudspeth (Princeton, NJ: Princeton University Press, 2013), 361–62.
25. To Harrison Gray Otis Blake, April 3, 1850, in Hudspeth, *Correspondence: Volume 2*, 55.
26. To Harrison Gray Otis Blake, March 27, 1848, in Hudspeth, *Correspondence: Volume 1*, 362.
27. To Harrison Gray Otis Blake, August 10, 1849, in Hudspeth, *Correspondence: Volume 2*, 31.
28. To Harrison Gray Otis Blake, May 28, 1850, in Hudspeth, *Correspondence: Volume 2*, 58–59.
29. Fletcher, *A New Theory*, 22.
30. Pound, *Gaudier-Brzeska*, 88.
31. I am indebted to Kenneth Gross for explaining this allusion to me.
32. Quoted in Howarth, *The Book of Concord*, ix.
33. Ralph Waldo Emerson, "Thoreau," in *Essays and Poems*, ed. Joel Porte, Library of America College Editions (New York: Library of America, 1983), 1024–25.
34. Cavell, *The Senses of Walden*, 20.
35. John Keats, "Ode to a Nightingale," in *The Poems of John Keats*, ed. Jack Stillinger (Cambridge, MA: Belknap Press, 1978), 372.
36. Keats, "Ode to a Nightingale," 371.

37. H. Daniel Peck, *Thoreau's Morning Work: Memory and Perception in A Week on the Concord and Merrimack Rivers, the Journal, and Walden* (New Haven, CT: Yale University Press, 1990), 43.
38. Specq, "Thoreau's Journal," 385.
39. Specq, "Thoreau's Journal," 387.
40. Specq, "Thoreau's Journal," 385.
41. François Specq, "Poetics of Thoreau's Journal and Postmodern Aesthetics," in *Thoreauvian Modernities: Transatlantic Conversations on an American Icon*, ed. François Specq, Laura Dassow Walls, and Michael Granger (Athens: University of Georgia Press, 2013), 221.
42. Anne-Lise François, *Open Secrets: The Literature of Uncounted Experience* (Stanford, CA: Stanford University Press, 2008), 153.
43. David M. Robinson, *Natural Life: Thoreau's Worldly Transcendentalism* (Ithaca, NY: Cornell University Press, 2004), 16.
44. William Shakespeare, *Hamlet*, ed. Cyrus Hoy, Norton Critical Editions, 2nd ed. (New York: W. W. Norton, 1992), 5.1.165–66.
45. For a concise account of Thoreau's combined scientific and philosophical response to his discovery, see Philip Cafaro, "Thoreau on Science and System" (paper presented at the Twentieth World Congress of Philosophy, Boston, August 10–15, 1998), https://www.bu.edu/wcp/Papers/Envi/EnviCafa.htm.
46. Thoreau puts it bluntly: "I want you to perceive the mystery of the bream" (J 11:359). As John Hildebidle argues, "The true naturalist . . . is interested in explaining the marvelous; Thoreau's concern is to make the ordinary marvelous." Hildebidle, *Thoreau: A Naturalist's Liberty* (Cambridge, MA: Harvard, 1983), 25.
47. William Wordsworth, "Preface to *Lyrical Ballads, with Pastoral and Other Poems* (1800 and 1802)," in *William Wordsworth: Twenty-First Century Oxford Authors*, ed. Stephen Gill (Oxford, UK: Oxford University Press, 2010), 73.
48. Kazin, "The Journal of Henry David Thoreau," 104.
49. See Daisetz T. Suzuki, *Zen and Japanese Culture* (Princeton, NJ: Princeton University Press, 1959), 215–68, and R. H. Blyth, *Haiku*, vol. 1, *Eastern Culture* (Tokyo: Hokuseido, 1971), 163–268.
50. Sharon Cameron, *Writing Nature: Henry Thoreau's Journal* (Oxford University Press, 1985; repr., University of Chicago Press, 1989), 5.
51. Sharon Cameron, *Lyric Time: Dickinson and the Limits of Genre* (Chicago: University of Chicago Press, 1979), 47.
52. Davis, *Ornamental Aesthetics*, 4.
53. "To George and Tom Keats," December 21, 27 (?), 1817, in *Selected Letters of John Keats: Revised Edition*, ed. Grant F. Scott (Cambridge, MA: Harvard University Press, 2009), 60.

CHAPTER 4

1. Susan Howe, *My Emily Dickinson* (Berkeley, CA: North Atlantic Books, 1985), 11.
2. Howe, *My Emily Dickinson*, 13.
3. Howe, *My Emily Dickinson*, 7.

4. Howe, *My Emily Dickinson*, 13.
5. Stanley Cavell, *The Senses of Walden: An Expanded Edition* (Chicago: University of Chicago Press, 1992), xv.
6. See, for example, the writer Helen Hunt Jackson's correspondence with the poet, especially L476a, L476c, L573a, L573b, and L573c, in which Jackson tries insistently to overcome Dickinson's resistance to publishing (though with only very partial success, much to her disappointment: see L937a).
7. Cavell, *The Senses of Walden*, 77.
8. Martin Heidegger, *Being and Time*, trans. John Macquarrie and Edward Robinson (New York: Harper, 1962).
9. This word again brings Heidegger to mind, in particular his essays "The Question Concerning Technology" and "The Origin of the Work of Art," as well as the famous passage in *What is Called Thinking?* (trans. J. Glenn Gray [New York: Harper, 1968], 44), where he bemoans the fact that human "thought has never let the tree stand where it stands."
10. Quoted in Laura Dassow Walls, "'The Value of Mutual Intelligence': Science, Poetry, and Thoreau's Cosmos," in *Thoreau at 200: Essays and Reassessments*, ed. Kristen Case and K. P. Van Anglen (Cambridge, UK: Cambridge University Press, 2016), 193.
11. Walls, "'The Value of Mutual Intelligence,'" 193.
12. Sharon Cameron, *Writing Nature: Henry Thoreau's Journal* (Oxford University Press, 1985; repr., University of Chicago Press, 1989), 150.
13. Heidegger, *What is Called Thinking?* 9.
14. François Specq, "Thoreau's Journal or the Workshop of Being," *Criticism* 58, no. 3 (Summer 2016): 376–77.
15. Ralph Waldo Emerson, *Nature*, in *Essays and Poems*, ed. Joel Porte, Library of America College Editions (New York: Library of America, 1983), 20.
16. Henry David Thoreau, *The Maine Woods*, in *A Week on the Concord and Merrimack Rivers, Walden, The Maine Woods, Cape Cod*, ed. Robert F. Sayre (New York: Library of America, 1985), 646.
17. An article by Robert Moor published by the Sierra Club, for instance, has the flippant title "When Thoreau Went Nuts on Maine's Mount Katahdin." *Sierra: The National Magazine of the Sierra Club*, August 19, 2016, https://www.sierraclub.org/sierra/2016-4-july-august/green-life/when-thoreau-went-nuts-maine-s-mt-katahdin. Moor omits the sentences in which Thoreau refers to the strangeness of his own body and to the strangeness of "be[ing] shown matter" on a "daily" basis (as opposed to during a single "epiphany" [Moor's word] upon a mountain). See also popular author Bill Bryson's openly contemptuous interpretation of this passage in *A Walk in the Woods: Rediscovering America on the Appalachian Trail* (New York: Broadway Books, 1998), 45.
18. Quoted in Cameron, *Writing Nature*, 4.
19. Cameron, *Writing Nature*, 5.
20. Thoreau, *Collected Essays and Poems*, ed. Elizabeth Hall Witherell (New York: Library of America, 2001), 552.
21. Cameron, *Writing Nature*, 5, 4.
22. Wallace Stevens, "The Plain Sense of Things," in *The Collected Poems of Wallace Stevens* (New York: Vintage, 1955), 502.

23. Laura Dassow Walls, "Romancing the Real: Thoreau's Technology of Inscription," in *A Historical Guide to Henry David Thoreau*, ed. William E. Cain (Oxford: Oxford University Press, 2000), 134; quoted in Specq, "Thoreau's Journal," 378–79.
24. Marianne Moore, *The Complete Poems* (New York: 1994), vii.
25. Thoreau, "Walking," in Witherell, *Collected Essays and Poems*, 229.
26. Thoreau, "Walking," 227.
27. Cameron, *Writing Nature*, 47.
28. Maurice Blanchot, *The Space of Literature*, trans. Ann Smock (Lincoln: University of Nebraska Press, 1982), 21–22.
29. Blanchot, *The Space of Literature*, 21.
30. Blanchot, *The Space of Literature*, 22. See also Paul Fry's account of literature as that which "bears . . . neither a symbolic relation to a referential register nor an iconic analogy to the existing world, but is merely indicial, disclosing neither the purpose nor the structure of existence but only existence itself." Paul H. Fry, *A Defense of Poetry: Reflections on the Occasion of Writing* (Stanford, CA: Stanford University Press, 1995), 11.
31. Thoreau, "Walking," 249.
32. To Harrison Gray Otis Blake, May 28, 1850, in *The Correspondence of Henry David Thoreau: Volume 2: 1849–1856*, ed. Robert N. Hudspeth (Princeton, NJ: Princeton University Press, 2018), 59.
33. Heidegger, *What is Called Thinking?* 9.
34. Thoreau, "Walking," 266.
35. Thoreau's direct allusion to the "Orienta[l]" theory and practice of "contemplation and the forsaking of works" reminds us that there is nothing accidental about the resemblance between Thoreau's model of disinterestedness and those found in the texts of Hinduism and Buddhism. See Branka Arsić, *Bird Relics: Grief and Vitalism in Thoreau* (Cambridge, MA: Harvard University Press, 2016), in particular the sections of her introductory chapter titled "How to Greet a Tree?" and "Contemplating Matter."
36. Rainer Maria Rilke, *The Sonnets to Orpheus*, I.3, in *The Book of Fresh Beginnings: Selected Poems of Rainer Maria Rilke*, trans. David Young (Oberlin, OH: Oberlin College Press, 1994), 81; brackets added.
37. Rainer Maria Rilke, *The Eighth Elegy*, in *The Duino Elegies*, in *The Selected Poetry of Rainer Maria Rilke: Bilingual Edition*, trans. and ed. Stephen Mitchell (New York: Vintage, 1989), 193.
38. Alfred Tauber, *Henry David Thoreau and the Moral Agency of Knowing* (Berkeley, CA: University of California Press, 2001), 4.
39. Tauber, *Henry David Thoreau*, 4.
40. Cavell, *The Senses of Walden*, 105–6.
41. Cavell, *The Senses of Walden*, 106–7n.

CHAPTER 5

1. Henri Meschonnic, "Rhyme and Life," trans. Gabriella Bedetti, *Critical Inquiry* 15, no. 1 (Autumn 1988): 90.

2. David Porter, *Dickinson: The Modern Idiom* (Cambridge, MA: Harvard University Press, 1981), 64.
3. Porter, *Dickinson: The Modern Idiom*, 50.
4. See Vivian Pollak, "Thirst and Starvation in Emily Dickinson's Poetry," in *American Literature* 51, no. 1 (March 1979): 33–49.
5. *Oxford English Dictionary*, s.v. "amaze (v.)," accessed May 16, 2024, https://www.oed.com/dictionary/amaze_v?tab=meaning_and_use#5664562.
6. Dickinson, quoted in Richard B. Sewall, "The Lyman Letters: New Light on Emily Dickinson and Her Family," *The Massachusetts Review* 6, no. 4 (Autumn 1965): 774.
7. Porter, *Dickinson: The Modern Idiom*, 37.
8. Yvor Winters, "Emily Dickinson and the Limits of Judgment," in *Emily Dickinson: A Collection of Critical Essays*, ed. Richard B. Sewall (Englewood Cliffs, NJ: Prentice-Hall, 1963), 30–31.
9. Porter, *Dickinson: The Modern Idiom*, 83.
10. Howe, *My Emily Dickinson*, 21.
11. Stéphane Mallarmé, "Un coup de dés jamais n'abolira le hasard," trans. A. S. Kline (2007), Poetry in Translation, accessed May 16, 2024, https://www.poetryintranslation.com/PITBR/French/MallarmeUnCoupdeDes.php.
12. "Le moderne se contente de peu," Valéry wrote. Paul Valéry, "Cahier B 1910," in *Tel quel* (Paris: Gallimard, 1996), 185; quoted in T. J. Clark, *Farewell to an Idea: Episodes from a History of Modernism* (New Haven: Yale University Press, 1999), 7.
13. Stéphane Mallarmé, preface to "Un coup de dés jamais n'abolira le hasard," trans. Kline.
14. Cristanne Miller, *Reading in Time: Emily Dickinson in the Nineteenth Century* (Amhers: University of Massachusetts Press, 2012), 40–42.
15. Miller, *Reading in Time*, 41.
16. Miller, *Reading in Time*, 41.

CONCLUSION

1. Rainer Maria Rilke, "The Eighth Elegy," in *The Duino Elegies*, in *The Selected Poetry of Rainer Maria Rilke: Bilingual Edition*, trans. and ed. Stephen Mitchell (New York: Vintage, 1989), 193.
2. Rudyard Kipling, *The Jungle Book* (New York: Viking, 1987), 71–72.
3. Thoreau, "Walking," in *Collected Essays and Poems*, ed. Elizabeth Hall Witherell (New York: Library of America, 2001), 244.
4. Sharon Cameron, *The Bond of the Furthest Apart: Essays on Tolstoy, Dostoevsky, Bresson, and Kafka* (Chicago: University of Chicago Press, 2017), 11.
5. Wallace Stevens, "The Plain Sense of Things," in *The Collected Poems of Wallace Stevens* (New York: Vintage, 1955), 502.

Index

Anderson, Douglas, 71, 73. *See also* scholarship, on Dickinson
Arsiç, Branka, 5, 83. *See also* scholarship, on Thoreau
art: absence of purpose and, 150; in "It would have starved a Gnat" (F444), 139; nature and, 16, 51–52
Association for the Advancement of Science, 18, 39
"At Half past Three, a single Bird" (F1099) (Dickinson), 70–71, 131, 140–41, 147

Beckett, Samuel, 13, 34
Benjamin, Walter, 61
Bennett, Jane, 5
"A Bird came down the Walk" (F359) (Dickinson), 144, 152
"The birds begun at Four o'clock" (F504) (Dickinson), 62–63, 95, 131, 141
Blackmur, R. P., 28–29, 30. *See also* scholarship, on Dickinson
Blake, H. G. O., 87–88
Blake, William, 65
Blanchot, Maurice, 8, 118–19, 124
"Blazing in Gold and quenching in Purple" (F321) (Dickinson), 144–45
Bloom, Harold, 41; on Dickinson, 45, 50, 52; on internalization of quest-romance, 64; on words, 48, 73
"Bloom opon the Mountain—stated" (F787) (Dickinson), 66–69, 71, 121, 131
boredom, 93, 126
bream, Thoreau's discovery of, 97–98, 110–12, 123
Browning, Elizabeth Barrett, 60
Burroughs, John, 77

Calvinism, Dickinson and, 140–42
Cameron, Sharon, 8, 10, 16, 22, 24–25, 30, 35, 40, 43–44, 58–60, 85, 97, 99, 104, 107, 113, 118, 150, 152. *See also* scholarship, on Dickinson; scholarship, on Thoreau
Cartesian dualism, 125
Case, Kristen, 34–36. *See also* scholarship, on Thoreau
Cavell, Stanley, 3, 8, 13–14, 22, 39–40, 42, 48, 83–84, 93, 103, 124–25. *See also* scholarship, on Thoreau
Celan, Paul, 20–21, 31
Channing, William Ellery, 81, 90–91
"Circumference," Dickinson's idea of, 69, 72–73, 123
classification, of Dickinson: 25–33
classification, of Thoreau: 34–37
confidence-despair dialectic, in Dickinson's poetry, 58–59, 61
"Conscious am I in my Chamber" (F773) (Dickinson), 63–66, 69, 71, 124, 131
context, Dickinson and, 27–28, 32, 47. *See also* referentiality
culture, 6–7; Dickinson and, 41, 101, 103; nature and, 6; Thoreau and, 103
Cunningham, J. V., 22

Darwin, Charles, 97, 151
Dasein, Heidegger's concept of, 104, 123
dashes, Dickinson's, 147–48
Davis, Theo, 7, 69–70, 75–76, 99. *See also* scholarship, on Dickinson; scholarship, on Thoreau
Dean, Bradley, 34, 38

Dickinson, Emily, asceticism and, 132; conception of poetry, 38; description of, 141–42; engagement with world, 31–32; fascicles, 24–25, 59, 61; fascination with words for their own sake, 55–56; innovativeness of, 32; lack of telos, 22–32; on "Possibility," 118; on Thoreau, 14; US and, 14. Poems: "At Half past Three, a single Bird" (F1099), 70–71, 131, 140–41, 147; "A Bird came down the Walk" (F359), 144, 152; "The birds begun at Four o'clock" (F504), 62–63, 95, 131, 141; "Blazing in Gold and quenching in Purple" (F321), 144–45; "Bloom opon the Mountain - stated" (F787), 66–69, 71, 121, 131; "Conscious am I in my Chamber" (F773), 63–66, 69, 71, 124, 131; "Four Trees - opon a solitary Acre" (F778), x, 9, 131, 152; "I am alive - I guess" (F605), 128–31, 134, 142, 153; "I dwell in Possibility" (F466), 117, 131; "I felt a Funeral, in my Brain" (F340), 148–149; "I heard a Fly buzz - when I died" (F591), 1–3, 139; "I saw no Way - the Heavens were stitched" (F633), 59–60; "I think I was enchanted" (F627), 60; "It would have starved a Gnat" (F444), 132, 137–40, 141–42; "A narrow Fellow in the Grass" (F1096), 54–57, 69, 141; "Some - Work for Immortality" (F536), 132–33; "A Sparrow took a Slice of Twig" (F1257), 141–44; "Sweet Mountains - Ye tell Me no lie" (F745), 4, 48–51, 54–55, 69, 131; "There's a certain Slant of light" (F320), 152; "They shut me up in Prose" (F445), 131; "This was a Poet" (F446), 133–36; "The Tint I cannot take - is best" (F696), 46, 48, 52, 89, 121, 131.

disinterestedness, 102–4, 123; Dickinson's model of, 127, 137; Thoreau's model of, 76, 115, 120–21. *See also* non-teleological writing

Egerton, Frank, 77
ellipsis, Dickinson's poetry and, 100, 128, 131, 148. *See also* language

Emerson, Ralph Waldo, 14, 52, 64, 91, 151; "Circles," 65, 66; eulogy for Thoreau, 90; *Nature*, 109
endings, Dickinson's, 144–45, 146–47, 149
ethics of Dickinson's poetics, 146–47
"*extra vagance*" Thoreau's idea of, 8, 106, 111

facts, 9–10, 71, 72; communication via, 106, 118; disinterested notation of, 117; insights into Thoreau's life and, 109, 113–16; meaning in, 128; poetry and, 80, 83–84, 89, 117
failure, 88, 96
fascicles, Dickinson's, 24–25, 59, 61
Fletcher, Angus, 8, 81, 83–84, 89
"Four Trees—opon a solitary Acre" (F778) (Dickinson), 131
fragmentary quality of Journal, 35–36, 75–76
fragmentation, of Dickinson's poems, 3, 23, 68, 145–46
François, Anne-Lise, 8, 44, 62–63, 95. *See also* scholarship, on Dickinson
Fry, Paul, 8, 44, 50–51, 53. *See also* scholarship, on Dickinson

gender: Dickinson's writing and, 40–41; language and, 41
gnomes: in Thoreau, 81–84. *See also* language
God: nearness of, 153; Thoreau and, 87, 111, 113
grammar, Dickinson's: in "Blazing in Gold and quenching in Purple" (F321), 144–45; invention of, 142; "A Sparrow took a Slice of Twig" (F1257) and, 143–44; Yvor Winters on, 146. *See also* language, Dickinson's; originality, Dickinson's
Granger, Michael, 18
Gross, Kenneth, 82

Hartman, Geoffrey, 51–52
Heidegger, Martin, 8, 71, 107, 110, 124, 152; on actuality, 121; on Dasein, 104; Dickinson and, 70

INDEX

Higginson, Thomas Wentworth, 14–15, 17, 141–42; correspondence with Dickinson, 17–18, 130

Hildebidle, John, 10, 39. *See also* scholarship, on Thoreau

Howe, Susan, 10–11, 14, 16, 30–31, 40–41, 102–4, 142; *See also* scholarship, on Dickinson

"I am alive—I guess" (F605) (Dickinson), 128–31, 142, 153; meaningfulness and, 134

"I dwell in Possibility" (F466) (Dickinson), 117, 131

"I felt a Funeral, in my Brain" (F340) (Dickinson), 148–49

"I heard a Fly buzz—when I died" (F591) (Dickinson), 1–3, 139

imagination, 52; imagining the absence of, 113, 152; Dickinson and, 53, 57; freedom of, 64; nature and, 51–52

Imagism, 82

immortality, Dickinson's poetry and, 65–66, 73

incompleteness: Dickinson's poems and, 145–46; of Journal, 118

indication, in Dickinson's language, 50, 57

insects, Dickinson and, 137–42

intention, intentional repudiation of, 16; Journal's renunciation of, 113

"I saw no Way—the Heavens were stitched" (F633) (Dickinson), 59–60

"I think I was enchanted" (F627) (Dickinson), 60

"It would have starved a Gnat" (Dickinson), 132, 137–42

Jackson, Virginia, 25, 26–31, 33, 35, 38. *See also* scholarship, on Dickinson

Johnson, Rochelle, 6

Journal (Thoreau), aims of, 74, 76–77, 85–86; alienness of nature and, 111; ambiguities in, 73; authorial control ceded to nature, 104; boredom and, 93; close readings of, 36; closure and, 36; comparisons in, 83; connection between poetry and natural fact and, 84; contradictions in, 75–79; description in, 112; evanescent quality of, 75–76; explanation and, 85–86; fragmentary nature of, 3, 36–37, 75–76; frame and content, 105–7; God in, 87; incomplete nature of, 118; interdependence of living and writing in, 107–9; interpretation of, 113; Kalendar and, 35–37; lack of ending, 19–20, 149; lack of organization, 22; as literary, 118–19; meaning in isolated facts and, 128; meditations of, 113; messiness of, 115; mind and, 104; mysteries and, 86–87; mystery in, 110; "mystery of life" in, 98; natural objects in, 88; nature and man in, 99; as non-teleological work, 3–4, 11–12, 78; omission of "I" in, 116; paradoxes in, 73; on perception, 74; perception and, 3–4; philosophy and, 83; as poem, 11, 73; poetry and, 78–81, 83, 117–18; as preliminary work, 36–37; prosaic passages in, 113; purpose of, 16, 43; reading, 91–92; renunciation of intentionality, 113; reputation of, 77; science and, 77, 83; scientific usefulness of, 11; self-expression and, 107; shift in Thoreau's thinking/writing and, 91; statement of purpose in, 89; syrup-making in, 114–16; telos renounced in, 94; theory of, 120; as Thoreau's chief literary outlet, 119; Thoreau's emotional involvement in subject, 99–100; Thoreau's inability to unite mind and nature in, 125; time in, 94; used for drafting passages, 80; value in isolated facts and, 128; value of, 35–36; *Walden* and, 37

Kafka, Franz, 86, 137
Kalendar (Thoreau), 35–37
Kant, Immanuel, 98, 125
Kazin, Alfred, 81, 98. *See also* scholarship, on Thoreau
Keats, John, 56, 82, 94, 100
Kipling, Rudyard, 151

knowledge: about nature, 95; forgetting, 74–75; in Journal, 96; "the thing-in-itself" and, 125; Thoreau on, 119
Krutch, Joseph Wood, 77

language: aura and, 48; conventional, Dickinson's renunciation of, 128; Dickinson and, 31, 131; Dickinson's inquiry into, 29; Dickinson's reinvention of, 15; Emerson on, 109; as form of life, 130; gender and, 41; meaning and, 131; in modernist poetry, 131; replacement of self by, 129; urgency in Dickinson's poems, 47. *See also* gnomes; words
language, Dickinson's, 53; Bloom on, 45, 50; "Circumference" of, 123; combination of grandeur and fragmentation in, 46; indication in, 50, 57; meaning and, 58; naming in, 57; non-teleological use of, 10–11, 68; "Ordinary Meanings" and, 42, 46; ordinary words and, 48; "Possibility" and, 123; "slant" of, 42, 45, 53–54, 56, 82; unnaming and, 52, 57; word-centered quality of, 45–58. *See also* grammar, Dickinson's
Loeffelholz, Mary, 34
Lyman, Joseph, 47
lyric poetry, 25–31

The Maine Woods (Thoreau), 110
Mallarmé, Stéphane, 147–49
man, nature and, 7–8, 99
materialism, 5–7; *See also* new materialism
meaning, 5, 16, 99; ability to see, xi; absence/negation of, 20; certainty and, 21; Dickinson's language/poetry and, 58; Dickinson's resistance to, 12, 20, 127; in experience of seeing, 2; in isolated facts, 128; language and, 131; nature and, 23; the ordinary and, 137; uncertainty of, 144; of words, 73
meaningfulness, "This was a Poet" (F446) and, 135–36
meditation, Thoreau and, 12, 113

Meschonnic, Henri, 130
Michael, John, 20–21, 30–31, 33, 53–54. *See also* scholarship, on Dickinson
Miller, Cristanne, 31–34, 47, 149. *See also* scholarship, on Dickinson
mind, nature and, 51, 125
modernism, 15, 147–48; language in, 131
Moore, Marianne, 116
Morris, Timothy, 30
mystery, Thoreau and, 86–87, 98, 110–11

naming, Dickinson and, 49–50, 52, 57, 83–84
"A narrow Fellow in the Grass" (F1096) (Dickinson), 54–57, 69, 141
nature, 59, 78; alienness of, 111, 153; art and, 51–52; authorial control of the Journal ceded to, 104; communication via, 89; culture and, 6; Dickinson and, 44, 46, 146, 151–53; difference of, 152; engaging, 120; exile of mind from, 125; function of art and, 16; imagination and, 51–52; inability to unite mind and, 125; inaccessibility/strangeness of, 109–12, 153; independence of, 51–52; knowledge about, 95; man and, 7–8, 99; meaning and, 20, 23, 44; mood and, 111; self and, 78; Thoreau and, 39, 93, 95; "The Tint I cannot take—is best" (F696) and, 89; turn to, 6; unknowability of, 20; value and, 152–53; writing about, 117–18. *See also* facts
negative capability, 5, 98, 100, 119
New Critics, 28–30
new materialism, 6–8. *See also* materialism; scholarship, on Dickinson; scholarship, on Thoreau
Nietzsche, Friedrich, 45, 55, 57, 73
Noble, Mark, 6–7
non-teleological writing, 43; absence/negation and, 20; choices and, 103; goal of, 4–5, 117–18; as minimalist, 9; vs. new materialism, 6–8; use of term, x, 5. *See also* disinterestedness
non-teleological writing, Dickinson's: "Bloom opon the Mountain—stated"

(F787) and, 68; Cavell and, 48; nature and, 46; pointed lack of story and, 53–57; unnaming and, 53. *See also* language, Dickinson's
non-teleological writing, Thoreau's, 48, 119–20; theory and practice of poetry and, 113

obscurity, Dickinson and, 61, 127
"the Open," Rilke's idea of, 123, 150–51
the ordinary, 8–9; Dickinson's poems and, 9, 49; relation with the extraordinary, 133; Thoreau's interest in, 81; value in, 133–37, 139–40
"Ordinary Meanings," Dickinson's idea of, 12, 42, 46, 133–36
organization, Dickinson and, 15, 17–18, 22–32. *See also* fascicles
organization, Thoreau and, 22, 23
originality, Dickinson's, 32, 142; Bloom on, 41, 52. *See also* grammar, Dickinson's; language, Dickinson's
Otterberg, Henrik, 34, 35, 36. *See also* scholarship, on Thoreau

Peck, H. Daniel, 36, 43, 94. *See also* scholarship, on Thoreau
Peel, Robin, 25, 26, 35. *See also* scholarship, on Dickinson
perception: Dickinson and, 1, 146; Thoreau and, 1–4, 74, 89; thought and, 120. *See also* seeing; seeing to see
poet, the, Dickinson on, xi, 132–33, 135–39; ethical task of, 134; Fletcher on, 89; introspection and, 109; Thoreau on, xi
poetic perception, 120, 137
poetics, Dickinson's: ellipsis and, 100, 128, 131, 148; impersonality and, 100; naming and, 49–50, 52, 57, 83–84; reticence and, 100; unnaming and, 52, 53, 57; as word-based, 4; words in, 127–28. *See also* non-teleological writing
poetry: business compared to, 101; Dickinson on, 38, 133–34, 136, 140; fact and, 80, 83–84, 89, 117; freedom and, 117; incommensurability of, 136–37; Journal and, 78–81, 83, 117–18; lyricization of, 27; philosophy and, 8, 9; prose and, 9–10; science and, 9–10; Thoreau's writing as, 109
pointlessness, Dickinson's poetry and, 53–57, 146
Pollak, Vivian, 34
Porter, David, 10, 16, 24, 30, 38, 40, 42, 44, 131, 142; on Dickinson-Higginson correspondence, 17; on Dickinson's lack of "the expected discourse," 26; on Dickinson's language, 45; on Dickinson's revisions, 143; *Dickinson: The Modern Idiom*, 41, 131; on fragmentation, 23; on simplicity, 132; on "A Sparrow took a Slice of Twig" (F1257), 143. *See also* scholarship, on Dickinson
"Possibility," Dickinson's idea of, 118, 123
post-structuralism, 30
Pound, Ezra, 82, 90
poverty, Dickinson's treatment of, 132, 136–38, 142
presence: absence and, 73, 88; defined by withdrawal, 70; in Dickinson's poetry, 71–72; distance and, 69, 72–73; place and, 73
privacy, 15–16. *See also* exile
process-oriented writing, 19–21
publication, 16, 17–18, 103. *See also* editors, Dickinson's
punctuation, Dickinson's, 147–48
purpose: lack of, 5, 22–32; obliqueness of, Dickinson and, 127. *See also* non-teleological writing

Qur'an, 153

reading of things, 91–92
referentiality, in Dickinson, 20–21, 29–30, 53, 55
renunciation, Dickinson's, 131; in "I am alive—I guess," 130; language and, 128; of self, 128, 130
revision: by Dickinson, 19, 140, 142–43; by Thoreau, 19

riddle: in Dickinson's poetry, 146; "A Sparrow took a Slice of Twig" (F1257) as, 142–43
Rilke, Rainer Maria, 102, 123, 150–51
Robinson, David M., 96. *See also* scholarship, on Thoreau
romanticism, 6, 64, 68, 94, 131
Rossi, William, 34
Ruskin, John, 142

sauntering, Thoreau's idea of, 5, 114
scholarship, on Dickinson: Anderson, 71, 73; Blackmur, 28–30; classification and, 20, 22–32; Davis, 7, 69–70, 75–76, 99; Deihl, 44; on Dickinson and culture, 34, 41, 101; earlier vs. recent, 10; François, 8, 44, 62–63, 95; Fry, 8, 44, 50–51, 53; historicist approach to, 31, 33, 38; individuality downplayed in, 32–33; Jackson, 25, 26–30, 31, 33, 35, 38; lack of goal/organization and, 17, 22–32; language-centered approach, 40–42; materialism and, 5–7; Michael, 20–21, 30–31, 33, 53–54; Miller, 31–34, 47, 149; New Critics, 28–30; non-teleological writing and, 44; Peel, 25–26, 35; post-structuralism, 30; recent, 29–30, 101; revisionist, 25–32; on scientific usefulness of Journal, 11; similarity to Thoreau scholarship, 32; skepticism about Dickinson's originality, 39; Stewart, 55; Stonum, 23; teleological prejudice in, 12; tone of, 34–37, 39; versions of Dickinson presented by, 39. *See also* Cameron, Sharon; Davis, Theo; Howe, Susan; Porter, David; Specq, François; Winters, Yvor
scholarship, on Thoreau: Arsiç, 5, 83; Blanchot, 8, 118–19, 124; Case, 34, 35, 36; classification problem and, 21–22; Davis, 7, 69–70, 75–76, 99; detractors, 77, 81; earlier vs. recent, 10; efforts to bolster Journal's reputation, 77; ends-oriented approach to Journal, 35–36; Hildebidle, 10, 39; historical/contextualized depiction of Thoreau, 38; individuality downplayed in, 32–33; on Journal's value, 35–37; Kazin, 81, 98; lack of goal/organization and, 23; language-centered approach, 40; materialism and, 5–7; non-teleological writing and, 44; on originality of Thoreau, 39; Otterberg, 34, 35–36; Peck, 36, 43, 94; recent critics, 43; representations of Thoreau, 39, 76–77; Robinson, 96; similarity to Dickinson scholarship, 32; Tauber, 7, 123–24; teleological prejudice in, 12; on Thoreau and nineteenth-century science, 33–34; Thoreau's recording of observations and, 34–38; tone of, 32, 34–37, 39; Walls, 32–34, 36–37, 72, 77, 105, 115. *See also* Cameron, Sharon; Cavell, Stanley; Journal (Thoreau); Specq, François; *Walden* (Thoreau)
science, 18; classification of Thoreau and, 37; Dickinson and, 25; difference of nature and, 152; nature and, 93; poetry and, 9–10; Thoreau and, 11, 18, 33–34, 38–39, 77, 83, 105, 108; truth and, 83–84. *See also* Journal (Thoreau); nature
seeing: Dickinson on, 1; meaning in experience of, 2; purpose of, x–xi; vs. seeing to see, 3; Thoreau on, 1. *See also* perception
seeing to see: Dickinson on, 1; vs. mere seeing, 3; reading Journal and, 91–92
self-consciousness, Thoreau and, 76, 123–24
Shakespeare, William, 52, 82
signification: conventional, Dickinson's renunciation of, 128; ordinary words and, 48
skepticism, 8, 125
"slant," Dickinson's idea of, 42, 45, 50, 53–54, 56, 82
Smith, Martha Nell, 34
Socarides, Alexandra, 34
"Some—Work for Immortality" (F536) (Dickinson), 132–33
"A Sparrow took a Slice of Twig" (F1257) (Dickinson), 141–44

Specq, François, 75–76, 84; on indefiniteness in Journal, 94–95; on Journal's lack of endpoint, 19–20; on non-teleological nature of Journal, 78; on Journal and self-expression, 107. *See also* scholarship, on Thoreau
spirituality, Thoreau and, 87–88
Stein, Gertrude, 30
Stevens, Wallace, 83, 113, 152
Stewart, Susan, 55. *See also* scholarship, on Dickinson
Stonum, Gary Lee, 23
subject matter, Dickinson's, 3, 19, 59, 61, 131; Dickinson mastered by, 146; ethics of Dickinson's poetics and, 146–47; grammar and, 146; insects, 137–42; meaninglessness and, 146; perception and, 146; temperament and, 146; treatment of, 140–41; vanishing quality of, 132. *See also* nature
subject matter, Thoreau's, 3, 19–20, 99–100, 108, 112. *See also* nature
"Sweet Mountains—Ye tell Me no lie" (F745) (Dickinson), 4, 48–51, 54–55, 69, 131

Tauber, Alfred, 7, 123–24. *See also* scholarship, on Thoreau
teleology: Dickinson's avoidance of, 4; resistance to, x; Thoreau's avoidance of, 3–4
telos, 5, 94. *See also* purpose
"There's a certain Slant of light" (F320) (Dickinson), 152
"They shut me up in Prose" (F445) (Dickinson), 131
"the thing-in-itself," Kant's idea of, 125
things: meaning of, 9–10; reading of, 91–92
"This was a Poet" (F446) (Dickinson), 133; meaningfulness and, 134–36
Thoreau, Henry David, ix; asceticism and, 132; on business, 101; correspondence with Blake, 87–88; Dickinson and, 70; Dickinson on, 14; as disinterested writer, 11; on experience of loss, 71; father of, 115–16; journal-writing practice, 90–100; Kalendar, 35–37; late career of, 10; on literature, 151; *The Maine Woods*, 110; negative capability of, 119; non-teleological writing of, 48; "Resistance to Civil Government," 91; science and, 38, 77; "The Succession of Forest Trees," 38; *Walden*, 63, 91, 93, 95, 120; *A Week on the Concord and Merrimack Rivers*, 102–3, 122. *See also* Journal (Thoreau); *Walden* (Thoreau). *See also* Journal (Thoreau)
"The Tint I cannot take—is best" (F696) (Dickinson), 46, 48, 52, 89, 121, 131
titles: of Dickinson's texts, 102; of Thoreau's texts, 102
Todd, Mabel Loomis, 14; Dickinson's punctuation and, 147; organization of Dickinson's poems and, 18

unnaming, Dickinson and, 52–53, 57

Valéry, Paul, 147–48
value, 5; ability to see, xi; of Dickinson's poetry, x, 139–40; Dickinson's protest against conventional ideas of, 12; in familiar, 136; inability to assess, 152; in isolated facts, 128; nature and, 152–53; in the ordinary, 133–37, 139–40; product-oriented, 16; Thoreau and, x, 104–5, 132

Walden (Thoreau), 63, 91, 93, 95, 120; actuality in, 121–22; "bloom" in, 122; drafts of, 19; gnomes in, 81–82; Journal and, 37; on meditation, 12; mind and, 104; mystery in, 110; neighboring in, 124; nextness in, 124; on speaking, 106; Thoreau refusing his culture his voice in, 103
"Walking" (Thoreau), 116–17
Walls, Laura Dassow, 32–34, 36–37, 72, 77, 105, 115. *See also* scholarship, on Thoreau
A Week on the Concord and Merrimack Rivers (Thoreau), 102–3, 122

White, Gilbert, 39, 97, 151
Whitman, Walt, 20, 39
Winters, Yvor, 12, 28–29, 146; on Dickinson's language, 146–47; on Dickinson's treatment of subject matter, 127, 140–41; on "At Half past Three, a single Bird" (F1099), 70. *See also* scholarship, on Dickinson

words: Bloom on, 48; connoisseurship of, 56–57; in Dickinson's poetics, 127–28; Dickinson's use of, 4; isolated, in Dickinson's poetry, 10; meaning of, 73; ordinary, in Dickinson's poetry, 49. *See also* language
Wordsworth, William, 7, 51–52, 62–63, 94, 100, 151

www.ingramcontent.com/pod-product-compliance
Lightning Source LLC
Chambersburg PA
CBHW032215230426
43672CB00011B/2560